MBA

Michael Cooper with a 28 kg Murray cod caught in the Murray River near Wentworth.

Fishing Techniques

by Steve Cooper

First published in 2002
Revised Edition 2006
Australian Fishing Network
1/48 Centre Way
South Croydon VIC 3136
Australia
Tel: (03) 9761 4044
Fax: (03) 9761 4055
Email: sales@afn.com.au
Website: afn.com.au

Copyright © Australian Fishing Network 2006
Designed by Joy Eckermann
Cover design by Katie Classon

ISBN No. 1 86513 1067

CONTENTS

FOREWORD

Amongst the mountains of books available on fishing, there's a Himalaya or so of titles that'll take readers to fishable waters and tell when to go and what to take. A less lumpy pile will broadly explain what to do once one is there—the steps that fit between removing a hook from tackle box and a fish mouth. When it comes to the hard core how-to however, the tackle and presentations cutting edge, we're talking a mere Kosciuszko.

Why are events such? Fishing's literary pool contains many able communicators and some eloquent wordsmiths who stand out, but very few who've played a defining role when it comes to the gear, rigs, and techniques for specific situations. The inspiration to write, to say nothing of the words wherewithal, descends with far less frequency on sport fishing's trailblazers and innovators, blokes with backgrounds more black singlet than academic black robe.

Steve Cooper is more than just a notable exception. The former boilermaker—an apprentice of the year—if that can be leaked—traded in his blowtorch and two pound hammer for a typewriter. As an investigative journalist, he went on to win two Walkley Awards, the Australian newspaper industry's highest accolade.

Scoop—now there's a nickname that does more than just roll off the tongue—fished hard as a kid. The snapper, whiting and flathead around his hometown of Geelong saw to the days when school wasn't on. And when the sportfishing revolution hit—the biggest new broom ever, driven by Ron Calcutt and the Australian Angler magazine—he was there from the start, casting and keeping chronicle.

Starting out on the stones—the ocean rocks are sport fishing's real school of hard knocks— Steve branched into boats and an exploration of sport fishing's other frontiers. Snapper to sailfish, mulloway to marlin, bream to barra, tuna to trout, fillets to fly, temperate waters to those tropical, Steve's latest book is the story of that pilgrimage. A signposted and information laden shortcut that others may follow. While Cooper adequately deals with tropical tuggers like barra, this work, wisely, has its species epicentre in the south—where most Australians live and fish.

Cooper's text is typically succinct. Few writers have the same knack of saying so much in not as many words. As for the accuracy of the technical gist, it's spot-on—and not a word of it about fish he hasn't caught. His skilfully woven theme captures the essence of sportfishing—one is primarily on the water to have fun and not have to justify the expense/time with a poultice of fillets.

Fishing Techniques is a smooth blend of the new, and the tried and true. The tools have changed, the targets haven't. In a scene where it sometimes seems a daily occurrence that some new tackle or rig is revealed, and where in the meantime anglers are compelled to fish harder and longer for smaller catches, the 10 per cent of anglers reckoned by most astute observers to be catching 90 per cent of the fish, are doing so through adopting a hi-tech approach to the non-variables like the way fish behave.

Fishing Techniques is a landmark contribution to the fisho think tank. Read and enjoy— somewhere, someway it will make your time on the water more enjoyable and more productive.

Rod Harrison
BRIBIE ISLAND, QUEENSLAND

INTRODUCTION

Like the ebb and flow of the tide, a fishing life changes and every day offers the promise of a new experience. To the dedicated angler, fishing is not sport or recreation. It is a discipline, serious and ever changing. Sure, there are basic rules to follow, but understanding and developing the necessary skills isn't dependent on strict adherence to convention.

Fish are a moving feast, a shimmering smorgasbord of life trying to eat (and not be eaten) in a harsh environment that is both different and the same. Some fish are migratory, others aren't, and some migratory fish are anadromous, ascending rivers to spawn on gravel beds known as redds after spending most of their lives in salt water. Fish that live on reefs are totally different to those thriving in river environments. Changes to the environments of fishes in the same water are as regular as the flow of water. This is what dictates changing techniques to catch the same species at different stages of the same tide phase.

Fishing is an evolutionary rather than revolutionary activity. While technology has come into play with new lines and space age rod materials the basic pursuit remains the same—getting a fish on the end of the line.

Most of us started out with small bait rods, sitting on the end of a pier or perhaps a riverbank. As often as not we knew what we wanted to catch because we could see them—small winks of silver in the water that indicated schooling fish like mullet, yellowtail scad or perhaps minnow or redfin. Catching those small fish from the end of a pier was an easy way of life. Back then the world was small, uncomplicated and, on good days on the pier, an exciting place. There was no need for doubt, the pieces making up the jigsaw of life fitted together easily in those days.

Our outfits were similar, el cheapo rods, sometimes made from steel coupled to reels with nylon gears, probably bought in a department store, during a sale, and then hidden away for a few months before being brought out and placed in a Christmas stocking. For some kids their enthusiasm to go fishing was relative to the lifespan of their el cheapo outfit. Like puppies and comic books, there was a use by date. For the rest of us, half our free time seemed to be engaged in keeping that little rod and reel going.

From dead bait and small fish the natural progression is to live baits, lures and bigger fish. For young, maturing anglers, recreational fishing is about size: big fish are a testosterone event. Similar feelings (not testosterone) overtake female anglers according to Robert Hughes who, in his classic book 'A Jerk On One End' writes about fishing bringing out the 'latent maenad' in women.

Remember your first serious fish? The way its struggles on the end of your line sent happy juices flooding through your body. That chemical reaction that followed told your brain this is something out of the ordinary. You want more. Big fish are addictive.

During this period, quantity is also likely to be used as a substitute for quality. If you can't catch big fish show off your prowess by landing a heap of smaller ones. The killing and bloodletting is something to reflect on in later years when you wonder why things are not as they used to be and ask: 'Where have all the fish gone?'

When size or quantity becomes dull and blood is no longer the crimson aphrodisiac it was, you seek out other glories. You fish for trophies and certificates in a competitive environment where you take comfort in knowing that winning makes you better than the people you have beaten.

One day you realise that perhaps there might be a new challenge out there. It's called fly-fishing and you see it as a method where fish are to be caught on uncomplicated tackle. This is an ethereal, some might even say blasphemous, thought at first. Like nicotine, it starts to take hold.

Some anglers take longer than others to change, which is understandable. Others are happy doing what they do and never change; this is also understandable. When you are used to high-tech, state-of-the-art, two speed, lever drag game reels with their stainless steel gears, ball bearings and double dogs, it can be hard to accept what looks like a light bait rod with a centre-pin reel as offering entry into a piscatorial Nirvana.

And what about the people who are into fly-fishing? Plenty of airs and graces; at least this is the perception. One day you realise that you know a few people who wave long wands; they aren't snobs, sissies, or weirdos. Well, most of them aren't anyway; there's always a couple with a touch of codswallop.

This is how many anglers move into fly-fishing. It's a bit like Caesar crossing the Rubicon; a point of committal from which there is no turning back. Fly-fishing is a discipline that is taken a lot further by some anglers than simply catching fish. Casting and fly tying becomes art form. Fly-fishing can develop into an obsession. In extreme forms it is almost religion: a search for the meaning of life, the Holy Grail and a barometer by which all of the world's ills are judged, rolled into one

In its purest form, fly-fishing is about trout, but saltwater fly-fishing is growing in size and stature. Some of us transgress and practise both. Eventually the arc of our cast becomes more focussed. Barometric pressures and Moon phases, tides and even algal blooms, and how all of these factors affect the feeding habits of fish, are researched. We know all there is to know about caddis flies and mayfly hatches and some anglers will even recite the Latin names of bugs. We are at peace with the world, casting tight loops and straight lines.

In practice, utmost effort in fly-fishing doesn't automatically realise maximum results. It is, to put it bluntly, the least efficient method devised to catch fish that I know of.

Moreover, one day it comes to pass that our theories and faith no longer fit as neatly as they once did. We knew everything we needed to know, only to find out that we know nothing at all, probably even less than we did all those years ago. When it comes to hooking fish well, they're more timid, finicky and hook shy these days. Of course, age has little to do with all of this.

You start to think that perhaps you should have stayed with bait or lures. Such is the life cycle of an angler. When our thoughts flow back to the font from where it all began we start again, rethink our theories and put new emphasis on ideas we discarded. Like the ebb and flow of the tide, a fishing life changes and every day offers the promise of a new experience. Anglers come to understand that knowledge is ethereal—the more we know, the less we understand.

Steve Cooper

ACKNOWLEDGEMENTS

The following people deserve credit for their input in this book: Michael Cooper, Jack Erskine, Dave Harrigan, Rod Harrison, Chris Palatides, Rod Mackenzie, Mark Rushton, Gus Storer, Jim Harris, Herbie Glacken, John Mitchell, Alex Julius, Dean MacFarlane, Cameron Whittam, Craig Smith, Jim Harnwell and Gordon Campbell.

Influencing Factors

CHAPTER 1

READING THE SIGNS

All fish are influenced by natural elements, and these can include tide, moon phase, salinity, and barometric pressure. But there are no set rules to what governs fish movement and habits.

The only way to gauge what natural event affects fish is by keeping notes and establishing patterns, but before you can do this, you must first understand what is happening. Successful anglers have to learn how to read the signs, understand environmental change, and be prepared to adapt existing methods to suit the circumstances on a given day. There is an order of efficiency in fishing that sees some methods produce consistently better results than others do.

As a rule of thumb, I rate live bait more productive than dead bait, lures, or flies. Sometimes the scenario reverses itself. Bream inhaling insects from the surface are unlikely to find a fresh nipper attractive. The same fish are more likely to attack a baitfish imitation lure rather than a dry fly when they are skulking in mid-water around an oyster lease.

A confluence of current where baitfish are likely to be swept out of control is a likely feeding area for predators so you would offer up a baitfish imitation or a live bait in that scenario. Take snapper. These fish are opportunistic feeders and when the school moves in over mud in 10 m of water, they are most likely to be scavenging an easy feed. Lures and flies are unlikely to work in that scenario; a fresh fish fillet is the best option.

The same fish off the rocks can be different again. A berley trail fed into a wash attracts all sorts of fish, snapper among them. Reds are usually well away from the rocks and down deeper so to catch them you toss a fillet out and allow it to sink down under the wash. Sometimes a lure brought in at mid-water through the wash also produces results.

SEEING IS BELIEVING

Anglers who achieve consistent success fishing estuaries and streams often have an acute sense of awareness in what to look for. The key ingredients to success, just as important as offering up the right bait or lure, is the ability to read the water and spot the telltale signposts of snags or weed beds, perhaps the odd wink of fish, and then understand what is happening. Fish aren't very difficult to find if you know where to start looking. Take a basic scenario like snags, or structures as some people prefer to call them. Structures come in lots of shapes and sizes. They can be sunken trees, boulders, rusting car bodies or shipwrecks. From the fish's point of view, these provide ambush points to pounce on any morsels that happen by. At the same time, the cover offers a haven from larger predators. Fish that make good use of this sort of cover include Murray cod, yellowbelly, trout and bream.

However, before you know what to look for you first have to be able to see and the best way to look into the water is via a good pair of polarising sunglasses. These days it is hard to find a serious angler who doesn't have at least one pair of polarising glasses; some have two or three pairs with different lens shades to suit conditions. An alternative is the photo chromic lenses that adjust to suit varying light conditions.

Offshore anglers use polarising glasses to spot current lines, rocks, reefs, and sandbars. When trolling, polarising glasses take the glint off the water and allow you to see fish making an inquiry on a lure. Even on dull days, the glasses reveal the shadow of a fish, as it will have a slightly darker colour tone to the water.

When fishing streams in valleys, or say estuaries heavily shaded by trees and brush,

Mangroves and overgrown bush along a river or estuary bank provide cover for predators and shelter for small fish.

Old piers are always worth prospecting. Pier pilings are little more than vertical reefs and offer shelter and food to a wide range of marine creatures.

A small pod of tuna busting on baitfish. Tuna move fast and hit hard so it pays to get ahead of the school

bird signs

Birds can often be one of the most effective ways of finding schools of pelagic fish, but they can also be deceiving. A flock of birds sitting close together on the water is not often the sign of fish, but birds flying in circles, and diving into the water is a sure sign that there are fish beneath the surface. Shearwaters or mutton-birds are great hunters and a favourite for anglers looking for schools of pelagic fish. But not all birds are as helpful. Seagulls can look like they are working when in fact all they are doing is haggling between themselves over a few scraps of orange peel.

yellow tinted glasses are good value as these increase light. Where you have constant changes of light and shade, photo-chromic brown or amber lenses also work well. Offshore or in an estuary, the water clarity is different, there are waves to reflect sunlight at constant changing angles, and many anglers prefer grey or the blue mirror style.

Polarising sunglasses will also help you distinguish a confluence of current, where baitfish are likely to be swept out of control. This is a likely feeding area for predator fish. It is a scenario always worth trolling or offering up bait to. The advantage of the glasses is that they will allow you to work that confluence by giving you the ability to see it. Fishing from the rocks, I have been able to observe salmon, sweep, and even snapper (albeit on rare occasions) in a berley trail that was fed into a wash.

But while polarising glasses help you spot fish, you still have to know what it is you are looking for. This comes with experience. Take

flathead: creatures that lie in ambush on the sea floor for an unwary prey to happen past. In an estuary where the bottom is covered in weed, these creatures are the masters of camouflage with their skin pigments adjusting closely to match the colours of the surrounding vegetation. What you have to look for then is a slightly different tone in a long shape; in my experience, these fish will usually appear

darker than their surroundings. I have seen flathead swim into weed and lie there with just their heads poking out. I would never have been able to see these fish if I hadn't watched them swim in first.

In the case of trout or estuary perch, sometimes it is the wink from the fish's flank as it turns after feeding that gives it away. Even in gin clear water trout, particularly the smaller fish are not always easy to spot. Sometimes you see the shadow of the fish on the bottom before you actually spot it. Without polarising glasses though, you won't see anything and will be fishing blind.

Estuaries, whether they are the mangrove-lined or bounded by flood plains and pastures, are the cribs of the marine food chain. This is where zooplankton develops into juvenile fish, and the lucky ones live long enough to learn about survival.

Tidal movement is the telling link in an estuary. The tides carry some fish to their feeding grounds and bring feed to other fish lying in ambush. For the alert angler, the tides are a pointer to where fish are and how well they're likely to be feeding. For example, on a flood tide baitfish and browsers like bream and whiting move with the rising waters. The higher

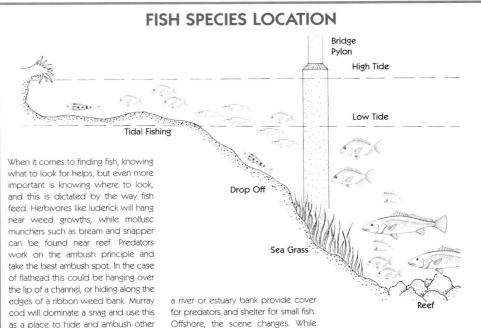

FISH SPECIES LOCATION

When it comes to finding fish, knowing what to look for helps, but even more important is knowing where to look, and this is dictated by the way fish feed. Herbivores like luderick will hang near weed growths, while mollusc munchers such as bream and snapper can be found near reef. Predators work on the ambush principle and take the best ambush spot. In the case of flathead this could be hanging over the lip of a channel, or hiding along the edges of a ribbon weed bank. Murray cod will dominate a snag and use this as a place to hide and ambush other fish, smaller predators may be located in the same snag, but the pecking order is dictated by size and the prime position, generally at the front, will be held by the biggest fish.

In salt water, tidal movement is a controlling factor, particularly in shallow areas like bays and estuaries. Tides bring fish to feeding grounds and carry feed to other fish lying in ambush. Low water sees fish congregate in deeper holes, channels, and choke points. Mangroves and overgrown bush along

a river or estuary bank provide cover for predators and shelter for small fish. Offshore, the scene changes. While bottom fish will still hang on reef structures and drop-offs, pelagic species are often found along current fronts and thermoclines. Even in lakes, windlanes attract fish like rainbow trout.

The pilings of piers are little more than vertical reefs and offer shelter and food to a wide range of marine creatures, and you know that wherever you find small fish, larger species are sure to be around somewhere. In the case of piers it is most likely to be

underneath in the shade or dark or, in the case of pelagic species, they will make a run along the front of the pier to hit unsuspecting baitfish that have moved out.

The up current side of structures such as reefs often fish best for large predators while on reefs being pounded by the sea many fish in the lee feed on food that is being washed over. Another top place is the up-current face of bridge pilings where large predators often take up feeding stations the tide gets the better the pickings tend to be for these fish as mud and sand banks that are exposed on low tide become covered by the incoming water. There is a downside though as high tides fragment fish, making them harder to find.

Low water has the opposite effect and fish tend to congregate in the deeper holes, channels and choke points, which become better defined as an estuary empties. Tide change is like night and day in an estuary. Whatever the location, prime time becomes those last hours of the runout and first hour or so of the flood tide.

When the tide turns to ebb a different complexion comes over the water and there is increasing urgency among baitfish. Instead of departing when there's sufficient water to do so safely, baitfish seem to wait, until it is almost too late, before departing for the sanctuary of deeper water. While there's a safety in numbers aspect about this postpone-ment, a delay that creates a peak hour near the bottom of the tide, for a relative few it is of no further consequence. By then, the predators have moved into ambush positions to prey on the passing baitfish trying to run the toothy gauntlet.

On spring tides, the water mix is more salt than fresh. Pelagic fishes such as tailor, salmon, bonito, trevally, queenfish, mackerel tuna and even longtails take advantage of this and invade estuaries in pursuit of anchovies, krill, and hardiheads. The action can extend through a six-hour cycle, half tide in to half tide out.

It is important to appreciate certain tides will lighten your burden, it's all about determining the tides that work best on your grounds and to organise your fishing times accordingly.

Most anglers agree that neap tides are kinder to their fishing than spring tides. The neap tide variation in the water level, a low high and high low, provides more constant water conditions compared with the volume contained in the high high and low low of a spring tide. In addition, the slower pace of change associated with a neap tide allows the angler time to identify and lock in on patterns. Spring tides on the other hand, simply mix more water with the fish.

ESTABLISH PATTERNS

To be successful you have to establish patterns, and the way to uncover patterns is to duplicate successful presentations rather than waste time. You can have a plan and experiment until you get presentation, lure or fly pattern or bait correct. However, two fish caught quickly doing the same thing is a pattern, and that is when experimenting should cease.

Head offshore and you are in another world entirely. For many anglers, first glance of the ocean gives a picture of a huge, empty expanse. After being on the water for a while you realise that there is more going on than you understand. There are signs in the form of current fronts, birds and bait, structure, water temperature and thermoclines.

Anglers, who go offshore in search of water temperature or blue water, are only filling in part of the overall picture. Predators are attracted to bait, and bait schools hang on structure. If there are known reefs nearby, go there and use your sonar to check out the piscine population in the depths. Bird activity is another sign. Mutton-birds for example can be a good indication of small tuna on or near the surface. If you believe the birds are following fish, then track their course.

In lakes, anglers fishing for rainbow trout

often find wind lanes productive. Off shore, what often appears to be wind lanes may be current fronts, a place where different water temperatures meet and bait schools often hold up along them.

Offshore also allows the angler to use his sense of smell. While off Cairns with Capt. Bobby Jones on Iceman I heard him asking me if I could smell the watermelon. This distinctive odour is a sure sign of a fish kill in north Queensland waters. Further south off New South Wales, I have motored through oil slicks that told a similar tale. We only started to look for the slick after we smelt the fish oil scent that drifted to us on the wind.

Finally, just to confuse the issue, there will always be fish that react differently. Some days you just can't take a trick as the fish act contrary to everything you have come to expect. That's part of the mystique of fishing, if it was too easy I think I'd probably take up golf or something just as dull.

Time and tide are always considerations for thinking saltwater anglers, and the overriding

LUNAR INFLUENCE

Whether you fish when a moon is waxing or waning, the lunar cycle plays an important role on the habits of fish; defining that role is the hard part.

influence on tide is the moon. So, whether you think moon phases or tides, you are still thinking in lunar terms. Even among freshwater anglers, many prefer to fish when the moon is down, or on the dark side.

Next to the sea, the moon is the strongest primeval urge in us and, when you think about it, moon, sea, and tide are one. This is the so-called 'rhythm of life'. If you can play the tune you'll catch more fish, or so the theory goes.

Science has proven that some living organisms respond to the moon's phases. The feeding cycle of oysters is influenced by lunar change, and fiddler crabs change colour in relation to the moon's position. Nor is it just animals: There are also studies that claim a relationship between the moon and odd human behaviour. The word lunacy derives from the Latin word for the moon: luna.

Lunar influence through the tides establishes a minute, but measurable, weight differential. George Darwin (son of Charles Darwin) put forward a theory that in pre-Cambrian times, more than a 1000 million years ago, the tides

A prime hunting scenario for marlin and tuna.

were tremendous and the weight differential would have been correspondingly large. At that time, the lunar force would have been the single most important environmental factor of littoral (region of the shore bounded by its highest normal submergence at high tide and most extreme emergence at low tide) animals.

Displacement and body weight then must certainly have decreased and increased dramatically with the rotation and phases of the moon, particularly if the orbit was at that time elliptic. The effect of a decrease in pressure on fish gonads bloated with eggs or sperm, already almost bursting and awaiting the slight extra pull to discharge, would have been considerable.

The moon has the greatest influence or effect on tides, governing speed and height as well as times of the tides. In contrast, the sun's effect on tides is only 40 per cent of the moon. During the full and new moon periods, both celestial bodies are exerting a gravitational pull in the same direction with the result that the tides with the highest and lowest ranges, spring tides, occur.

Neap tides are those that have the least variation between high and low water and occur when the sun and moon are working against one another, during the first and last quarter phases of the moon. When the moon is full or new, rips will be stronger and evident over longer periods than during the first and last quarters.

We can safely assume then that fish that move around when tidal currents are strong will be more active during the period of spring tides. Most game fish fall into this category.

Swift currents are not easily navigable by some small fish species. Larger predators handle these conditions more easily and feed on the smaller offerings as they are swept by.

This is not a hard and fast rule. Sometimes, in an estuary for example, larger species find that spring tides are not always acceptable. There are influencing factors behind this. Excessive tidal currents can, for example, roil the water, stirring up the sand and mud on the bottom; this reduces visibility and makes hunting harder. Spring tides, while they can be very high, can also be extremely low leaving only channels and gutters navigable for large species. Often it is better to concentrate on neap tidal periods when your quarry will be able to cruise about in relative safety, at least from the elements, at all stages of the tides.

Following a bright, moonlight night fish that feed between sunset and sunrise tend to rest in the depths to digest their nocturnal meals. Anglers who prefer daylight fishing therefore should select the dark of the moon periods for their sport since the fish will not have gorged themselves. Days following overcast nights offer much the same conditions.

Many game species are not nocturnal in their feeding habits so when feed is there the gamefish will also be when dawn breaks. Other fish are notable in that they appear to feed when the mood hits them, day or night. Couta are a species that often fits this category.

In hot weather the angler should concentrate on moonlight fishing because both forage and predator species seek the cooler depths to avoid warm, sun-lit surface waters—this does not apply to pelagic species such as tuna.

I have worked on the 29-day lunar cycle for my fishing with enough success to believe it worth passing on. To fish by the lunar phases means keeping a diary of the events over many years and then establishing a pattern of movements for a species in a particular area. It is important to avoid confusion by not recording irrelevant anecdotes. The main points to note are the moon phase and the month.

Maintain an accurate log and don't lose sight of the objective. If you do this than eventually you will build up a diary that on some species will enable you to reduce your fishing time while increasing your catch rate per outing.

TIDES

The rise and fall of water levels around our coastline is tidal movement, however, tides are divided into categories other than spring and neap. I am grateful to Tim Smith for much of the following information.

SEMI-DIURNAL TIDE is the most common tide type. Mainly the summing of the gravitational effects of the Moon over the Earth influences the tide, and the centrifugal force produced by the rotation of the Earth and Moon. These last a half-day, completing a full cycle about every

Some areas in northern latitudes experience tidal extremes.

12 hours. Most days we usually see two near equal high tides and two near equal low tides. Diurnal Tides last a full day, completing a full cycle about every 24 hours so that each day there is one high tide and one low tide.

SEMI-DIURNAL TIDES with Diurnal Inequality Attributes occur with characteristics based on both semi-diurnal and diurnal tides. For example, two unequal high tides and two unequal low tides, all unequally spaced in time.

MIXED TIDES occur with characteristics loosely based on both semi-diurnal and diurnal tides so that there are two unequal high tides and two unequal low tides, all unequally spaced in time, and occasionally cycling through one high tide and one low tide per day.

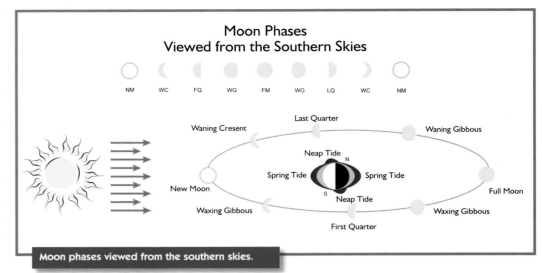

Moon phases viewed from the southern skies.

HOW TIDES WORK

The Moon and Sun generate tides. The Sun generates diurnal tides every 24 hours and semi-diurnal tides every 12 hours. The Moon on the other hand generates its tides at different intervals to the Sun. The diurnal tide generated by the Moon occurs on average every 24 hours 53 minutes and semi-diurnal tides on average every 12 hours 26 minutes. The time spans for the Moon are average figures as these figures change depending on the season.

The effects of gravity fade with distance, so the Moon pulls weaker on the far side of the Earth and harder on the near side. The Moon does not orbit the centre of the Earth. Actually both orbit their aggregated centre of mass called the Barycentre, a point approximately 1600 km below the Earth's surface, on the line between both the Earth's and Moon's centres. As the Earth swings around the Barycentre, centrifugal force is strongest on the side opposite the Moon. Thus, gravity and centrifugal force combine to make the Earth's surface protrude outward in two directions—toward the Moon and away from the Moon (see diagram below).

The Sun also creates semi-diurnal tides, however, although the Sun's mass is much greater than the Moon's, it is much further

away from the Earth. In theory the Sun's tidal influence is approximately half that of the Moon's.

The diagram below also depicts a theoretical model of the Earth with an ocean of equal depth covering a perfect sphere, with the Moon on the Earth's equator. In this model the line of zero net tide generating force goes through the Earth's poles, this is because the Moon is exactly above the Equator (it has a zero declination angle, see diagram above).

Select a point on the Earth. On the Moon side of the Earth, we can see that as the Moon traverses to a point directly overhead (its highest point in the sky) the tides also increase to their highest level. As the Moon begins to drop from the overhead position so

tides

Taking note of the tidal conditions is of great value when fishing. Rigs can be adjusted to suit different current speeds and conditions. For example, it is of little use using a small sinker to fish on the bottom in a strong flowing current.

too do the tides begin to decrease until they reach their lowest point when the Moon sets. On the opposite side of the Earth (directly below; where the Moon don't shine) we can see similar affects. Therefore using our model, over the course of a 24-hour period we will experience two high and two low tides.

The combination of centrifugal force produced by the Earth's rotation and the Moon's daily crossing of the sky generates our tides. Such enormous force is produced by these phenomena that it causes the Earth's surface to bulge up to 16 centimetres.

SPRING AND NEAP TIDES

Generally speaking tides go through a cycle known as the spring/neap cycle approximately every fortnight; the spring tides are larger than average and the neap tides are smaller than average. In general, spring tides coincide with the Full and New phases of the Moon, while the neap tides coincide with the First and Last Quarter phases of the Moon.

Many ports do however, exhibit a tide lead or a lag time of a few hours or perhaps even days, this phenomenon is commonly called the age of the tide. Diagram 3 depicts how the position of the Moon and Sun either combine to reinforce each others gravitational pull on the Earth during the New and Full Moon phases to generate spring tides, or act against each other during the First and Last Quarter phases to generate Neap tides. The inner blue bulge highlights the Sun's tidal influence while the outer bulge highlights the Moon's influence.

EXTERNAL INFLUENCES

Other factors outside astronomical influences and landmasses, such as meteorological changes can significantly affect tidal flow, e.g., storm surges, fluctuating atmospheric

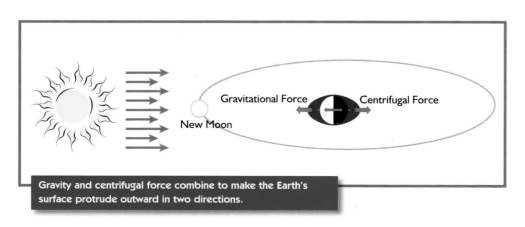

Gravity and centrifugal force combine to make the Earth's surface protrude outward in two directions.

pressure, wind patterns, and poor data analysis techniques. In simple terms, barometric pressure has an inverted effect on the level of the sea. As storms approach the barometric pressure falls and so the level of the sea rises. During high barometric pressure the level of the sea decreases. Movement in sea level height due to barometric pressure may be as much as 300 millimetres. As the change in atmospheric pressure also generates wind, the effects can be quite noticeable—higher than normal tides during a storm, or lower than normal tides during a high-pressure spell. Because of these and other factors, actual tide levels can vary dramatically from predicted values.

WATER TEMPERATURE

Knowing what the preferred water temperature is for your target species may be of critical importance.

If the water is too warm trout, for example, will take up a lie in a deep pool where there is shade. Snapper prefer the water to be at least 16o Celsius, while species like tuna prefer the water to be even warmer.

Trout suffer during warm water flows in excess of 20 degrees, and fish kills in shallow lakes often occur at the height of summer because of the water warming. Native fish such as yellowbelly and Murray cod thrive as the water warms.

Sometimes the water can be too warm, and this has the same effect on fishing as when it is cold.

Science has been entering the field of fishing increasingly in recent years; this is especially relevant for both landbased and offshore sport fishers along the eastern seaboard where there is a heavy reliance on the East Australian Current.

Research by oceanographers has shown that this current is not a continuous stream. Rather it is a series of eddies, about 200 km wide that move in a southerly direction at a speed of about 80 km per month. The currents around these eddies have been measured at a depth of 1500 metres. The total flow around the eddy is about half that of the Gulf Stream—enough to fill Lake Eucumbene, in the Snowy Mountains, in two minutes!

The East Australian Current transports warm water, poor in nutrients and of low salinity, from the Coral Sea southwards into the Tasman Sea. Coral Sea derived water has been found as far south as the eastern end of Bass Strait. A feature of this current is the presence of temperature fronts in its surface waters in the latitudes between Sydney and Eden. Water poor in nutrients occurs on the warm side of the fronts. For some years the Division of Fisheries and Oceanography has been issuing maps of these fronts to tuna fishers as southern bluefin tuna tend to congregate on them.

fact box

TEMPERATURE

Here is a list of some of the most popular sportfish, and their preferred temperature range.

FISH	TEMP (°C)
FRESHWATER	
Australian Bass	15 – 25
Chinook Salmon	10 – 18
Macquarie Perch	10 – 17
Murray Cod	16 – 25
Saratoga	25 – 31
Silver Perch	14 – 26
Trout	
– Brown	13 – 20
– Rainbow	10 – 18
Yellowbelly	21 – 24
SALTWATER	
Atlantic Salmon	10 – 18
Barramundi	24 – 29
Black marlin	19 – 26
Bonito	16 – 24
Cobia	19 – 29
Dolphinfish	24 – 30
Frigate mackerel	19 – 24
Sharks	
– Black whaler	11 – 31
– Bronze whaler	11 – 31
– Tiger	17 – 31
– Mako	15 – 31
– Hammerhead	15 – 31
– Blue	15 – 26
– Thresher	15 – 24
Snapper	12 – 16
Spanish mackerel	23 – 30
Tuna	
– Big-eye	15 – 29
– Longtail	18 – 21
– Mackerel	15 – 29
– Southern bluefin	11 – 25
– Striped tuna	15 – 27
– Yellowfin	15 – 29
Wahoo	23 – 30
Yellowtail kingfish	13 – 25

BAROMETER

Many anglers believe fish are affected by the rise and fall in barometric pressure. I'm not so sure. When it comes to nailing down the tangibles, proof can be difficult to define.

Barometric pressure is something we all experience everyday of our lives. At sea level the air pressure around is 32 pounds to the square inch, which is rated as one atmosphere. Descend five metres beneath the surface and you experience two atmospheres of pressure, or 64 pounds per square inch. At ten metres, the pressure is three atmospheres and so on.

The big question is whether or not a creature that lives in an environment with a higher atmospheric pressure can feel the weather change and, more importantly, whether or not it reacts to this. Fish have all five senses that we have—sight, sound, taste, touch and smell—although these are developed in a slightly different manner more suited to their environment.

Fish have another sixth sense, which is unique to them and is operated by a system of nerve organs located in a canal beneath the skin. It can be seen quite clearly along the flank of the fish and is called the lateral line. No one fully understands all the functions of the lateral line. What is known is that its basic function is connected with monitoring movements and water currents. It is because of the lateral line that fish are able to recognise when other fish are swimming near to them and it is used to locate obstacles—all well before the fish can actually see what the lateral line has sensed. And it is through the lateral line that fish are able to sense changes in pressure.

In fresh water the barometer is a tangible pointer to a good day's fishing in lakes and impoundments. When the air pressure is rising, so too are the fish. Trout fishers have long believed that barometric fluctuations mirror their success or otherwise.

The barometric equation is not as tangible in salt water. The only positive example I have been given of a marine creature being affected by the barometer occurs in the Caribbean and involves the Caribbean spiny lobster. This animal lives on shallow reefs but marine biologists say it can detect changes in atmosphere, even though it doesn't have a swim bladder, lateral line, or obvious sensory organ to detect change with. When the barometric pressure changes indicating the onset of the winter weather pattern the lobsters gather together in single file and march on down off the reef and into the deep water.

In my experience, there have been excellent days fishing when the barometer was rising. Other days have been equally as good as the pressure was falling. The only solid evidence I have based on experience has been that the day before a weather change the fish often come on the bite. And the few hours before a change arrives can offer up some memorable fishing.

UNDERSTANDING THE FORECAST

Ever been out fishing and had the wind and sea get up when you didn't expect it to happen? I know I have. It is better to be forewarned than to have a squall thrust upon you unexpectedly.

I have heard many anglers blame this sort of even on the weather bureau. But sometimes the warnings are there; it's more a case of the people not understanding what they are being told. For example, the bureau puts out a forecast for moderate to fresh winds. I know that on the bay that this means some discomfort on the water. But how many other anglers realise what the bureau's forecasts, in terms of wind speeds and sea conditions, really mean?

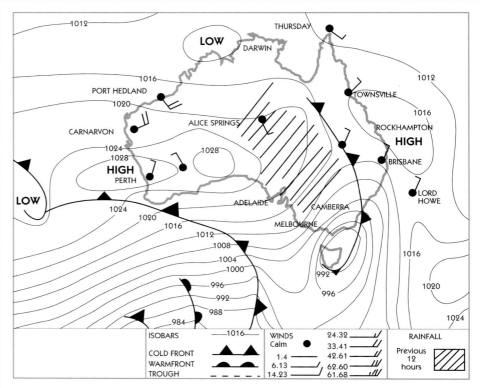

ISOBARS	———1016	WINDS Calm	●	24.32	⟋⟋	RAINFALL
COLD FRONT	▲▲▲		1.4	33.41	⟋⟋	Previous 12 hours
WARMFRONT	●●●		6.13	42.61	⟋⟋	
TROUGH	– – –		14.23	62.60 61.68	⟋⟋⟋	

Interpreting weather maps.

Interpreting a weather map is not a difficult procedure and the best way to learn about reading these maps is to go to the weather bureau web site at www.bom.gov.au, and follow the links. Another excellent reference to the weather is The Users Guide to the Australian Coast by Greg Laughlin, published by Reed books. The following is a rough guide only, much of the information gleaned from the Bureau of Meteorology.

The most obvious features of weather maps published in newspapers or seen on television are the patterns of high and low pressure, and the barbed lines identifying cold fronts. In the southern hemisphere, the earth's rotation causes air to flow clockwise around low-pressure systems and anticlockwise around high-pressure systems. So, during a high pressure the wind direction will most likely have a north or easterly influence.

Wind strength is inversely proportional to the distance between isobars — the closer the lines, the stronger the winds. However, this rule doesn't apply in the tropics where the effect of the earth's rotation is weak. For this reason, tropical meteorologists usually replace isobars with streamline arrows that indicate wind and direction without directly relating to the pressure gradient.

Shaded areas on weather maps show where there has been rain in the previous 24 hours, and wind direction is shown with arrows that have a series of barbs on their tails to indicate speed.

Being caught at sea in a squall can be an unpleasant experience. When the sea turns white and there is a rainbow across your rods ypou know it is wet!

fact box

WIND SPEED

When most people hear the weather forecast and it is for moderate to fresh winds, not too many would know how fast the wind speed will be. The Beaufort Wind Scale is the standard measure and gives you some idea of what conditions will be like on the water.

	Units in km/h	Units in knots	Description on Land.	Description at Sea
CALM	0	0	Smoke rises vertically.	Sea like a mirror.
LIGHT WINDS	19 km/h or less	10 knots or less	Wind felt on face; leaves rustle; ordinary vanes moved by wind.	Small wavelets, ripples formed but do not break: A glassy appearance maintained.
MODERATE WINDS	20–29 km/h	11–16 knots	Raises dust and loose paper; small branches are moved.	Small waves - becoming longer; fairly frequent white horses.
FRESH WINDS	30–39 km/h	17–21 knots	Small trees in leaf begin to sway; crested waveless form on inland water.	Moderate waves, taking a more pronounced long form; many white horses are formed—a chance of some spray.
STRONG WINDS	40–50 km/h	22–27 knots	Large branches in motion; whistling heard in telephone wires; umbrellas used with difficulty.	Large waves begin to form; the white foam crests are more extensive with probably some spray.
	51–62 km/h	28–33 knots	Whole trees in motion; inconvenience felt when walking against wind.	Sea heaps up and white foam from breaking waves begins to be blown in streaks along direction of wind.
GALE	63–75 km/h	34–40 knots	Twigs break off trees; progress generally impeded.	Moderately high waves of greater length; edges of crests begin to break into spindrift; foam is blown in well-marked streaks along the direction of the wind.
	76–87 km/h	41–47 knots	Slight structural damage occurs—roofing dislodged; larger branches break off.	High waves; dense streaks of foam; crests of waves begin to topple, tumble and roll over; spray may affect visibility.
STORM	88–102 km/h	48–55 knots	Seldom experienced inland; trees uprooted; considerable structural damage.	Very high waves with long overhanging crests; the resulting foam in great patches is blown in dense white streaks; the surface of the sea takes on a white appearance; the tumbling of the sea becomes heavy with visibility affected.
	103 km/h or more	56 knots plus	Very rarely experienced—widespread damage.	Exceptionally high waves; small and medium sized ships occasionally lost from view behind waves; the sea is completely covered with long white patches of foam; the edges of wave crests are blown into froth.

If you take the forecast off the late news details are often scarce. As likely as not, the forecast will be about capital cities around the country. Even the normal evening news can be ordinary when it comes to giving any depth in weather and sea conditions predicted.

The wind and sea definitions can be a little confusing, or intimidating, when the weatherman comes on the television and says something like 'moderate winds' or 'moderate seas', or maybe there will be a 'storm'. At least the terminology will be correct, but what does it really mean?

Here's a run down on what it all means, first there is wind descriptions: Calm is no wind, light winds are up to 19 km/h, and moderate winds are from 20 to 29 km/h. It's when you get into fresh winds that the fun starts; this is a 30 to 39 km/h blow. Strong winds range from 40 to 62 km/h, gale force is from 63 to 87 km/h and storm 88 km/h and more.

The 'storm warning' is severe but for many anglers looking at being on the water even fresh winds can cause difficulties, although much depends on whether or not you are fishing in the lee.

Seas range from calm, which is obvious, to phenomenal and these are rated as 'over 14 metres, precipitous and only experienced in cyclone'. In between these two extremes are smooth and slight, with waves ranging from 0.1 to 0.5 metres. Slight seas are to 1.25 m and waves rock small boats; moderate seas are in the 1.25 to 2.5 m ranges with the sea becoming furrowed. A rough sea is from 2.5 to 4 m and deeply furrowed, very rough is 4 – 6 m with the 'seas much disturbed with rollers having steep fronts'.

And, like the television marketing guy says, there is more. High seas range from 6 – 9 m and then there is very high, this comes with 9 – 14 m waves and 'towering seas'. It's all a matter of knowing your limits. What is uncomfortable in a six-metre boat can be downright dangerous in a three-metre tinnie. So, keep this in mind when making any assessment on whether or not to go out. My advice is to err on the side of caution.

PART 2
Tackle

CHAPTER 2

RODS AND REELS

The choice of rod and reel depends on where you are fishing, the method, and the species. There is no universal outfit to suit all needs. Like food though, different anglers prefer different tackle.

My preference has always been for overhead reels wherever practical, yet some anglers have only threadline reels in the kit. Among fly fishers, particularly saltwater aficionados, the direct drive reel is generally preferred to the anti-reverse models, and yet there are those who prefer the latter type.

The term "balanced outfit" is bandied about a fair bit. It's a sort of vague reference to the combination rod and reel that works. At least that's how I read most peoples' understanding of the term. If your in a tackle store and ask the salespeople to define what constitutes a balanced outfit you are likely to come out with some surprising answers.

For what it's worth, my definition of a balanced outfit is one that offers firepower without causing fatigue. It is a rod and reel that sits comfortably with the angler, casts the lure or bait easily, and has enough grunt to load up on a fish without causing an extreme physical burden to the angler. Unbalanced outfits feel awkward, maybe even heavy. And what constitutes a balanced outfit to the casual angler is often a long way short of what a skilled, serious angler will accept.

RODS

Rod technology, particularly the use of space-age graphite materials has brought completely new actions into rods built on old mandrels. When the Shakespeare rod company released its Ugly Stiks a couple of decades ago, they were a sensation. The solid glass tip in a tubular blank was a brilliant innovation. I still have my 1100B Ugly Stik, and I still use it. Those rods were almost indestructible: how much further could rod technology go?

Well companies like Sage and G.Loomis made a quantum leap when they started producing state-of-the-art fly rods so good that some of the world's best fly casters doubted their own abilities to get the most out of the rods. Other rod manufacturers, not just

Large centrepin reels are popular with anglers bottom bouncing offshore reefs.

fly rod makers but surf, spin and baitcast, have adopted that technology.

It's hard to tell where it will all end. I grew up with Rangoon cane and solid fibreglass rods, shoddy equipment by today's standards. Even the cheap combo outfits sold by the thousands in supermarkets are offering reasonable quality at a price kids with paper runs can afford easily.

The technological advancements have created two distinct markets for fishing rods. There is the traditional market catering for anglers who want serviceable rods that will cover their needs. The other market is for the sportfishing-orientated angler wanting to fish lighter, try different methods, and make fishing more challenging.

Snapper rods are an example of the former. The market dictates that a snapper rod should be about 2.2 metres long, and have a solid tip. These rod works well for casting whole fish with small amounts of lead, and the design features are such that they have plenty of low down power. The shock absorber characteristics of a solid tip reduces the chances of busting a big red off near the boat, and does help when casting a soft, unweighted bait such as a whole pilchard.

It's a similar scenario when you look at surf, bream, whiting, or trout anglers. There are traditional standards preferred by the bulk of the market, and there is no denying the rods work. However, given an education on fishing rods and limitless funds to buy what they want many would change over to higher modulus graphite or graphite composite rods, which are my preference when the budget can afford it.

Graphite construction rods are more expensive and fragile than tubular fibreglass rods, but graphite rods are lighter, easier to cast and offer more overall control. Graphite construction rods have a sharper recovery factor than normal fibreglass rods. And don't be fooled into thinking this is simply an optimum light tackle configuration. The performance characteristics transcend all methods, working just as well on light lures or unweighted baits as when heavier lures or rigs are employed.

Back in the 1970s, jigging was in vogue and short, heavy walled, fast taper rod were the popular choice to handle the heavy lures (up to 200 grams) that were needed to get down deep fast. The Japanese have taken over the development of cutting edge jig sticks and companies like Daiwa with their Saltiga rods are leading the field. Today's angler can buy a graphite rod barely thicker than a pencil, weighing half as much as the old traditional jig sticks but with three or four times (up to 30 kg) the pulling power.

Rod fittings are just as important, and

Australia's favourite tropical sportfish, the barramundi, will test tackle to the limit.

just as diverse in terms of quality, as are rod blanks. Cheap guides are a potential disaster. Inserts pop or lack the hardness to handle gelspun lines. Speed and power, and the resulting friction, are major hurdles that have to be overcome if you are working high-speed pelagics such as tuna, mackerel, marlin and sailfish. Speedsters can literally burn anglers, or more to the point, their lines away. The problem is twofold: abrasion and heat dissipation. Guides that groove or over-heat (or both) when the going gets tough are a recipe for disaster.

Another aspect of rod building, particularly light spin, baitcast and fly rods, is that single

foot guides are less of a damper on the recovery power of a rod than are double-footed guides. Single foot guides have their limitations. You can use them on 12 – 15 weight fly rods, but they are not as effective for heavy spin or baitcast tackle above 4 kilograms.

Silicon carbide was the high tech guide material of the 1980s. And these guides are still top of the line in value today. Nevertheless, there have been other developments. The Gold Cermet guides made by Japanese rod component manufacturer Fuji is a good example. These low friction, ceramic rings found a ready market among the swoffing [saltwater fly fishing] fraternity particularly anglers who are looking for performance. Fuji claims that Gold Cermets are lighter and harder than contemporary silicon carbide varieties, dissipate heat better, are smoother, and never corrode.

The bottom line is that the cermets are expensive. But supporters say the extra dollars are well spent as the guides hold their value and apart from breaking, they can't wear out and the titanium frames won't corrode.

Reel seats are in the same boat and you get what you pay for. The better reel seats are manufactured from a graphite material, but there are always alternatives. Victorian fly reel maker Terry Hayden started to manufacture titanium reel seats. Again, they are expensive but they will certainly outlast the life of the fishing rod.

REELS

Technology has given anglers lighter, stronger rods and thinner lines. Many anglers have failed to adapt or perhaps realise how to take advantage of the changes to improve their fishing.

What the new rods and lines have done is give anglers the ability to downsize if they want to. Take overhead reels. You can spool up a medium sized baitcaster like a Penn International 955 or the Daiwa Millionaire CV-Z253A with about 300 metres of 30-pound gelspun. This is more than enough line for most light tackle sportfish including snapper, small kings, striped tuna, and mackerel. Despite this, most snapper anglers will continue to use larger reels, the Shimano Calcutta 400 or the ABU 7000 for example.

It's the same with threadline reels, technology has given anglers the opportunity to downsize in reels and still catch the same fish. As you would expect, there are situations where downsizing isn't practicable. Sometimes you need the large spool diameter for a high retrieve when spinning, or perhaps the cranking power available with a larger reel due to variables like big sinkers in deep water. It is a matter of selecting the reel to suit the situation.

Reel development has also seen the introduction of anti-reverse needle rollers, magnetic backlash controls, free spooling for threadlines and independently floating spool spindles. By far the best innovation has been the waterproof drag housing and trend towards heat dissipation materials for washers. Penn uses a patented HT100 material for its drag systems, Teflon is popular and so is cork impregnated Teflon.

Reel quality often comes down to little things, like stainless steel ball bearings and metal inserts in graphite frames for metal thread screws. There has been a trend at the top of the market to manufacture reel housings from marine grade aluminium bar stock and, instead of screws, the side plates are threaded onto the housing. Threadline reels even come with bail arm roller bearings and sealed gearbox compartments.

And when it comes to buying a reel, check out the specifications closely. Put the reel on the rod you intend using to see that it is suitable, and when you decide on the model ask about the warranty. You wouldn't spend big bucks on a stereo system without getting a warranty so why not do the same with a reel? Remember, there are still many cheap end reels being sold at top end prices. If you feel the need to spend big bucks, then go with the top brands.

CHOOSING A LINE

Buying a fishing line is no longer a simple procedure. Gone are the days when you went to a tackle store and the only decisions you made were about breaking strain and colour.

Times have changed. These days fishing lines come in a wider range of materials. When you walk into a shop and ask for a line the chances are you that probably won't know what it is you are getting. The days of buying monofilament, regardless of label, and receiving the same product are over. There is a lot more to line differences these days than colour. Nylon fishing lines come under several different classifications: homopolymers, co-polymers, and tri-polymers, gelspun braids and even fusions.

A homopolymer line is made of one type of nylon: There aren't many homopolymer lines on the market and most are at the cheaper end. As a rule of thumb, cheap, bargain–basement lines made in Asia are, more often than not, a homopolymer.

Co-polymers and tri-polymers are structured from more than one nylon and most quality

leaders

When fishing with braids a leader is required to give some stretch and absorption factor to counteract the minimal 3 per cent stretch of braid. But remember, shorter leaders mean crisper lure actions and more strikes.

lines available in tackle shops are co-polymers. These range from affordable lines for the weekend angler to expensive, specialised lines for serious sport fishers. Products in this category include most pre-test lines and those sold as being tough, like Penn 10X or designed for specific purposes, like Lureline.

For the past four or five years, it is the super braids or gelspun lines that have made the most impact, establishing niche markets due to distinctive advantages they deliver in many fishing situations.

Super braids are made from Dyneema or Spectra, the two brand names for the high modulus, gelspun polyethylene material used. Multiple fibres of the polyethylene material are braided together to produce a line with a much smaller diameter than monofilament of the same braking strain. And, where monofilament lines have an average stretch factor of about 25 per cent braids stretch less than 5 per cent.

The differences between various super braids come about because the line manufacturers braid the fibres to their own specifications.

The value of braid lines is in their sensitivity and fine diameter. Due to their lack of stretch, you can detect a subtle strike in deep water or heavy crosscurrents more easily than you will with monofilament line. And because they are thinner in diameter than monofilament of the same breaking strain there is less water drag. This means you can use lighter sinkers when fishing strong currents, and it preserves the action of lures and allows trolled lures to swim deeper.

The stronger breaking strain for a finer diameter can also be an asset. For example, a 5 kg mono line has about the same diameter as a 24 kg super braid, which means you can get more line of the same breaking strain on your reel. If you were game fishing with 24 kg tackle and your reel held 750 m of mono, you would get almost 3000 m of braid on the same spool.

There are also disadvantages. The lack of stretch in a braid that gives the bite sensitivity also means it is less forgiving than mono so you may experience more break-offs or pulled hooks when you are not used to using this material. To counter this it is necessary use a lighter drag setting on your reel. Using monofilament leaders and rods with softer tips also helps.

Braid lines need to be wound on firmly to avoid the line spinning on the spool. Some anglers put a bed of monofilament on the bottom of the spool before winding the braid on.

Several of my friends now fish exclusively with braid lines. On whiting, they claim a hook-up rate up to five times better than using monofilament. The value with snapper is the ability to use lighter sinkers in fast water. Most braid devotees employ terminal monofilament rigs, saying that the finer diameter of braid means less abrasion resistance. A braid line of the same diameter as a monofilament has been shown to be more abrasion resistant than monofilament. But when you do the comparison on breaking strain then monofilament, due to its larger diameter, wins easily.

Knots are also an issue. Super braids have resulted in a need for a range of new knots. Australia's leading authority on knots and rigging, Victorian angler Geoff Wilson, has even put out a book on this subject. *Geoff Wilson's Guide to Rigging Braid, Dacron and Gelspun Lines* is an essential tool in the kit of any angler deciding to use one of the new lines.

Other fishing line materials include: nylon co-filament, polyethylene gelspun with monofilament core, braided dacron, braided nylon, braided gelspun with monofilament core, twisted linen and twisted cotton.

---

fact box

LINE OPTIONS
The following are suggested line options based on scenario.

SPECIES	SCENARIO	METHOD	LINE
Whiting/flathead	Beach/bay	Bait	Mono 3–5 kg
	Deep water/current	Bait	Braid 10 kg
Snapper	Beach/bay	Bait	Mono 8 kg
	Deep water/current	Bait	Braid 15 kg
Mulloway	Estuary/surf	Bait	Braid 15 kg
			Mono 10 kg
Australian Bass	River	Bait	Mono 3 kg
Estuary perch		Spin/troll	Braid 10 kg
Salmon/tailor	Beach/bay	Bait	Mono 3–5 kg
		Spin/troll	Braid 10 kg
Murray cod	Lakes/rivers	Trolling	Braid 10–15 kg
Yellowbelly		Spinning	Braid 10 kg
		Bait	Mono 8–10 kg
Trout	Lakes	Trolling	Braid 5 kg
		Bait	Mono 3 kg
	Rivers	Bait	Mono 3 kg
	Lakes/rivers	Spin	Mono 2–3 kg
Barramundi	Beach/estuary	Troll	Braid 10 kg
		Spin	Braid 10 kg
		Bait	Mono/Braid 8–10 kg
Mangrove jack	Estuary	Spin	Braid 10 kg
		Bait	Mono 8 kg
	Offshore reefs	Bait	Braid 15 kg
Small tuna	Offshore/Landbased Game	Trolling	Mono 5 – 10 kg
		Spin	
		Bait	
Big tuna	Offshore	Trolling	Mono 10–15 kg
		Cubing	Braid 15 kg
	Landbased Game	Live bait	Mono 15 kg
		Spinning	Mono 10 kg
Marlin	Landbased Game	Live bait	Mono 15–24 kg
			Braid 24 kg
	Offshore	Trolling	Mono/braid 15–6 kg
Sharks	Offshore	Bait	Braid/Mono 15–24 kg
	Landbased Game	Bait	Braid/Mono 15–24 kg

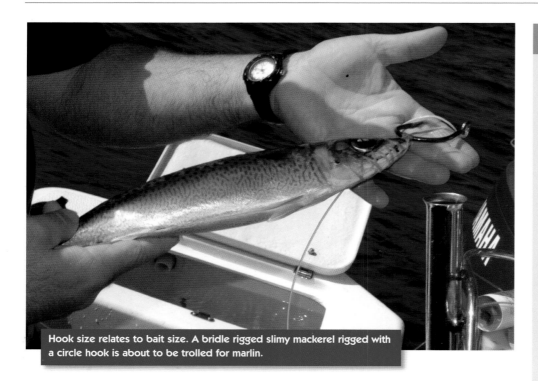

Hook size relates to bait size. A bridle rigged slimy mackerel rigged with a circle hook is about to be trolled for marlin.

coloured hooks

Don't fall into the coloured hook trap. Red, blue, and so-called invisible hooks are, in my humble opinion, a selling gimmick based on a shallow idea that had its roots back in the 1980s. Red hooks were purported to match the bloodied colour of a fish fillet and, so the claim went, when the bait was in the water the hook would blend in with the flesh. That lasts for all of about the five seconds it takes for the blood to leach out and the flesh turn pale.

I use coloured hooks, but not for any reasoning relating to their so-called invisibility. It just happens that my favourite hooks are chemically sharpened and come in either red or black. Mind you, users who believe in the magical disappearing powers of coloured hooks, and probably look for fairies under toadstools as well, gain a psychological edge. As for the fish, they're sub-reptilian; reasoning and logic are beyond their capabilities. It's a scenario not too far removed from political practice where the less scrupulous members, upon seeing a head sticking out, kick first and ask questions later. No time to waste when it comes to political point scoring, or getting in first for a feed for that matter.

UNDERSTANDING HOOKS

The business end of fishing is the pointy end, and using the correct hook will have a bearing on hook-up rates.

Deciding on a hook pattern is a lot more difficult than many people think. When you first start out fishing, you use a couple of different patterns, like Suicides or Kirbys. But as your fishing develops and you become more aware of improve techniques and presentations you start to look more closely at what is available. And the range of hooks that are on the market can be mind blowing.

In any single pattern, there are generally at least 20 sizes of hooks and even the way these hooks are sized can be a problem as different manufacturers have different sizes for the same numbers. For example, a 6/0 Big Red Mustad hook is slightly smaller than say a Gamakatsu Octopus pattern 6/0.

If you went for a basic run of hooks then Kirbys with Baitholder barbs are popular for bait fishing, Suicides for live baiting and bigger fish such as snapper or mulloway where the hook is needed to twist and turn slightly to penetrate. Long shanked, straight O'Shaughnessy hooks suit most trolling needs and saltwater fly enthusiasts look kindly on Gamakatsu Trey Coombs hooks. The last named are gaining popularity among keen snapper anglers.

In a feature for Saltwater Sportfishing magazine, Mustad consultant Dave Harrigan said the fishing tackle industry has accumulated tens of thousands of hook patterns around the world. 'At one stage Mustad had about 100,000 patterns on its books before it decided to rationalise,' he says.

SNAPPER HOOKS

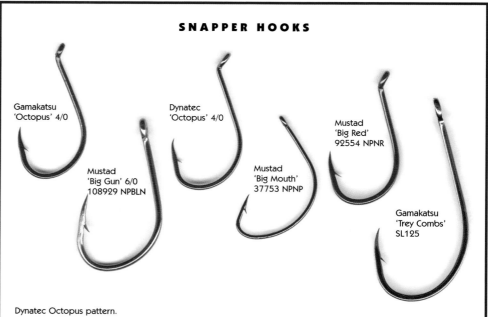

Gamakatsu 'Octopus' 4/0

Dynatec 'Octopus' 4/0

Mustad 'Big Red' 92554 NPNR

Mustad 'Big Gun' 6/0 108929 NPBLN

Mustad 'Big Mouth' 37753 NPNP

Gamakatsu 'Trey Combs' SL125

Dynatec Octopus pattern.
Gamakatsu Octopus pattern.
Gamakatsu SL 12S (Trey Combs) similar to 7766 Mustad finer wire chemically sharpened.
Mustad Big Red, chemically sharpened version of 92554 Suicide.
Mustad Big Mouth (4/0 is ideal) chemically sharpened. Excellent with large cube baits.
Mustad Tuna Circle.

The Big Mouth, Tuna Circle and Trey Coombs hooks do not have a bent back eye and are best rigged as single hooks.

When the fish are a reasonable size, say from about 4 kg up, use two 4/0 hooks on the same leader with one sliding to act as a keeper to retain the bait's shape. For smaller fish use a single hook.

SALTWATER CHEMICALLY SHARPENED HOOKS

MANUFACTURER: MUSTAD

MODEL	STYLE	SIZE RANGE	POINT STYLE
1. Big Red (92554NPNR)	Heavy Beak	8/0–6	Needle Suicide Point
2. Hoodlum (10827NPBLN)	Heavy Line Bait	11/0–1/0	Needle Straight Point
3. Bloodworm (90234NPNR)	Extra Long Shank Beak	3/0–6	Needle Point
4. Needle Sneck (3331NPG)	Square Bend	2/0–12	Needle Point
5. Big Gun (10829NPBLN)	Heavy Saltwater	12/0–6	Kirbed Needle Point
6. Big Mouth (37753NPNP)	Wide Gap	7/0–6	Needle Point
7. Red Baitholder (92668NPNR)	Baitholder	4/0–1/0	Needle Point
8. Aberdeen (3261NPBLN)	Light Gauge	1/0–8	Needle Bend Point
9. Needle Tarpon (7766NPNR)	Heavy Straight	7/0–6	Turned-in Needle
10. Needle Tarpon (77662NPBL)	Open Eye Gang	1–6	Needle Point
11. Demon Fine Wire (39952NPBL)	Circle Style	11/0–2/0	Kirbed Point
12. Saltwater Fly (34039NPSS)	Extra Long Stainless	4/0–1/0	Needle Point
13. Saltwater Fly (34005KESS)	Stainless	2/0–1	Knife Edge

MANUFACTURER: DAITCHI

MODEL	STYLE	SIZE RANGE	POINT STYLE
1. 2546 Stainless	Straight Eye O'Shaughnessy	6/0–6	Needle Point
2. 3000 Red	2x Short Shank Beak	10/0–4	Turned-in Needle Point
3. 3111 Black	2x Short Shank Beak	10/0–4	Turned-in Needle Point
4. 2451 Black	Straight Eye O'Shaughnessy	4/0–8	Needle Point
5. 7000 Stainless Steel	Extra Heavy Duty Game	10/0–6	Knife Edge
6. 1720 Red	4x Long Shank	2–12	Needle Point
7. 1750 Bronze	4x Long Shank	2–12	Needle Point
8. 2174 Green	Short Shank Weed/Shrimp	2–12	Needle Point

MANUFACTURER: YOUVELLA

MODEL	STYLE	SIZE RANGE	POINT STYLE
1. Octopus (121462XB)	2x Beak	10/0–1/0	Turned-in Needle Point
2. Baitholder (11716B)	Baitholder	4/0–4	Turned-in Needle Point
3. Kirby (424142XB)	2x Strong Kendall Kirby	10/0–1/0	Needle Point
4. Carlisle (11605B)	4x Long Shank	2/0–12	Needle Point

MANUFACTURER: TRU-TURN

MODEL	STYLE	SIZE RANGE	POINT STYLE
1. Bait Holder	2x Long Shank	1/0–6	Spear Point
2. XX Strong	2x Strong	4/0–2/0	Spear Point
3. Long Shank	Forged	4–10	Spear Point

MANUFACTURER: SAIKO

MODEL	STYLE	SIZE RANGE	POINT STYLE
1. Special Sea Hook	Long Shank	6/0–4	Needle Point
2. Extra Strength	Micro Barb, Heavy Wire	8/0–3/0	Needle Point

MANUFACTURER: VMC

MODEL	STYLE	SIZE RANGE	POINT STYLE
1. Octopus (7299SS)	Stainless Octopus		Cone Cut Point
2. O'Shaughnessy (7255SS)	Stainless O'Shaughnessy		Needle Point
3. Baitholder (7292RO)	Baitholder		Cone Cut Point
4. Octopus (7299RD)	Octopus		Cone Cut Point

MANUFACTURER: MCLAUGHLIN'S

MODEL	STYLE	SIZE RANGE	POINT STYLE
1. Snapper	Heavy Duty Beak	4/0	Turned-in Needle Point
2. Mulloway	Heavy Duty Beak	6/0	Turned-in Needle Point
3. Whiting	4x Long Shank	6	Needle Point
4. Blackfish	Extra Short 200 Shank Bend	8	Needle Point
5. Gar/Yakka	4x Long Shank	12	Needle Point

MANUFACTURER: GAMAKATSU

MODEL	STYLE	SIZE RANGE	POINT STYLE
1. Octopus	Octopus	10/0–12	Needle Point
2. Octopus Circle	Circle	8/0–2/0	Turned-in Needle Point
3. Baitkeeper	Double sliced long shank	4/0–8	Needle Point
4. Baitholder	Double sliced long shank	4/0–14	Needle Point
5. Oceania Long Shank	2x Long Shank	2/0–12	Needle Point
6. Worm Hook	Fine Gauge Long Shank	1–6	Needle Point
7. O'Shaughnessy	Heavy Duty Straight	10/0–8	Needle Point
8. SL 12S Big Game	Fine Gauge Tinned	10/0–4/0	Needle Point
9. Big Bait	Extra Strong Offset	10/0–1/0	Needle Point
10. Big Bait Circle	Circle	8/0–2/0	Turned-in Needle Point
11. Shiner	Super Bend Circle	1–6	Turned-in Needle Point

SALTWATER CHEMICALLY SHARPENED HOOKS (continued)

MANUFACTURER: **MARUTO**

MODEL	STYLE	SIZE RANGE	POINT STYLE
1. MS-4310	Beak	10/0–12	Needle Point
2. 3300	Long Shank Carlisle	6/0–6	Needle Point
3. DS-4310	Baitholder	10/0–10	Needle Point

MANUFACTURER: **EAGLE CLAW**

MODEL	STYLE	SIZE RANGE	POINT STYLE
1. LT6088R	Long Shank Double Barb	2–8	Needle Point
2. LT226RD	Suicide Double Barb	9/0–6	Needle Point
3. LT141	Kahle Wide Gap	7/0–8	Needle Point
4. L318N	Live Bait Straight	9/0–6/0	Needle Point
5. L7042	Wide Bend	2/0–8	Turned-in Needle Point
6. L741	Kahle Wide Gap	5/0–10	Needle Point
7. L054SS	O'Shaughnessy Stainless	4/0–1/0	Needle Point
8. L057	Straight	5/0–6	Needle Point

MANUFACTURER: **DYNATEC**

MODEL	STYLE	SIZE RANGE	POINT STYLE
1. Long Shank	2x Long Shank	4/0–12	Needle Point
2. Suicide	Offset Point	8/0–8	Turned-in Needle Point
3. Wide Gap	Super Bend Circle	4/0–6	Turned-in Needle Point
4. Baitkeep	Double Slice Offset	6/0–10	Turned-in Needle Point
5. O'Shaughnessy	Straight	5/0–6	Needle Point

MANUFACTURER: **ALPHA**

MODEL	STYLE	SIZE RANGE	POINT STYLE
1. Bait Holder	Forged Shank	2/0–10	Turned-in Needle Point
2. Long Shank	4x Long Shank	2/0–12	Needle Point
3. Suicide	Forged Shank	6/0–8	Needle Point

MANUFACTURER: **GLOBAL**

MODEL	STYLE	SIZE RANGE	POINT STYLE
1. 1.44007S	O'Shaughnessy	6/0–8	Needle Point

MANUFACTURER: **PARTRIDGE**

MODEL	STYLE	SIZE RANGE	POINT STYLE
1. Sea Prince (C552)	Stainless O'Shaughnessy	6/0–10	Turned-out Needle Point

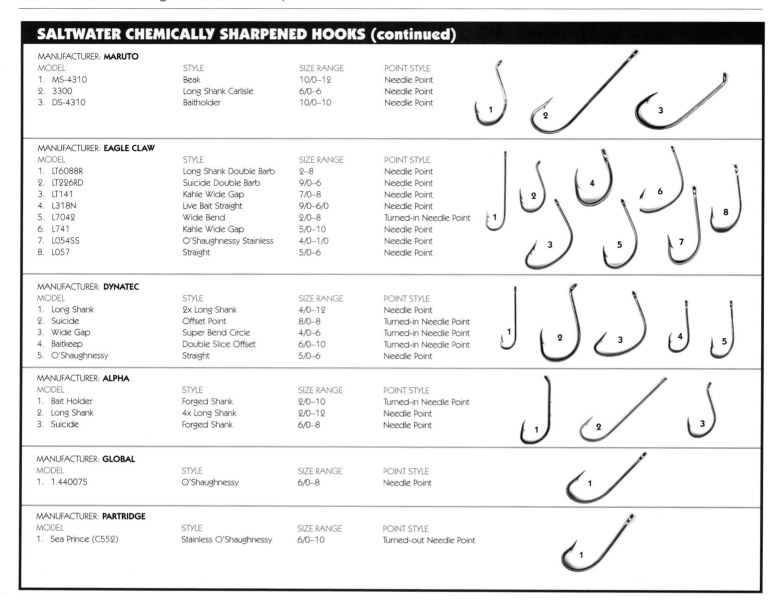

Chemically sharpened hooks are able to maintain their keen point despite hours in the water. For example, I have used Gamakatsu Octopus hooks for days on end while live baiting off the rocks without the need to hone the point. Stainless steel hooks also maintain their points longer in the salt. Normal tinned hooks though require constant attention, as the point will become dulled and blunt after a couple of hours in the water.

There's nothing new about chemical sharpening, Mustad first used it in 1953, but better quality, more consistent materials, plus more finite control in the heat treatment process have enabled the process to make a comeback. This is particularly so on needlepoint hooks, which had a reputation for brittleness.

Dave says that contrary to what some anglers might think, chemicals do not create the point on chemically sharpened hooks. Rather, a brew of corrosive chemicals is applied to hooks to get rid of irregularities and produce a nice, smooth needlepoint that maximises penetrating power. It is more like polishing than sharpening, although by improving the penetration power of the point it can accurately be said to sharpen the hook.

'You can't form a sharp point by using corrosive chemicals to attempt to do what a grinding apparatus would otherwise do,' he explains. 'This would actually produce an extremely blunt point, as the tip of the point would be the first thing to be dissolved. In other words, needle points are formed by grinding, then finished off by chemicals.'

Electrolysis is a problem for hooks in some fishing situations, particularly bluewater trolling. It causes rapid corrosion on non-stainless hooks and any hooks moving at speed through water are more prone to electrolysis than stationary hooks. Serious lure trollers prefer stainless hooks with either knife-edge points, or standard points.

Many chemically sharpened hooks are lighter than their standard counterparts, and have somewhat thinner wire for a given tensile strength. That is due to improved heat

fish hooks

If by chance you do get lightly hooked and are having difficulty in removing it, try pressing the eye of the hook firmly down onto the skin, place a piece of fishing nylon through the bend of the hook and pull backwards with the fishing line so that the hook has the chance of coming out on the same path as it went in. If unsure, seek medical advice. For deep hook penetration, seek medical help.

CIRCLE GUIDE

MANUFACTURER: **MUSTAD**

MODEL	STYLE	SIZE RANGE	POINT STYLE
1. Demon Circle (39960BL)	Circle	12/0–16/0	Turned-in Straight
2. Demon Fine Wire (39952 NPBL)	Circle	11/0–2/0	Turned-in Needle
3. Commercial Circle (39952NPBL)	Circle	10/0–16/0	Turned-in Straight
4. Commercial Circle (39965D)	Circle	10/0–16/0	Turned-in Straight
5. Tainawa Commercial (20202R)	Circle	18–15	Turned-in Needle

MANUFACTURER: **GAMAKATSU**

MODEL	STYLE	SIZE RANGE	POINT STYLE
1. Big Bait Circle	Circle	8/0–2/0	Turned-in Needle
2. Octopus Circle	Circle	8/0–2/0	Turned-in Needle

MANUFACTURER: **BLACK MAGIC**

MODEL	STYLE	SIZE RANGE	POINT STYLE
1. KI Series	Circle	1/0–6/0	Turned-in Needle

MANUFACTURER: **WASABI**

MODEL	STYLE	SIZE RANGE	POINT STYLE
1. Puka Hook	Circle	13/0	Turned-in Needle

treatment and wire consistency.

Tuna Circles are the buzz hooks of the new Millennium. While chemically sharpened hooks dominated the 1990s, the curved in point of Tuna Circle patterns has grown in popularity. Most of us have grown up with the convention J-shaped hook where the point runs parallel, albeit sometimes slightly offset to the shank, as in the case of Suicide pattern hooks. Therefore, you can understand the reluctance of anglers to readily accept Tuna Circles, after all having a point set at right angles to the shank you have to wonder how they work. Nevertheless, catch rates in trials with gamefish show an increased hook-up rate and a reduced mortality rate compared with fish caught on conventional hooks.

My first experience of these hooks was on a Bermagui charter boat, Headhunter, skippered by Steve Tedesco. Steve is a skipper who thinks about his fishing and is as concerned about hooking a marlin as he is about releasing the fish quickly in a healthy state. Nothing wrong with that. On Headhunter, we trolled skirted lures as teasers and ran a large Witchdoctor attractor. The Witchdoctor, basically a mirror that swims, emits a huge intermittent flash in the wake while the skirted lures simply leave a trail of bubbles, or 'smoke' as the game gurus say. As well as this array were two lines of plastic squid on outriggers that also acted as teasers.

When a marlin came up and looked at a lure or teaser a live slimy mackerel, bridle rigged with a tuna circle hook, was slipped back and the lures pulled from the water. It worked for me. I missed one marlin and landed another, albeit a small striped marlin of about 30 kg that was quickly tagged and released.

Steve likes the Tuna Circle hooks and says he gets more marlin hooked in the corner of the mouth, something that bodes well for the fish. These hooks are designed to be swallowed and then pull back out of a fish's gullet without hooking up. It is when they turn the corner, so to speak, that the hook

Snapper caught on a 5/0 Eagle Claw Circle pattern. There is, however, a major structural difference in that a 20 mm long piece of wire comes off the back of the hook near the eye, at a right angle to the hook shank.

WIDE GAP GUIDE

MANUFACTURER: **MUSTAD**			
MODEL	STYLE	SIZE RANGE	POINT STYLE
1. Wide Gap (37160S)	Wide Gap	2–5/0	Needle
2. Big Mouth (37753NPNP)	Wide Gap	7/0–6	Needle

MANUFACTURER: GAMAKATSU			
MODEL	STYLE	SIZE RANGE	POINT STYLE
1. Shiner	Wide Gap	6–5/0	Turned-in Needle

MANUFACTURER: **DYNATEC**			
MODEL	STYLE	SIZE RANGE	POINT STYLE
1. Wide Gap	Wide Gap	4/0–6	Turned-in Needle

MANUFCTURER: **WASABI**			
MODEL	STYLE	SIZE RANGE	POINT STYLE
1. Wide Gap	Wide Gap	3/0–5/0	Needle

MANUFACTURER: **EAGLE CLAW**			
MODEL	STYLE	SIZE RANGE	POINT STYLE
1. I741G	Wide Gap Heavy	8–5/0	Needle
2. L141	Wide Gap	10–5/0	Needle
3. LT141	Wide Gap	7/0–8	Needle

MANUFCTURER: **MARUTO**			
MODEL	STYLE	SIZE RANGE	POINT STYLE
1. 2151	Wide Gap	1–8/0	Needle

MANUFACTURER: **YOUVELLA**			
MODEL	STYLE	SIZE RANGE	POINT STYLE
1. Wide Gap	Wide Gap	1/0–6/0	Needle

point goes home—right into the corner of the fish's mouth. There is no exposed point to snag on a fish's internal organs. It is when the hook shank begins leaving the corner of a marlin's mouth that it is induced to rotate. As the shank no longer shields the point, it penetrates the mouth.

Test this by tying line on a Tuna Circle hook, putting the point against your thumb and pulling. The hook shank will tip downward so the point of the hook will be angled to penetrate at an angle parallel to that at which you are pulling the line.

As well as bridle rigged baits, Tuna Circles are now being used in saltwater flies and many anglers have taken to them for normal live and dead bait situations. It is important when these hooks are used not to strike hard or jerk the line. Let the fish swallow the bait, tighten the line, and allow the fish to swim off. The hook will come out and lodge in the mouth under the fish's own motion of swimming away against the drag.

Shark hooks are commonly from 8/0 to 12/0, but that can vary with patterns. Many anglers prefer to run two hooks on their wire trace and fly fishers do likewise for best results.

The pattern most commonly used for shark fishing with conventional baits, such as a fish fillet, is the Mustad Sea Master, ref. 7699. This comes in sizes 20/0 down to 4/0 and is a forged offset hook (kirbed) with a knife-edge point and special tin finish. There is also a Needle Eye version of the Sea Master. This is the 7690, available in sizes 20/0 to 4/0.

If you wanted a straight (non-offset) shark hook, the choice would be the 7698B, which is similar in shape and characteristics to the 7699, but straight, and available 12/0 to 6/0. There is also the 7691, which is also a forged straight hook; it is the non-stainless version of the 7691S and available 14/0 to 1/0.

All these three patterns have a turned-in style point and special tin finish. None of the hooks referred to has a 'chemically sharpened' point. When you get to hooks of this size and type, the advantages of a needlepoint with chemical sharpening are doubtful.

TERMINAL FLEXIBILITY

Fishing can be as complicated or as simple as you want to make it. Wherever possible, my fishing technique is simple, being based as it is on the KISS principle— Keep It Simple Stupid.

Ever wondered why some anglers, regardless of species, current, and water depth, always use sinkers? Or, for that matter, why some anglers have a fixation with floats, or smaller items like brass rings, swivels, luminous beads, and tubing. Anglers can become too set in their ways, developing a fixation with certain rigs or a method is a one-way tide: the results are predictable and there is little challenge.

The reality of terminal tackle is that success is more achievable through flexibility. More often than not, this means minimising the amount of gear you use at the business end of your string. Put another way, the less complicated your terminal set up is the better your results.

SINKERS

I use sinkers only when I have to get bait down to fish or to hold bottom in current. Even then, I employ the minimum weight I can get away with and, as the current abates, will often reduce sinker size. I also use floats and have tried a variety of terminal trinkets with varying degrees of success. As a rule though, if I can get away without sinkers, floats and other gizmos, then I will. The trick is not in knowing when to use sinkers and floats rather, the skill is in knowing when not to.

For example, you wouldn't dream of fishing a free-swimming mudeye along a weed bank unless you could maintain complete control. Let a mudeye do what it wants and you'll be waiting all day for a bite that will never happen.

A free-range mudeye doesn't lie around like a chook egg in the back yard. Mudeyes head straight for the cover of vegetation where they are less likely to be found by hungry trout on dinner patrol. But free-swimming mudeyes can be effective if you keep them under control, away from weed banks or work them in streams and allow the current to push them through prime feeding zones.

FLOATS AND UNWEIGHTED BAITS

Let's start with those bread and butter species that hang around pier pilings and other objects such as snags, weed banks, and the like. Depending on where you fish you probably know these fish by names such as mullet, yakkas, roughies, garfish, luderick, etc.

These fish are mainly mid-water to surface feeders so you would probably think a float is an obvious starting point. A quill or pencil float, a couple of small pieces of shot below the float and a No. 6 long shank hook is a fairly standard rig in this scenario. Anglers using floats will tell you it is the way to go. They can see a take and the float keeps the bait off the bottom and enables them to control the depth they want their bait to be at. All of which are valid reasons and, if you are happy to fish that way, then my advice is to continue doing so.

However, there is a more effective alternative. If you have a reasonable number of fish around and are teasing their taste buds with a fine berley mist then chances are your float is superfluous to the exercise. An unweighted bait cast into the berley and allowed to sink slowly and naturally is often a better option.

I have often used this method in shallow weed bed areas at the southern end of Port Phillip Bay. Setting up a berley trail often brings salmon, garfish, mullet, and King George whiting. Of these species, only the whiting have to be fished for on the bottom.

The method involves casting a short distance from the boat and then allowing the bait to dribble out and down at the speed of the tide. This can vary, depending current, from as little as an inch at a time to very fast. The trick is to maintain a tight line without impeding the progress of the bait. To do this you keep the line between your fingers as you feed it out, feeling for nibbles it sinks.

The advantage is that instead of relying on a delayed signal from a float, the angler can feel a bite the instant it happens. That millisecond or so of time lag between a bite indication on a float and one felt directly through the line can make a big difference in hook-up rates.

The next best scenario is to polaroid the fish, watching them take the bait and then

Ganged hooks can be used for more than casting pilchards at tailor. This bait has been rigged for surf fishing, the small water bomb balloon designed to keep the bait off the bottom and away from crabs.

GAFFS

Landing nets are popular for catch and release fishing, but when it comes to landing big fish such as mackerel or marlin, the gaff is the only sensible option.

Anyone who has fished for big fish at some time or another will have had cause to use a gaff. Never use a gaff unless you intend keeping the fish, as it will surely die after being impaled on the gaff hook.

Nets on the other hand are the choice for smaller fish. If you are into tag and release or want to remove a hook without harming the fish then a net is second choice. First choice for this operation should be picking the fish up by hand and holding it. Not all fish lend themselves to this exercise though as they are well endowed with spines.

Gaffs come in three basic forms, these are fixed head, flying and cliff gaff and come with three different point styles: round, diamond and triangle.

The circumstances regulate the desired length of the gaff pole. In a boat it probably would never need to be longer than about two metres, most of the time only about half this. Fishing from the shore though, say from a rock ledge or a pier, and the length of the gaff pole needs to be able to reach the water at low tide and the bottom of the swell.

Ideally, the gaff should be a single piece unit with fittings at one end for a flying gaff and a screw fitting at the other end for a fixed head gaff. Aluminium of 3 mm wall thickness and 25 mm diameter is both strong and light and should be considered when a gaff is being made.

Any gaff needs some sort of handle. This could be simply taped or, in the case of aluminium, a knurled grip. As well, gloves

setting the hook. Garfish for example are easily spotted in a berley trail when the water is clear. Put bait into the trail and allow it to drift out. It's a bit like nymphing for trout in a stream. Even if you don't feel the take, you will often see it as garfish turn when they take bait: the telltale winks as the sun reflects on the elongate silver body are a dead give away.

If you are working an oil-based berley then sometimes a fine line will float on the trail. If not simply add floatant to your line, but keep the floatant well away from the hook. This is a variation on the sink-tip lines fly fishers have 'discovered' in recent years.

Floating baits work for a range of bigger fish as well. Fishing offshore near rocky exposed reefs or islands I have often found snapper sitting back at the end of the wash. Unweighted bait put into the surge, allowed to drift back, and down naturally is often taken. The nearest I can liken it to is cubing for yellowfin: feed out a few 'freebies' into the wash and then offer up a bait that comes complete with bonus hook. A wide range of species can be caught on free drifting baits from a boat; among them are tuna, snapper, salmon, couta, and sharks.

Live baits can also be used to good effect when allowed to swim free but they are more difficult to keep in check. It can be desirable to put a sinker above the leader on a live bait to send it down into the depths. How much lead you use depends on current strength and, to a lesser degree, the size of the live bait. This is where flexibility comes into play.

If you are using a berley trail then putting bait below a sinker may negate its value. Berley doesn't sink immediately: instead, it drifts down slowly. The incline becomes steeper the further it is from the boat. Putting live bait down under a sinker below the boat and allowing it to swim too deep can keep the baitfish out of the prime-feeding zone. Sometimes it doesn't matter, but there will always be days when it does.

Conversely, putting bait out under a floater at a set depth and allowing it to swim away from the boat can also be futile. First you have to keep the baitfish in the trail and second, if it is any distance from the boat, it might be swimming above the trail. How can you tell? Like I said, it's important to stay in control at all times.

There is a way around this but it depends on attitudes. I know some anglers don't like the method I am about to describe believing it to be cruel. What it involves is removing one of the lobes of a baitfish's tail fin. If you remove the top lobe the bait will stay high in the water, near the surface; take off the bottom lobe and it swims deep. I'll let you make up your own minds about the ethics or otherwise of that one.

Flexibility is the key to success but there is another factor that can come into play—Murphy's Law. According to Murphy, the number of fish caught by an angler is in inverse proportion to how much the angler deserves them.

with a ridged diamond pattern with Silastic will ensure a better grip. A sheath of plastic tubing over the point should be used to cover and protect the gaff points when they are not in use.

gaffing

Two methods can be used to gaff a fish. The best is to reach over the fish and pull the hook in. This is the easiest method as the weight of the gaff brings it naturally in towards the fish. The second method is to have the gaff in the water and allow the fish to swim in to it and then lift the gaff into place and secure the fish inboard or on shore. Never take a wild swipe at a fish, or try to gaff one that is still lively and has not been played out properly.

This mako shark is being held by the trace. Note the squid tentacle protruding from its mouth.

A gaff can be used to hold a fish while the hooks are removed, demonstrated here by Alan Cort who maintains control over this dogtooth tuna by leaving the gaff in its jaw.

GAFFS

Size Range Available

Length (gape)	Head Size	Item	Length (gape)	Head Size	Item
General Use			**SWF**		
600 mm NEW	62 mm	(000)	2400 mm	75 mm	(006A)
	75 mm	(000A)		100 mm	(006A)
1200 mm	75 mm	(001)		150 mm	(007)
	100 mm	(002)	**NEW**		
Tuna & General Use			1800 mm	62 mm	(044)
1800 MM	75 MM	(003)	Gaff head	75 mm	(045)
	100 mm	(004)	for 12 ft two		
	150 mm	(005)	piece gaff pole.		

CHAPTER 3

TACKLE MAINTENANCE

All tackle, regardless of quality, must be properly maintained and serviced for optimum performance.

Here are a few tips on what to do to make sure your gear won't let you down. Many of the listed tasks should be done after each outing. If this wasn't the case, then now is a good time to roll your sleeves up and get into it.

RODS

- Use a soft cloth to help remove any scales stuck on your rods. Avoid using abrasive scrub cloths as this may damage the rod finish.
- To help preserve that new rod sheen, apply and wipe off a furniture polish (Marveer is a good one) periodically.
- Visually inspect your rod guides for any nicks or cuts that could damage or fray your line. An effective method to check for guide damage is to run a pair of women's stockings through the guides. The nylons will snag on any significant imperfections.

Most of the work when maintaining tackle is about having an eye for detail.

- When storing your rods, avoid leaning them against walls as this may cause the rods to bend and warp. Instead, store them vertically in a rod holder, or hang them horizontally, in a cool, dry location.

REELS

- If you plan to overhaul your reel yourself, organization is extremely important. Select a level, uncluttered, well-lit work area. Keep your manual handy as a reference guide when disassembling and reassembling your reel. Arrange your tools, lube, grease rags, brushes, cleaners, etc. ahead of time, and prepare a place to put parts, sub-assemblies, etc. Many anglers arrange parts in the order they disassemble them, often placing parts in empty egg cartons or similar containers to avoid mix-ups.
- Once a reel is disassembled, you will need to break the oil/grease down. Degreasing agents range from kerosene to mineral spirits to detergents. Remember to remove the degreaser before re-assembling.
- Use quality marine grade grease for gear teeth, bearings, and other internal frictional surfaces.
- Once reassembled, apply a coating of protective oil, such as CRC or WD-40 to your reels. Take care not to spray your line. If you do, be sure to wipe it off immediately.
- Apply light grease to oil ports on handle knobs and outside frictional surfaces on reels. Resist the temptation to apply too much grease, as it is better to lubricate sparsely and often.

DRAG SYSTEMS

Reel makers have improved their drags, but improvement is a long way short of perfection. Gun anglers always check their drags thoroughly, regardless of the make or model of the reel. Many game fishers have the drag bearing surfaces of a new lever drag reel machined before even thinking about using the reel. They do this as a matter of course, not always, because it is necessary.

To service a reel drag the first step is to ascertain the type of drag. If it is a dry drag then ensure all washers are clean and free from grease or dirt. Wet drag systems will require lubricant so check this with the manufacturer's specifications.

Sometimes it isn't the drag but loose tolerances of reel makers allowing too much spool movement that is the problem. In a lever

Tackle maintenance is an essential part of angling, something that should be undertaken regularly.

drag reel for example, when the spool moves off the horizontal plane the drag bearing surfaces move out of alignment. A threadline reel that has too much lateral spool movement under pressure is also a problem. Instead of the line peeling off at 90 degrees to the bail arm the tilted spool means line runs off at an angle. As well as affecting drag smoothness, this increases line friction.

Drags should be set at 25 per cent of the line's breaking strain with a full spool of line. To make sure that the setting is correct use an accurate spring scale, with the rod pointing straight along the line at the scale. Do this no less than 10 times to ensure that the friction surfaces of the drag components are bedded together and heated up the way they would be when playing a big fish.

As the angler it is up to you to ensure your drag is smooth and correctly tensioned. It is also important to monitor the performance of your drag during a fight. During a fight with a fast, powerful fish, be prepared to adjust the drag, particularly as your spool diameter decreases.

A series of tests by Aftco demonstrated the importance of reel dynamics. The tests

STAR DRAG ASSEMBLY

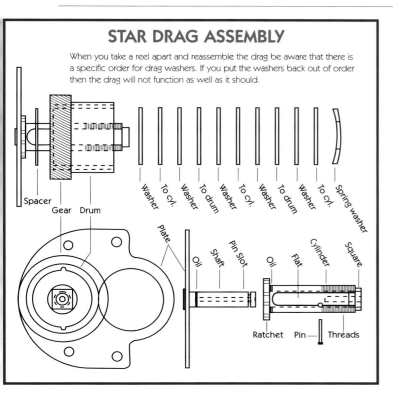

When you take a reel apart and reassemble the drag be aware that there is a specific order for drag washers. If you put the washers back out of order then the drag will not function as well as it should.

and made a 135-degree turn at 9 knots. Less than 2 kg of pull was felt at the reel, but at the 'fish', the pull registered 10 kg, four and a half times the strain at the reel. Intelligent adjustment of the drag setting to counter these effects comes with experience. Keep it in mind for the day the XXOS gamefish comes along.

Preventative maintenance on drags is an insurance policy. When storing reels, the golden rule is to back the drag lever to the free spool position, This removes any pressure and allows the washers to relax. This also ensures that the drag components won't fuse and become bonded to the pressure plate, resulting in a frozen drag. When doing this, back the drag completely off and turn the reel handle while holding the spool and crank for ten or twenty seconds. This ensures that the washers are all totally free and clear of each other.

LINES

- Fishing line is the most import link as it connects you to the fish. Over exposure to sunlight and ultra violet light can cause deterioration in monofilament line so always store your lines away from fluoro lights and sunlight.
- It is good practice to constantly check for

fraying, cuts, nicks or fading. If you find evidence of any of these, either cut the problem section of the line off or, if there is too much line involved, top shot the reel. Sometimes it is better to replace the whole line.

- Check line for abrasion, cuts, nicks by running through your fingers. If you find it hard to detect abrasion this way, try feeling the line by running it between your lips.
- When abrasions are detected check all rod guides, bail arm roller on spinning reels and level wind mechanism on overhead reels for grooving or fractures that can quickly destroy a line.
- Main reasons to change a line are: The line is too low on the spool, old age, abrasion, severe discolouration, poor knot strength and over-stretching, as when snagged and excessive force is used to break line.
- Due to the fine diameter and danger of cuts with gelspun braided lines it is imperative that they be seated properly. When tying braid always allow plenty of line so that you can seat the knot firmly by wrapping a cloth around your hand or fingers to protect them from the braid.
- When installing new line on your reel wind the line firmly on the spool. With overhead reels, the line should come directly off the spool holding the line. For spinning reels, line should come off the side of the line spool in the opposite direction to the reel spool rotation. This is done to eliminate line twist. For example, if a reel turns clockwise when viewed from the front, the line must come off the spool holding the line in an anti-clockwise direction.

TERMINAL TACKLE

- Terminal tackle such as hooks and swivels should be kept clean and dry. Hooks, even the chemically sharpened and stainless steel types should always be checked for sharpness—regardless of whether they have been in the water. My advice is never to trust rusty hooks and as they are not an expensive item in terms of tackle costs overall, it is better to replace them.
- Lures can be a hassle, particularly the likes of minnows with two sets of trebles held on with tiny key rings. It is good policy to check all rings, hooks, bibs, even lure bodies for damage, and set about making repairs, or replacing whatever needs to be replaced.

And finally, terminal tackle is the messy, least organised aspect of most tackle. Why not set about re-organising your tackle so that there is a place for everything so, at least on your next outing anyway, everything will be in its place.

found that as the diameter of line on the spool decreased more force was needed to pull line off the reel. When the diameter of the spool is halved, the true drag setting on the reel will have doubled. To put it another way, when the line diameter on the spool is down to one-quarter its original size the amount of drag setting on your reel will have increased fourfold. Therefore, if you set your strike drag at 25 per cent of the breaking strain of the line, your line will now be at breaking point.

Other tests showed how much stress water friction can add to fishing line. A boat simulating a fish took out 220 m of 24 kg monofilament

DRAG QUADRANT

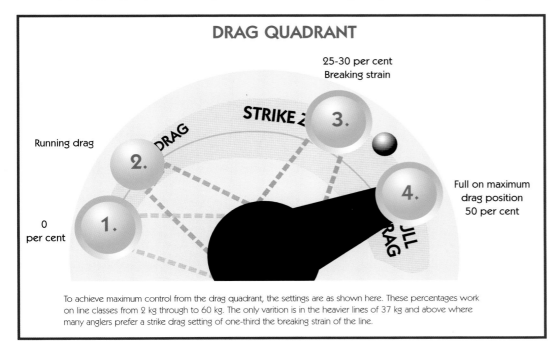

To achieve maximum control from the drag quadrant, the settings are as shown here. These percentages work on line classes from 2 kg through to 60 kg. The only varition is in the heavier lines of 37 kg and above where many anglers prefer a strike drag setting of one-third the breaking strain of the line.

CHAPTER 4

FAVOURITE KNOTS

Knots are such a vital element in angling that books have been written about them, complete with tying illustrations. There are hundreds of knots but in many cases, it is a matter of re-inventing the wheel for the sake of doing so. For example, the Blood Knot, Improved Clinch, and Uni-Knot are all variations of the Clinch Knot.

Any knot used in fishing should be the most uncomplicated and secure system you can find. There are some golden rules with knots:

- The more complicated a knot is, the more likely you are to tie it incorrectly.
- The more knots you use, the greater the chances are that one of them will let you down.

If this was an equation, you could multiply a 'degree of difficulty' factor in tying a knot by the number of knots tied to understand how this potential problem can compound. The solution is simple. Use the KISS principle (Keep It Simple Stupid), and use knots that are easy to tie, and don't use any more than you absolutely have to.

It has been written many times by knowledgeable anglers that knots form potential weak links in the line between angler and fish, the general acceptance being that the more knots you include the more potential weak links you have. In practice though, if the knot you tie is only 70 per cent of the breaking strain of the line it should not be a problem provided your drag is set correctly at about 25–33 per cent of the breaking strain of your

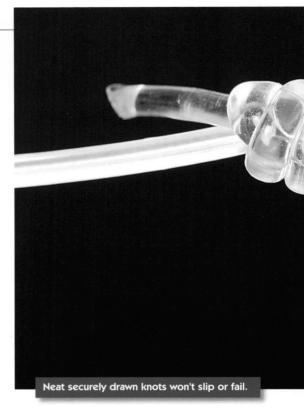

Neat securely drawn knots won't slip or fail.

WIRE LEADER CONNECTION

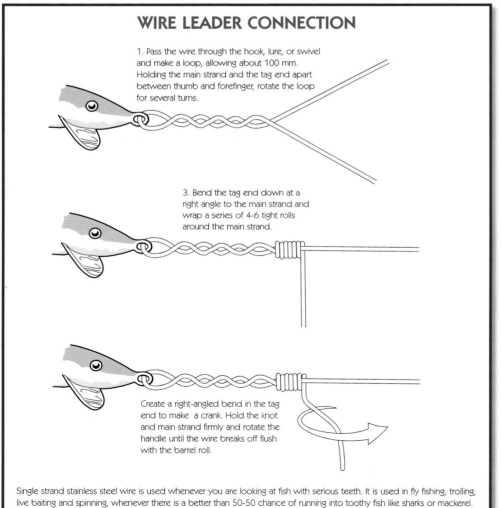

1. Pass the wire through the hook, lure, or swivel and make a loop, allowing about 100 mm. Holding the main strand and the tag end apart between thumb and forefinger, rotate the loop for several turns.

3. Bend the tag end down at a right angle to the main strand and wrap a series of 4-6 tight rolls around the main strand.

Create a right-angled bend in the tag end to make a crank. Hold the knot and main strand firmly and rotate the handle until the wire breaks off flush with the barrel roll.

Single strand stainless steel wire is used whenever you are looking at fish with serious teeth. It is used in fly fishing, trolling, live baiting and spinning, whenever there is a better than 50-50 chance of running into toothy fish like sharks or mackerel.

Multi-strand wires are not as adaptable for sportfishing, and bulky crimps make them ungainly when presentation is important.

The advantage in making up your own leaders rather than buying them is that you can custom fit them to suit what you want. For example, you may want a 25 cm leader for fly-fishing for sharks or a 6 cm leader for spinning for barracouta.

MONO TO WIRE CONNECTION

1. First start by bending a piece of wire over and kinking the bend up slightly (approx. 45°). Then start the knot by passing the tag end through the loop and over the outer side of the two parallel straight sections of wire.

2. Now pass the tag end under and back over the two straight pieces of wire.

3. Continue wrapping the line around back over itself working back toward the kinked section.

4. After a minimum of 10 wraps pass the tag end back through the bend in the wire.

Tough estuary fish like the mangrove jack will test knots to the max.

VARIATION OF THE ALBRIGHT KNOT)

5. Pull the knot tight so that it slides forward and locks itself up against the kind, and then roll the tag end back creating another loop.

6. Thread the tag end back around the main line in the loop previously created (minimum five times). Pull this knot tight and slide it back down locking itself down onto the other knot created earlier. Trim the excess off the tag end and you're complete.

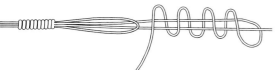

The Albright knot used to be called the shock leader knot in the early 1970s but its main problem is the potential to slip under extreme load. To overcome that I tie a Jim Rizutto finish, named after American angler and game fishing writer Jim Rizutto who publicised its use by Hawaiian game fishing skippers.

Attaching mono to wire without using rings or swivels gives better presentation and allows more control. A swivel in a connection creates an unwieldy link in the terminal end, which is something you need to avoid. This is a particularly effective method for saltwater fly fishers and lure casters.

The key factors in the connection are the upward kink in the looped wire. This gives the line a stopper to keep the knot firm and prevent it slipping over the end. The second important factor is the Rizutto finish, which is better explained as a reverse Uni. This locks the knot and ensures it won't slip.

LEFTY KREH LOOP KNOT

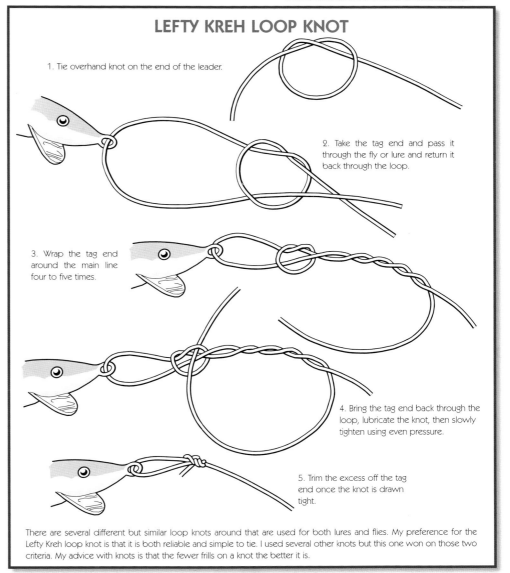

1. Tie overhand knot on the end of the leader.

2. Take the tag end and pass it through the fly or lure and return it back through the loop.

3. Wrap the tag end around the main line four to five times.

4. Bring the tag end back through the loop, lubricate the knot, then slowly tighten using even pressure.

5. Trim the excess off the tag end once the knot is drawn tight.

There are several different but similar loop knots around that are used for both lures and flies. My preference for the Lefty Kreh loop knot is that it is both reliable and simple to tie. I used several other knots but this one won on those two criteria. My advice with knots is that the fewer frills on a knot the better it is.

main line. When this setting is used, the knot is still twice the strength of the drag setting required to break it.

If you have a system of knots that you have used, knots that you tie well and don't let you down then there is no reason to expand the range, unless you happen to have a specific need.

There are no secrets to good knots because there is only one way to tie them, and this is correctly. Most knots break because they slip, and the reason they slip is that they haven't been tied correctly. To put it more succinctly there are either too many turns or the knot hasn't been pulled up securely.

Putting too many turns around the standing line is a common problem. What happens is that the more wraps there are the harder it is to draw the knot down securely. And on dry lines, knots that haven't been lubricated can resist being pulled snug. The way around that is to lubricate the line (including gelspun) with saliva, and when this is done the line will drawn down more easily and snug up tight.

An old standard with many anglers is the Improved Clinch or Locked Half Blood knot. It is a knot I rarely tie these days because some lines are not suited. I stopped tying Blood Knots when line manufacturers started to introduce co-polymer lines and tri-polymer lines. I found the blood knot wasn't always the best to use so I discarded it for most of my fishing.

A major failing of this knot though is that some anglers attempt toomany turns around the standing line. The maximum turns this knot needs for lines to 3 kg are five, for lines to 7 kg it is four, and if you are using 24-kilogram line then three turns will suffice. A problem with the Blood Knot comes when you decide to lock it. Pulling the tag end can force the last wrap to 'roll over' the next wrap and create a twist or stress point in the knot.

While many anglers still employ this knot successfully, my preference is the Uni Knot, an easy to tie 100 per cent knot that can also be used to join two lines of equal diameter. Its value as a joining knot is that there is no hinging, the lines lie parallel, and the pull is longitudinal along the lines.

Double knots are essential to learn. In this regard my preference is for the Bimini Twist for creating a double line that can be used as a leader from a main line to a swivel, for loop-to-loop connections in fly leaders or when you want to join two lines of unequal diameter using a Uni-Knot. The Plait is a neat and tidy knot. Like the Bimini, it is a 100 per cent knot, and despite looking complicated, I have a friend who can weave a Plait faster than I can tie a Bimini. Sometimes you feel like you need three hands to tie a Bimini, but once you get the hang of this knot you will find it is simple and straightforward, a knot that is difficult to build incorrectly.

Loop to loop connections are used when fly fishing. These also come in handy when attaching a mono leader to a gelspun main line, although in that case the connection is a Cats Paw arrangement with the mono leader threaded over the

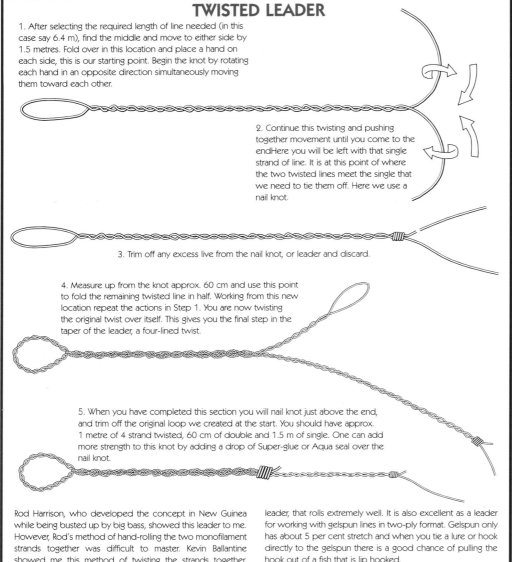

TWISTED LEADER

1. After selecting the required length of line needed (in this case say 6.4 m), find the middle and move to either side by 1.5 metres. Fold over in this location and place a hand on each side, this is our starting point. Begin the knot by rotating each hand in an opposite direction simultaneously moving them toward each other.

2. Continue this twisting and pushing together movement until you come to the endHere you will be left with that single strand of line. It is at this point of where the two twisted lines meet the single that we need to tie them off. Here we use a nail knot.

3. Trim off any excess live from the nail knot, or leader and discard.

4. Measure up from the knot approx. 60 cm and use this point to fold the remaining twisted line in half. Working from this new location repeat the actions in Step 1. You are now twisting the original twist over itself. This gives you the final step in the taper of the leader, a four-lined twist.

5. When you have completed this section you will nail knot just above the end, and trim off the original loop we created at the start. You should have approx. 1 metre of 4 strand twisted, 60 cm of double and 1.5 m of single. One can add more strength to this knot by adding a drop of Super-glue or Aqua seal over the nail knot.

Rod Harrison, who developed the concept in New Guinea while being busted up by big bass, showed this leader to me. However, Rod's method of hand-rolling the two monofilament strands together was difficult to master. Kevin Ballantine showed me this method of twisting the strands together, although he had never used it to make a leader.

These are fast fix leaders made up in critical situations. The ultimate development in Twisted Leaders is in the Knotted Dog range where the degree of expansion and contraction in the tight machine-applied helical weave provides a measure of give and abrasion resistance that cannot be duplicated by hand.

The leader has many applications. It can be sectioned into four-ply, two-ply, and one-ply for a tapered saltwater fly

leader, that rolls extremely well. It is also excellent as a leader for working with gelspun lines in two-ply format. Gelspun only has about 5 per cent stretch and when you tie a lure or hook directly to the gelspun there is a good chance of pulling the hook out of a fish that is lip hooked.

A two-ply mono leader provides 'give' at the business end of the rig where it's needed. This is a better option than softer rods and means more striking fish are hooked, and less hooked fish are lost. In the two-ply configuration, used mainly for working lures or bait fishing, a cats paw loop-to-loop connection is used between the gelspun and monofilament. This allows the mono/gelspun connection to flow out smoothly through the rod guides, something that doesn't always happen when you use knotted connections.

UNI KNOT

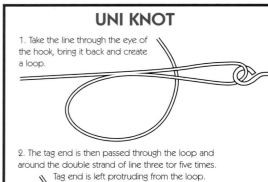

1. Take the line through the eye of the hook, bring it back and create a loop.

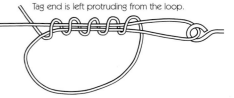

2. The tag end is then passed through the loop and around the double strand of line three tor five times. Tag end is left protruding from the loop.

DOUBLE UNI KNOT

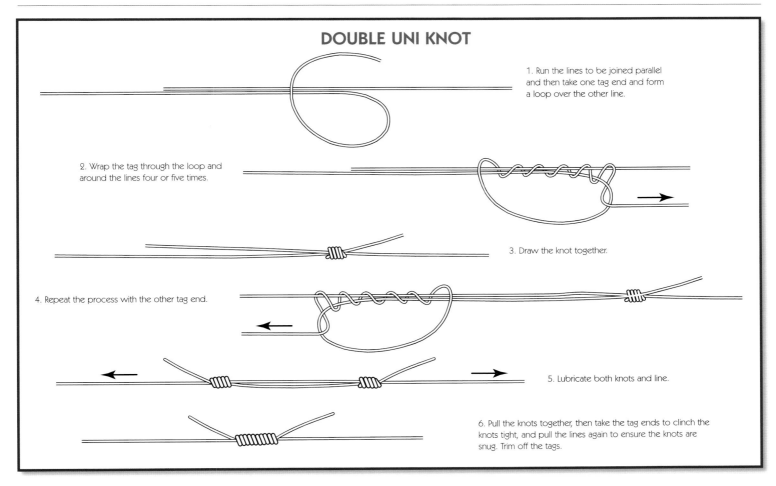

1. Run the lines to be joined parallel and then take one tag end and form a loop over the other line.

2. Wrap the tag through the loop and around the lines four or five times.

3. Draw the knot together.

4. Repeat the process with the other tag end.

5. Lubricate both knots and line.

6. Pull the knots together, then take the tag ends to clinch the knots tight, and pull the lines again to ensure the knots are snug. Trim off the tags.

gelspun and then passed through the gelspun loop in a figure eight configuration several times. The advantage in doing this is to more evenly distribute the load area on the both the gelspun and the monofilament.

Anglers who want to bottom bounce, or say fish the surf, and use a Paternoster rig will sometimes make the mistake of employing a three-way swivel. These swivels are weak in their design in that the extension that leads from the swivel at right angles is in 'sheer'

HEAVY DUTY ALBRIGHT KNOT

1. Form a loop in the tag end of the heavier. line or wire making sure you allow 15 cm to overlap.
Take the lighter line and pass the tag through the formed loop.

2. Pinch both lines about 8 cm from the end, and at the same time allow about 8 cm of the lighter line to protrude beyond this point to tie the knot. Start winding the lighter line back towards the end loop over the doubled section. Pass the lighter material through the end loop on the same side of the loop that the lighter line originally entered.

3. Very slowly pull on the lighter line ends while grasping the heavier section and working the coils of the knot towards the loop end. Do not allow the coils to slip off the loop. Take special care when tying this knot as it is very prone to slipping if it is not tightened correctly.

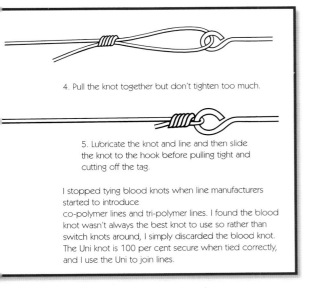

4. Pull the knot together but don't tighten too much.

5. Lubricate the knot and line and then slide the knot to the hook before pulling tight and cutting off the tag.

I stopped tying blood knots when line manufacturers started to introduce co-polymer lines and tri-polymer lines. I found the blood knot wasn't always the best knot to use so rather than switch knots around, I simply discarded the blood knot. The Uni knot is 100 per cent secure when tied correctly, and I use the Uni to join lines.

IMPROVED ALBRIGHT KNOT

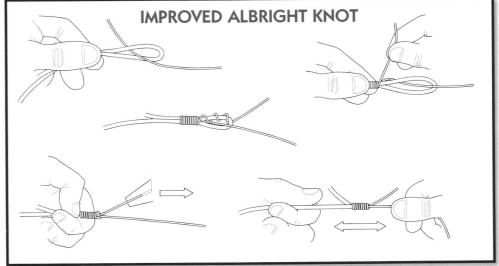

BIMINI TWIST

To tie this knot more easily have someone holding the line or else have your line running off the rod with the reel locked up.

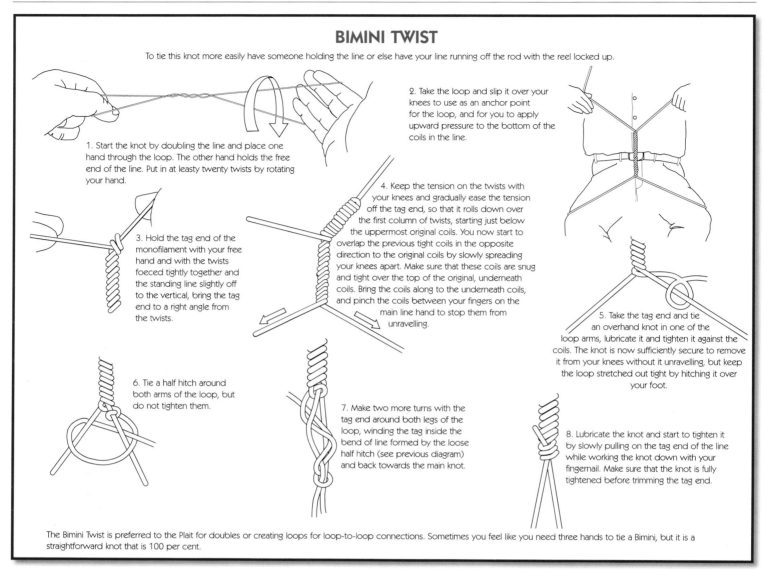

1. Start the knot by doubling the line and place one hand through the loop. The other hand holds the free end of the line. Put in at leasty twenty twists by rotating your hand.

2. Take the loop and slip it over your knees to use as an anchor point for the loop, and for you to apply upward pressure to the bottom of the coils in the line.

3. Hold the tag end of the monofilament with your free hand and with the twists foeced tightly together and the standing line slightly off to the vertical, bring the tag end to a right angle from the twists.

4. Keep the tension on the twists with your knees and gradually ease the tension off the tag end, so that it rolls down over the first column of twists, starting just below the uppermost original coils. You now start to overlap the previous tight coils in the opposite direction to the original coils by slowly spreading your knees apart. Make sure that these coils are snug and tight over the top of the original, underneath coils. Bring the coils along to the underneath coils, and pinch the coils between your fingers on the main line hand to stop them from unravelling.

5. Take the tag end and tie an overhand knot in one of the loop arms, lubricate it and tighten it against the coils. The knot is now sufficiently secure to remove it from your knees without it unravelling, but keep the loop stretched out tight by hitching it over your foot.

6. Tie a half hitch around both arms of the loop, but do not tighten them.

7. Make two more turns with the tag end around both legs of the loop, winding the tag inside the bend of line formed by the loose half hitch (see previous diagram) and back towards the main knot.

8. Lubricate the knot and start to tighten it by slowly pulling on the tag end of the line while working the knot down with your fingernail. Make sure that the knot is fully tightened before trimming the tag end.

The Bimini Twist is preferred to the Plait for doubles or creating loops for loop-to-loop connections. Sometimes you feel like you need three hands to tie a Bimini, but it is a straightforward knot that is 100 per cent.

LOOP TO LOOP CONNECTION

1. Tie a loop in each end of the line to be connected. The best loop knot for this is the Bimini Twist.

2. Pass one loop through the other, and then bring the tag from the loop that has gone over the line, down through the loop that passed through. Draw slowly tight, ensuring the loop connection lays correctly.

Loop to loop connections are used when fly fishing. These also come in handy when attaching a mono leader to a gelspun main line, although in that case the connection is a Cats Paw arrangement with the mono leader threaded over the gelspun and then passed through the gelspun loop in a figure eight configuration several times. The advantage in doing this is to more evenly distribute the load area on the both the gelspun and the monofilament.

force and can part under a heavy load. The simple and surest way around this is to tie a Twisted Dropper Loop. These can be set at any distance above the sinker on the main line. Separate snoods are made up and connected in loop-to-loop fashion. This is not a big fish rig, but it is easy and fast for surf species such as Australian salmon.

When you read a knot book, you will find an array of 'new' knots. Some of the so-called 'old knots' are still as good or better than the later variations. An example of this is the Albright Knot that was developed in the 1950s. During the high speed spin boom of the late 1960s and early 1970s, it became known as the shock leader knot. It was commonly employed by anglers chasing tuna on lures from the rocks who wanted an easy heavy to light line connection. These days it is commonly employed to join braid to monofilament, or LC 13 shooting heads to braided on saltwater fly outfits. Once again, this is an easy knot to tie; the main problem with it is the potential to slip under extreme load if it isn't locked.

The best way to ensure it won't slip is to tie a Jim Rizutto finish, which is better explained as a reverse Uni-Knot. This locks the knot and ensures it won't slip. I am not sure of the rating of the Albright, but it won't fail you when you lock it so I guess it is up around the 90 per cent mark.

The loop knot used for flies is best for small species up to about 5 kilograms. Be careful when choosing leader when this style of knot is to be used as some materials, and fluorocarbon is the best example, are brittle and the constant wear from the swinging fly can cause the line to fracture. Nail Knots are handy for more than simply attaching leader to fly line. When I tie a twisted leader, I use a nail knot to lock it off, which eliminates a knot from the leader. This knot can also be used when putting a braided loop on the end of a fly line to lock the loop to the line as added security. Nail Knots can also be used to create loop knots, although the downside is that they tighten up under load and the loop closes, although this doesn't matter once the hook has gone home.

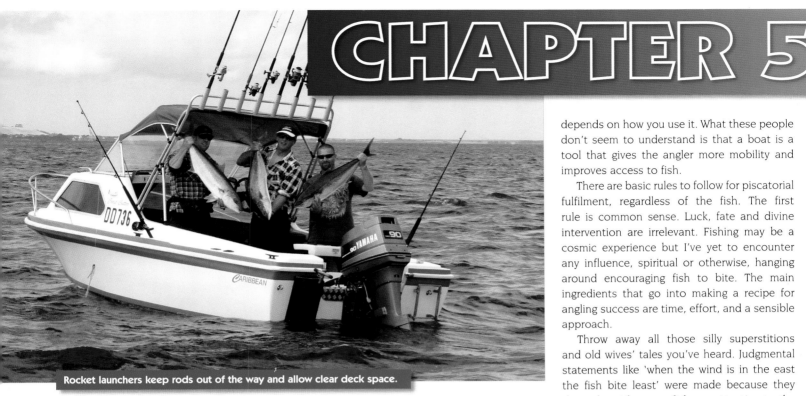

CHAPTER 5

Rocket launchers keep rods out of the way and allow clear deck space.

BOAT FISHING

A boat can be a bonus or a liability; it depends on how you use it. Having a boat isn't a licence to catch fish. To achieve the best results you have to know how to use the boat properly as a fishing tool.

Imagine you are fishing late at night in a deep little backwater and it's dead calm. Snapper have been nosing about but they are finicky and easily spooked. To compensate you are fishing light, keeping noise to a minimum and ensuring no torchlight shines into the water. All is still and quiet, just as you want, as you sit and wait in anticipation of that first run.

Suddenly, out of the dark you hear the roar of an outboard. A dipstick in a flash looking cuddy cab starts circling the bay. Zigging and zagging his way around with his sounder on, he is trying to find a school of snapper. He might as well be riding a Harley motorcycle for there's nothing subtle about this person's approach. Suddenly the motor quietens down as he reduces speed, then it stops altogether. Peace at last? No way! Above the noise of a blaring radio, there is much clanking and banging followed by a huge splash. The anchor has gone overboard. Problem is, every snapper within a couple of kilometres also knows.

Meet the angler from hell! I've run across these people in many places, lakes, bays, estuaries and even offshore. They are the characters that anchor half a rod length away when you are on a hot whiting bite. Alternatively, they are the types who follow so close behind when you are trolling that your lures are almost scraping the bow of their boats, or else come motoring past in a pea soup fog.

Anglers from Hell are indisputable proof that owning a boat isn't a recipe for angling success. At least in Victoria and, Heaven knows, things are tough enough down south without added handicaps.

A boat can be a bonus or a liability; it depends on how you use it. What these people don't seem to understand is that a boat is a tool that gives the angler more mobility and improves access to fish.

There are basic rules to follow for piscatorial fulfilment, regardless of the fish. The first rule is common sense. Luck, fate and divine intervention are irrelevant. Fishing may be a cosmic experience but I've yet to encounter any influence, spiritual or otherwise, hanging around encouraging fish to bite. The main ingredients that go into making a recipe for angling success are time, effort, and a sensible approach.

Throw away all those silly superstitions and old wives' tales you've heard. Judgmental statements like 'when the wind is in the east the fish bite least' were made because they rhymed, not because fish pay attention to the wind. Irish pessimist, Murphy, is credited with saying 'anything that can go wrong will.' If you believe that one you are likely to experience a self-fulfilling prophecy.

FINDING FISH

The shadow of a boat hull looming over a lair can spook fish and discourage feeding. Anchoring away from a snag and fishing to it is generally more productive. Another advantage is that fish that hide in snags will head straight back to them when hooked. Putting yourself

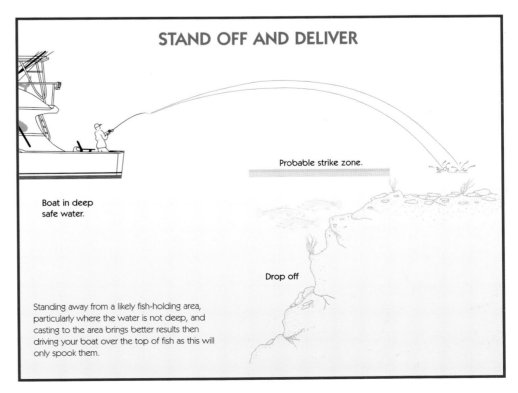

STAND OFF AND DELIVER

Probable strike zone.

Boat in deep safe water.

Drop off

Standing away from a likely fish-holding area, particularly where the water is not deep, and casting to the area brings better results then driving your boat over the top of fish as this will only spook them.

in a position to apply pressure that steers the fish away from the problem area improves your chances of landing them.

A different approach is adopted around pier pilings. After a few seasons immersed in the water, pilings become barnacle encrusted and develop into vertical reefs. Alive and vibrant, these pilings become a mini marine smorgasbord full of fresh takeaways.

The psyche of pier anglers is invariably to throw baits as far from the structure they are standing on as they can. Experienced boat anglers, seeking species including silver trevally, warehou (trevalla), John Dory, leatherjackets, and mullet, know better. Rather than fish away from the pier, these people often elect to tie up to the structure and fish between the pilings.

Old pilings offer anglers a fresh bait source for tasties like mussels, cunjevoi, and crabs. The act of bait gathering, scraping mussels off with a rake for example, results in a neat little berley trail that enhances the piscatorial quality of the neighbourhood. Oddly enough, I've seen anglers scrape a piling for bait then move 20 m along the pier before wetting a line.

Rock fishers often adopt a similar approach to their pier-based counterparts. You don't have to travel several kilometres offshore in search of reef systems. Sometimes they are right under your nose. If you don't believe me

fads

Ever wonder why so many boats seem to congregate around channel beacons and old pilings? The answer is simple. Old pilings have collected all manner of vegetation and crustacean life over the years and the natural build up creates a vertical reef. Small fish come to feed on even smaller marine animals, and wherever you find small fish, you are sure to find bigger fish eventually.

then the next time you're near a pier look at the kids. Invariably they'll be fishing for the baitfish, yakkas, mullet and the like, then ask yourself what attracts large predators? The conclusion is obvious.

Some very big fish often linger below piers. Baitfish often stay under the lights and predators, like big mulloway, barracouta and squid, will work the twilight zone between light and dark, feeding on them.

Close to my home base, snapper often school up under a particular pier. Knowing anglers go right on under and fish for them. It is illegal, difficult, and dangerous due to live power lines. Many anglers though find the rewards too good to pass up.

Inexperienced King George whiting anglers

working Victorian bays and inlets have a sure fire method of finding fish: they look for other boats. It is then a simple matter of motoring over and dropping the pick as close as they can. Not only does this annoy the people who put in all the work finding the fish, it doesn't work all the time. Sometimes the fish are in a hole or over a patch of ground directly behind one of the boats. Drop bait a metre either side and there are no fish.

So how do the anglers in the boat continuously drop their baits in the hole with the fish? It is called controlled casting. The way to achieve it is to ignore the mechanics of your reel and fish as though using a handline. When whiting are found, instead of reeling the fish in, hand line it through the rod, carefully coiling the line in a bucket at your feet as you go. After unhooking the whiting and rebaiting simply cast out again. The line will travel exactly the same distance. Provided the cast is straight, your bait will be back in the happy hunting ground.

You can't do this with bigger fish such as snapper but it works a treat on smaller battlers. Mind you, it always pays to have insurance. Even though you are not using your reel always set the drag in case you happen to hook something that doesn't suit hand lining.

Melbourne rod builder Gary Marsh has specialised in trolling in recent years; particularly in lakes. The thing that most irks him is the habit of some anglers who troll with their rods pointing skywards. He points out that the lures are meant to dive. To get the best out of the lures, rods should lie horizontal and the lures troll at least 50 m astern.

Then there are the people who forget to tie their electric motors down, hit a snag and over it goes. The wire connections to the battery are to conduct electricity to the motor, not to stop the motor from going overboard.

Fishing in an aluminium boat without soundproofing the hull against the clanking echo of a sinker on the bare metal is another way of scaring fish. This is especially true in calm waters when the fish are timid. I've heard anglers who pound away at their berley buckets in the middle of the night during a snapper run complain of catching nothing. Other anglers, well away from the noise, did all right.

From an outsider's viewpoint there appears to be a wide gulf between the fish-producing abilities

Multi-directional rod holders are essential fro bait fishing as they help keep lines out of the way of each other as the boat swings.

ANCHORING

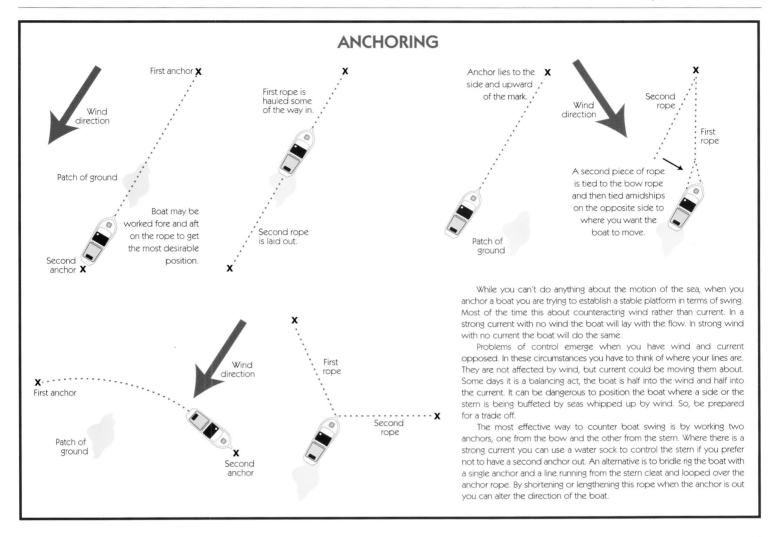

First anchor **X**

Wind direction

Patch of ground

Boat may be worked fore and aft on the rope to get the most desirable position.

Second anchor **X**

First rope is hauled some of the way in.

X

Second rope is laid out.

X

Anchor lies to the side and upward of the mark.

X

Wind direction

Patch of ground

Second rope

X

First rope

A second piece of rope is tied to the bow rope and then tied amidships on the opposite side to where you want the boat to move.

X

Wind direction

First anchor

Patch of ground

Second anchor

X

First rope

X

Second rope

X

While you can't do anything about the motion of the sea, when you anchor a boat you are trying to establish a stable platform in terms of swing. Most of the time this about counteracting wind rather than current. In a strong current with no wind the boat will lay with the flow. In strong wind with no current the boat will do the same.

Problems of control emerge when you have wind and current opposed. In these circumstances you have to think of where your lines are. They are not affected by wind, but current could be moving them about. Some days it is a balancing act, the boat is half into the wind and half into the current. It can be dangerous to position the boat where a side or the stern is being buffeted by seas whipped up by wind. So, be prepared for a trade off.

The most effective way to counter boat swing is by working two anchors, one from the bow and the other from the stern. Where there is a strong current you can use a water sock to control the stern if you prefer not to have a second anchor out. An alternative is to bridle rig the boat with a single anchor and a line running from the stern cleat and looped over the anchor rope. By shortening or lengthening this rope when the anchor is out you can alter the direction of the boat.

---

of top anglers and the rest. These gulfs are narrow streams of learning through which a little common sense flows.

Anglers who specialise, whether it is bream or mulloway, will generally achieve success more consistently than those who swap and change. By concentrating on a species you develop a closer affinity and begin to understand its habits. All this of course means using a bit of grey matter. Fishing is about thinking. The result of thinking is success and being an angler in paradise is a lot better than being an angler from hell.

ANCHORING

If you intend to fish for long periods at anchor my advice is to have two sets of anchors, for soft bottoms and reef. For example, the popular double bladed Danforth style anchor is not suited for reef, while multi-pronged anchors will not take hold in sand or mud. A recent anchor design that uses a large triangle shaped blade has been the Sarca, which is designed to work in all terrain.

The secret of effective anchoring lies in the use of a long length of heavy chain and a heavy rubber ring that is tied off at the bow

and attached to the anchor rope. As the boat rises and falls the ring stretches but there is no lifting action on the anchor. If raising the anchor presents problems the way around this is to use a large polystyrene ball or heavy plastic float. When it comes time to raise the anchor the float is placed on the anchor rope via a shackle. The boat is motored forward forcing the float down the anchor rope to lift the anchor off the bottom.

In my experience it is preferable to carry at least two anchors, as a swinging boat can be a problem. The most effective way to counter this is to employ a stern anchor. An alternative is to bridle rig the boat with two anchors off the bow. Stern anchors can be a problem as there is a need to tether the anchor short to the boat. If you have too much anchor rope trailing astern, there is always a high risk of a good fish fouling your line. Regardless of which anchoring method you chose it is important that you anchor to allow for tide, wind and the distance you will cast your baits from the boat.

TROLLING

Trolling is one of the most successful methods devised for catching many of our sport fish

in both fresh and salt water. Whether you are chasing trout or Murray cod or perhaps Australian salmon or marlin, trolling will sometimes prove the most successful method.

I used to believe that trolling was a lazy way of fishing and that anybody could catch a fish towing a lure behind a boat. That perception was wrong, on both counts. If you are lazy and simply toss a lure out without thinking about what you are doing then it is a lazy procedure and if you happen to catch a fish well, that's just a bonus. Anglers I have met who are seriously into trolling are far from lazy. Success comes through thinking about the approach, the type of lures and colour, plus a hundred and one other little things.

Some lures simply cannot be trolled at anything more than walking pace while others need speeds of six knots or more to get the best results.

High speed trolling lures include big bibless minnows and skirted lures that are used for bluewater pelagics such as marlin and mackerel. Big bibbed deep divers such as the Halco Poltergeist are trolled much slower for the likes of Murray cod, yellowbelly and estuary perch while in between these come the likes of

TROLLING LURE PATTERNS

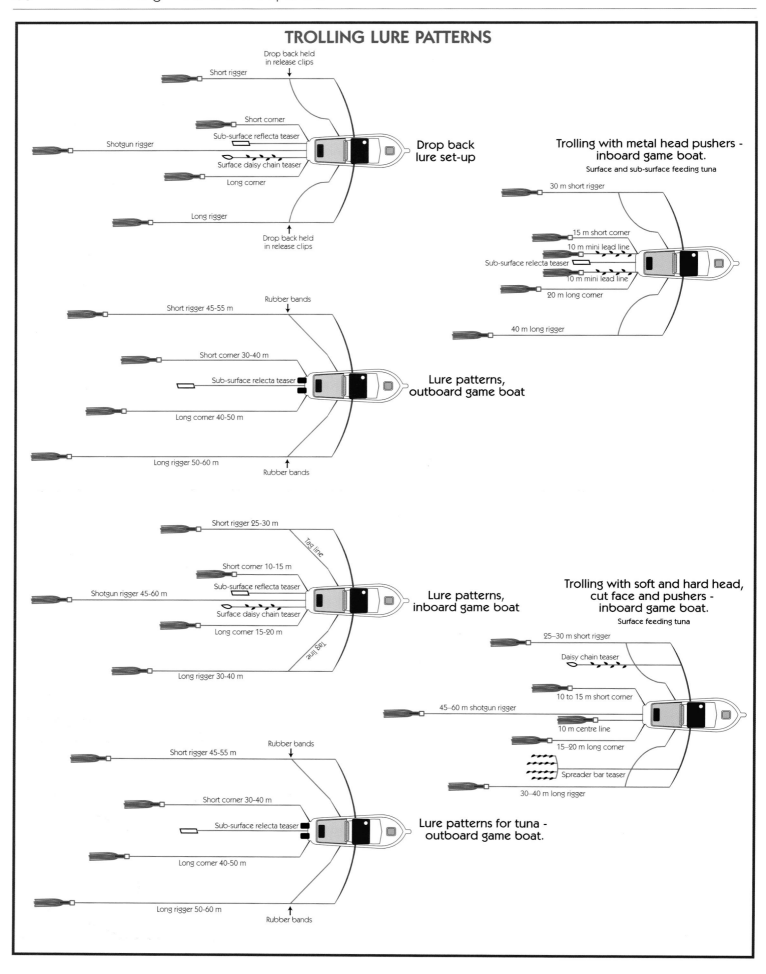

Drop back held
in release clips

Short rigger

Short corner

Shotgun rigger

Sub-surface reflecta teaser

Surface daisy chain teaser

Long corner

Long rigger

Drop back held
in release clips

**Drop back
lure set-up**

Rubber bands

Short rigger 45-55 m

Short corner 30-40 m

Sub-surface relecta teaser

Long corner 40-50 m

Long rigger 50-60 m

Rubber bands

**Lure patterns,
outboard game boat**

Short rigger 25-30 m

Tag line

Short corner 10-15 m

Sub-surface reflecta teaser

Shotgun rigger 45-60 m

Surface daisy chain teaser

Long corner 15-20 m

Tag line

Long rigger 30-40 m

**Lure patterns,
inboard game boat**

Rubber bands

Short rigger 45-55 m

Short corner 30-40 m

Sub-surface relecta teaser

Long corner 40-50 m

Long rigger 50-60 m

Rubber bands

**Lure patterns for tuna -
outboard game boat.**

**Trolling with metal head pushers -
inboard game boat.**
Surface and sub-surface feeding tuna

30 m short rigger

15 m short corner
10 m mini lead line

Sub-surface relecta teaser

10 m mini lead line

20 m long corner

40 m long rigger

**Trolling with soft and hard head,
cut face and pushers -
inboard game boat.**
Surface feeding tuna

25–30 m short rigger

Daisy chain teaser

10 to 15 m short corner

45–60 m shotgun rigger

10 m centre line

15–20 m long corner

Spreader bar teaser

30–40 m long rigger

WHERE FISH ARE

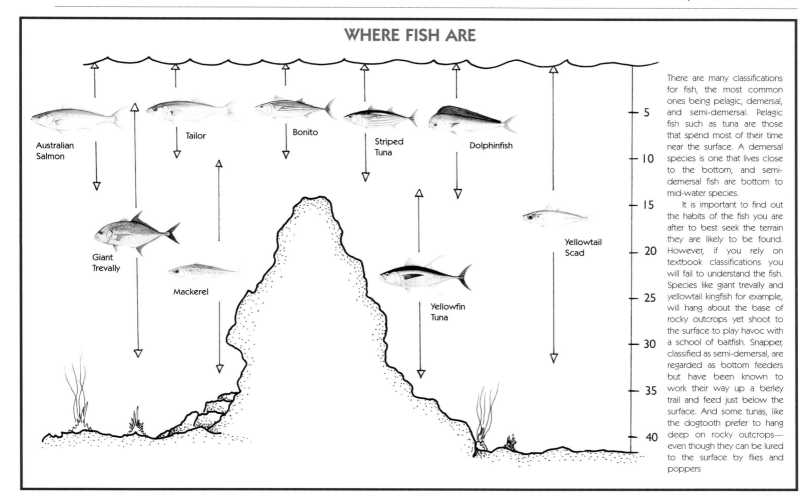

There are many classifications for fish, the most common ones being pelagic, demersal, and semi-demersal. Pelagic fish such as tuna are those that spend most of their time near the surface. A demersal species is one that lives close to the bottom, and semi-demersal fish are bottom to mid-water species.

It is important to find out the habits of the fish you are after to best seek the terrain they are likely to be found. However, if you rely on textbook classifications you will fail to understand the fish. Species like giant trevally and yellowtail kingfish for example, will hang about the base of rocky outcrops yet shoot to the surface to play havoc with a school of baitfish. Snapper, classified as semi-demersal, are regarded as bottom feeders but have been known to work their way up a berley trail and feed just below the surface. And some tunas, like the dogtooth prefer to hang deep on rocky outcrops— even though they can be lured to the surface by flies and poppers

'winged' lures such as Tassie Devils for trout and wobblers for salmon.

In lakes, rivers and estuaries, trolling is generally a slow procedure, one where noise is a factor in success. Outboard motors can be noisy so many anglers opt to use electric motors to cut down on noise and give a slower trolling speed. Downriggers, which take a lure down to the depth you want to run at, are more common in fresh water.

Many species caught in these environments prefer to hang around snags or structure so it is critical for anglers to hold their rods and 'feel' their way through when fishing this sort of territory. One way of doing this is to use a braid line. Braided lines have limited stretch and are much thinner—about one-third—the diameter of monofilament line of the same breaking strain. The finer diameter allows lures to run much deeper while the minimal stretch factor gives the opportunity to feel when a lure is hitting snags. In the case of monofilament line, which can have a stretch factor of more than 25 per cent, the hooks on lures will sometimes jag a snag before there is time to realise the danger.

Offshore and in our bays trolling is different. Along the east coast trolling lures for pelagic species including marlin, tuna and even mackerel depending on how far north you venture, involves minimum speeds of six knots and sometimes as fast as 10 knots. Lures are often run on the surface, or just below and noise in the form of a rattle and bubble trails can be important. In southern waters barracouta and salmon are the most common saltwater fishes sought after. These require slower speeds of less than six knots, but not as slow as those used in fresh water.

Current lines, which can be seen on the sea surface as calm strips of water between the ruffled surfaces are often worked. Just as important are reefs and structure where predatory species are most likely to be found hunting out smaller fish.

Braided line isn't so important but sometimes traces need to be made from wire, especially when you are chasing toothy critters such as couta. Some anglers prefer material such as Twistweld. This wire has a coating of a plastic-like substance, which is heated up with a lighter to fuse together. My preference is for piano wire using a haywire twist to hold it together.

Finally there is the issue of changing lures. Clip swivels make life easy in this regard but you can also buy the clip minus the swivel and this in my opinion is a better way to go.

TECHNOLOGY

Most seasoned anglers have their marks. The smart people keep a record of these mrks for future reference. Past practice has been to establish a mark by triangulation, lining up at least two distinctive shore-based objects to position the boat. The advent of Global Positioning Systems has done away with this and has unerring accuracy that cannot be beaten by eyesight triangulation.

As well as giving latitude and longitude, some GPS units come with inbuilt maps, and

marks

If you find a good fishing ground in a bay or estuary, it is a good idea to take note of where it is so you can return to the exact spot. If you have a Global Positioning System unit then it is easy: simply mark the Waypoint. An alternative is to use landmarks. By lining up three or four items on the land, be they a tree, a house roof or alike, you can easily return to the same position on another occasion. Just make sure that the marks you use are not going to move.

most can be set to track a course or show you where you are on the map. The trend has moved away from satellite positioning systems to 'differential' or DGPS units.

Unlike standard GPS, the DGPS units are free from interference and can place you within one metre of a desired spot. A DGPS unit gets its signal from a land based Differential Beacon Receiver.

The true value of a GPS unit though is not in finding fishing spots. If you are ever out at night and fog rolls then you will come to understand that these units are worth their weight in gold, particularly if you remembered to mark the boat ramp as a Waypoint.

SONAR

While being able to position yourself over a particular location within a metre is fine, seeing the bottom and whether or not there are any fish in the vicinity is even better. A good sounder enables the angler to find fish, terrain and know the depth of water.

There are many types available on the market and some have features including digital compass, water temperature, boat speed, and distance travelled. A good sounder will show clear definitions that the angler can easily decipher including the type of bottom, structure, and weed.

Fish come up as arches or boomerangs, the

bigger the arch the bigger the fish. Arches are created when the fish enters the cone of the transducer signal. When the fish first enters the cone the signal at the outer edge has to travel a slightly greater distance to strike the fish than it does in the centre of the cone. In the centre of the cone the signal is travelling a shorter distance to reach the fish so the signal rises to form the top of the arch. Leaving the cone the signal has to travel further to reach the fish so the screen trace drops to complete the arch.

A perfect arch is only formed when a fish passes straight through the cone. Sometimes you only get half or part of an arch. A change of direction, speed, or depth by the fish will alter the shape of the signal. Perfect arches form only if the face of the transducer is level with the bottom, if tilted it will only ever display half arches. The size of the arches received can be influenced by the size of the fish.

FINDING FISH

Being able to see the bottom and whether or not there are any fish in the vicinity is of more value to anglers than most other technologies available. Being on a mark or sitting in the right water temperature zones means nothing if there are no fish in the vicinity, or even likely fish holding structure.

A good sounder will show clear definitions that the angler can easily decipher, these will include reef, mud, and weed. On some sounders fish come up as red blotches or may be indicated by fish symbols, but the most common reading is that which shows fish as arches or boomerangs, the bigger the arch the bigger the fish.

Arches are created when the fish enters the cone of the transducer signal. When the fish first enters the cone the signal at the outer edge has to travel a slightly greater distance to strike the fish than it does in the centre of the cone. In the centre of the cone the signal is travelling a shorter distance to reach the fish so the signal rises to

form the top of the arch. Leaving the cone the signal has to travel further to reach the fish so the screen trace drops to complete the arch.

A perfect arch is only formed when a fish passes straight through the cone. Sometimes you only get half or part of an arch. A change of direction, speed, or depth by the fish will alter the shape of the signal. Perfect arches form only if the face of the transducer is level with the bottom, if tilted it will only ever display half arches. The size of the arches received can be influenced by the size of the fish arch, a sign that a fish is on the side of the cone of signals emitted by the transducer.

In seven metres of water the transducer signal cone stretches out to about two metres in diameter. One thing about echo sounder is that there is less clutter and a clearer reception when you are sounding with a sea rather than motoring into it.

A sonar or depth sounder unit operates as the eyes of an angler underwater. Understanding how to read one of these units will improve your results.

BAIT FISHING
BERLEY

Berleying is perhaps the single most effective way of creating a feeding scenario tailored to suit your particular methods.

Slow fishing can be frustrating. Worse still are those days when you know there are a few fish about but you either can't find them or, you can find them but they won't bite. Sometimes all it takes is a change of tide to stir up some action. Unless you can walk on water, that is

berley recipe

An easy berley mix to make up consists of chook pellets, tuna oil, bread, cat food and pilchard pieces. These should be mulched in a large plastic container and mixed in with water and allowed to soak for a day before use. Chook pellets and bread will soak the oil up. When this is done pour the berley into milk cartons and freeze.

When you go fishing remove one of the frozen berley blocks from the carton and put it into the berley bucket as you are travelling out. This will help to start the thawing process. An alternative is to place the frozen berley in an onion bag and leave it hanging over the side of the boat, but preferably off the bottom. The simple process of lifting and dropping the bag while it is in the water will start freeing up berley. The slow disintegration as it thaws will create a neat trail.

Coral trout like this beauty held by Steve Earle are susceptible to a well-laid berley.

beyond your capability. The best alternative is to induce the fish to feed by tantalising their taste buds. In other words, use berley.

Using berley is not rocket science. It is a simple procedure that can be fine-tuned to suit different situations. The only circumstance I know of in salt water where berley cannot (or should not) be used is close to swimming beaches, for obvious reasons. Other than that, you can work up berley trails in any saltwater scenario.

I am surprised at how few shore-based anglers deploy a berley. In most situations, berley is an advantage regardless of whether you are fishing in a boat or from a pier. Making the effort to gear up and go fishing is only part

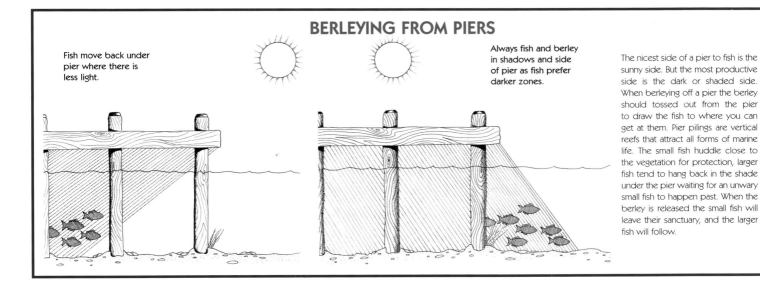

BERLEYING FROM PIERS

Fish move back under pier where there is less light.

Always fish and berley in shadows and side of pier as fish prefer darker zones.

The nicest side of a pier to fish is the sunny side. But the most productive side is the dark or shaded side. When berleying off a pier the berley should tossed out from the pier to draw the fish to where you can get at them. Pier pilings are vertical reefs that attract all forms of marine life. The small fish huddle close to the vegetation for protection, larger fish tend to hang back in the shade under the pier waiting for an unwary small fish to happen past. When the berley is released the small fish will leave their sanctuary, and the larger fish will follow.

BERLEYING FROM THE ROCKS

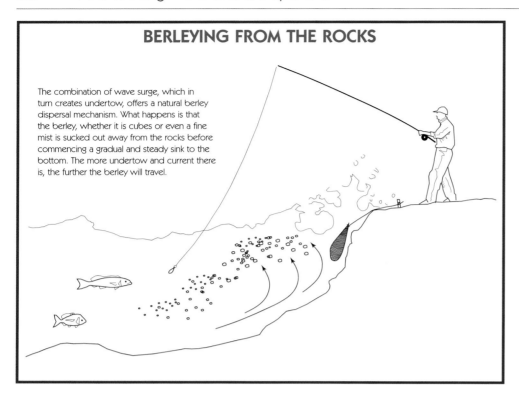

The combination of wave surge, which in turn creates undertow, offers a natural berley dispersal mechanism. What happens is that the berley, whether it is cubes or even a fine mist is sucked out away from the rocks before commencing a gradual and steady sink to the bottom. The more undertow and current there is, the further the berley will travel.

of the battle. Sometimes not running a berley trail can mean a wasted effort.

Methods of deploying a berley vary and depend on the scenario. The only sure thing about employing any berley is that it will at the very least attract small fish, and you know what follows small fish around.

Nor is berley the be all to end all. You do need to be in a feeding zone. In an estuary, you may want to work along a drop off, or a combination snag and drop off. Offshore for tuna you need to find the right water before starting a cube trail while in the surf pick out the best gutters and rips close to the beach.

ROCKS

Many anglers regard working a berley trail on the rocks as being too hard. Based on personal experience, the best ever sessions I was involved in were in combination with a berley trail. Fishing the stones on the New South Wales south coast one year, we experienced a hot run of longtails. While many fish were returned, one was always kept to be tail roped and hung over the edge of the ledge. The action of the waves pushing the body of the tuna against the rocks created a mincing effect and the trail lasted as long as the fish.

Of course you do not always have a tuna lying around to do this with, and not everyone wants to hook up with gamefish either. One of the most effective techniques I have used is free floating baits drifted down a wash spiced with berley. In this case, a berley is made up of pilchard or fish scraps, chopped, and mixed with chook pellets and tuna oil. Whenever

chook pellets are to be employed, it is better to allow time for the pellets to soak up the oil to ensure that the oil breaks up below the surface in the water column.

The optimum way to present berley is to use a ladle or large spoon and scoop some out of a bucket, throwing it into the wash at regular intervals as a wave is receding. This method has accounted for a range of fish including snapper, salmon, and trevally. It's a simple, effective method but the berley has to be maintained for it to effective, for when the berley stops, so too do the fish.

Stan Wright at Apollo Bay on the Great

Ocean Road in Victoria uses a berley of bran to attract the large garfish. But that is only part of the story. He also selects areas where he believes there is a naturally occurring berley trail. On a rock ledge, he tells why a certain area will produce fish by pointing to a pile of rotting bull kelp in a corner. His explanation starts with a run down on the life cycle of flies that lay eggs, which turn into maggots that feed on the rotting weed. On high tides the waves pound over the kelp and maggots are washed back into the ocean. A natural food trail brings in fish to feed. Adding the bran to the trail brings the fish higher in the water column where they can be caught.

BAYS AND ESTUARIES

Fishing in bays and estuaries, berley can be used to attract the likes of bream, flathead, gummy sharks, silver trevally, mullet, garfish and a host of other species. It works from a boat or shore, although there is more scope for boating anglers.

A key factor in shallow water berley operations is the terrain. The first thing to do is find an area where there is both current and a slight drop off. Current is essential to disperse berley and dead flat ground is not as productive as uneven areas. A slight drop off, even if is only 10 or 15 cm, can make all the difference.

It is important that a shallow water berley trail consist of a fine mist. Avoid using large chunks of fish as it defeats the object of the trail, which is to give the fish a taste, then offer up a meal with a hook inside.

In this case fish like garfish, mullet, trevally and salmon will come right up to the berley pot and hang about anywhere from the surface to

BAYS AND ESTUARIES

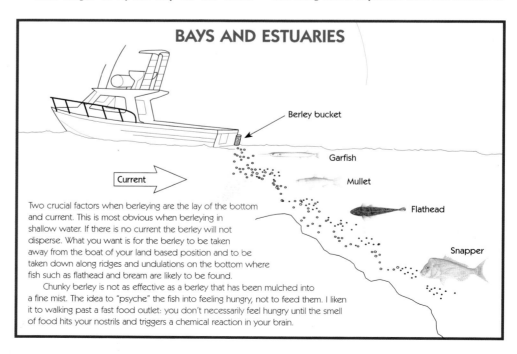

Berley bucket

Garfish

Mullet

Current

Flathead

Snapper

Two crucial factors when berleying are the lay of the bottom and current. This is most obvious when berleying in shallow water. If there is no current the berley will not disperse. What you want is for the berley to be taken away from the boat of your land based position and to be taken down along ridges and undulations on the bottom where fish such as flathead and bream are likely to be found.

Chunky berley is not as effective as a berley that has been mulched into a fine mist. The idea to "psyche" the fish into feeling hungry, not to feed them. I liken it to walking past a fast food outlet: you don't necessarily feel hungry until the smell of food hits your nostrils and triggers a chemical reaction in your brain.

light bites

If you are after fish that are finicky and bite lightly, consider using a solid tip rod as this type has an increased degree of sensitivity than totally hollow fibreglass rod tips. A selection of interchangeable solid tips makes one rod more suited to different applications of fishing methods. When fishing turbid water those baits that smell such as shellfish like mussels and worms will often prove the better choice.

mid-water. Gummy sharks will hang well back during the day, but move in close at night.

Flathead can be a lot of fun. When they arrive, they will be in predator mode and agitated. Sometimes sitting directly below the berley pot, flathead prop on their pectoral fins and remain motionless and poised ready to strike at anything that moves. Now is the time to offer up an unweighted bait, or else pass a fly or lure past the flathead you want. When the fish sees your offering its dorsal spine will arc up and it will shoot off the bottom and devour it.

An old luderick angler who was giving

estuary

The weed line is an area where food is at its most abundant for some fish. Decaying vegetation and softer sand attracts many burrowing creatures, which provide meals for many fish. Whiting, flathead and luderick are some of the many fish that you may catch fishing on the weed line.

the local luderick population a solid workout showed a variation on this method to me in the harbour at Bermagui. The concept was the same, the application slightly different. In this case, his berley mix consisted of lettuce weed gathered from the rocks and mixed with damp sand to help it sink. Each time before he threw his berley out, the old angler crunched the weed and sand in his hands to make sure the lettuce weed was shredded.

SURF

Anglers who work the surf often spice the beach by tossing berley into the wash of a receding wave. This system works extremely well for the likes of mullet, Australian salmon, and tailor. While the method has been successfully practised for many years, it falls short of achieving optimum results.

There is a better way but it takes more effort. Geoff Wilson showed me the better way on the beach at Pt Addis. Geoff has developed a large berley cage that relies on wave action to mince up fish and establish a trail. The berley cage is cylindrical, about 1 metre in diameter and 1.5 m long and covered all over with 20 mm square birdcage wire. Fish scraps are placed inside the cage, which is anchored on the beach by two ropes at the edge of the wash. What happens is that as a wave comes in the cage rolls up the beach and is then pushed back down again. The force of the outgoing water rushing through the cage pushes the fish scraps against the wire and minces them. Simple design, brilliant application.

OFFSHORE

Berley is an essential ingredient when fishing offshore. A good berley slick will attract a range of species including marlin, tuna,

mackerel, sharks, and a host of other species like Australian salmon, barracouta, snapper, and even arrow squid. It all depends on what is available in the area you happen to be fishing.

When making up the berley for sharks in Victoria, given that barracouta and arrow squid are a by-product, a higher proportion of tuna oil is used. I normally get fish scraps, old pilchards and crunch them in the pot. As well as mixing oil in with the berley, some shark fisherman like to hang the tuna oil off the stern of the boat and allow it to drip feed into the trail. One way to ensure the oil goes where it is meant to is to pour it onto pieces of bread and place them in the berley pot.

Ironically, anglers fishing for yellowfin tuna off Bermagui tend to minimise their berley because of sharks, preferring instead to rely on a cube trail to bring fish to the boat. Berleying offshore in Queensland is a way of attracting mackerel to the boat, and bringing reef fish like coral trout on the bite. Again, this is more a cubing than a berley exercise.

CUBING

It's slightly different method to berleying, and gives the angler the opportunity to sightfish for the species being sought.

At least that is my definition of what is one of the most effective and exciting fishing methods used today. Let me give you an example of what cubing is really like.

Conditions couldn't be better. My fishing partner Richard Carr and I are more than 20

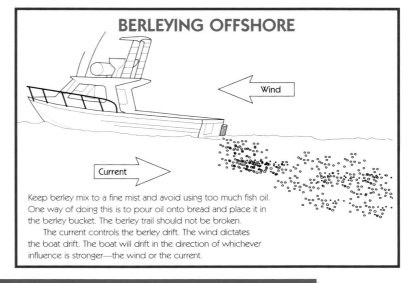

BERLEYING OFFSHORE

Wind

Current

Keep berley mix to a fine mist and avoid using too much fish oil. One way of doing this is to pour oil onto bread and place it in the berley bucket. The berley trail should not be broken.

The current controls the berley drift. The wind dictates the boat drift. The boat will drift in the direction of whichever influence is stronger—the wind or the current.

A berley cage developed for the surf has proven effective. As the waves wash in through the cage, and then recede the force of the water minces the berley against the wire.

Tuna like these southern bluefin will follow a cube trail up to the stern of the boat.

nautical miles northeast of Narooma on a calm, purple-hued sea. The cloud cover is high and thin. An ageing temperature gauge gives a digital reading of 17.4 degrees Celsius. We aren't concerned; the gauge is a degree out. Around us small grey mutton-birds and gannets are working. The light slaps of water echoing against the fibreglass hull of our 18-foot cuddy cab and the occasional squawking birds are the only sounds.

Slimy mackerel (blue mackerel) caught a little over an hour earlier and sliced neatly into cubes, lay spread across the bait board. I pump the berley as Richard starts feeding the cubes into the water. Few words are spoken. To quote Charles Dickens, this is a time of 'Great Expectations'.

Less than half an hour into the exercise and we have visitors. Whoosh! Whoosh! You think you can hear them as they come tearing through the berley trail. But, of course, you can't. And you don't see the yellowfin coming. It is always a back or gilded flank as they dive through the slick to inhale a cube. On the surface a figure of eight eddy appears where a yellowfin has taken a cube barely two metres astern. You expect to see the top lobe of a

yellowfin tail and the pointed tip of a yellow sickle breaking the water. But you don't. It is the torpedo-shaped bulk of a fin, displacing, and sucking water down, which causes the vortex.

Richard takes a cube off the bait board and threads it on the sharpened 9/0 hook attached to his 24 kg outfit. Another cube goes out, followed by the one with a hook in it. Matching the drift and sink rate of the free cubes, he inches out line. It is an urgent take. Richard pushes the lever on his reel up to strike mode, the line pulls tight, and the fish's momentum sends the point of the hook home into the jaw and 45 kg of tuna races away at full steam and the battle begins.

This is fishing for tuna on the east Australian coast, about 350 miles south of Sydney in the State of New South Wales. Yellowfin are one of the toughest and most

sought after fish in these parts. Spectacularly colourful in the water, they're a fast action, eating machine with enough grunt enough to give the strongest angler a double hernia. Sizzling line-burning runs, sometimes in the vertical plane, are a trademark while the fight that ensues can be more like an all in brawl with fish and angler trading blow for blow. Yellowfin show a predilection to lug down deep; a stand-up fight in a rocking boat makes balance difficult and anglers earn every kilogram, bit by bit.

Hooking and landing a yellowfin can take anywhere from 15 minutes to more than a couple of hours. It depends not just on the size of the fish and the weight of tackle used. Determining factors also include the size of the fight in the fish and where the hook is, down deep or in the jaw. I've seen 50 kg yellowfin hooked deep take less than 15 minutes to bring to gaff. The same size fish hooked in the mouth is a different proposition and can fight two or three times as long. On big fin, 75 kg plus fish, fights lasting two hours or more are not unusual with the fish often winning out as the angler runs out of steam. Even a 20-minute encounter with a yellowfin that wants to lug deep straight down below your boat can be a backbreaking exercise. Two hours of winding, pumping and hanging on is a masochistic experience requiring single-minded resolve by the angler to push through the pain barrier.

You can catch yellowfin on lures and flies but the big action on the south coast is drifting using berley in conjunction with cubes or live baits. People who advocate using lures and trolling in these waters are on a different wavelength to experienced hands. Lure caught yellowfin are almost a by-catch for anglers seeking billfish. Generally these fish are smaller and it is a hit and miss option not

CUBING

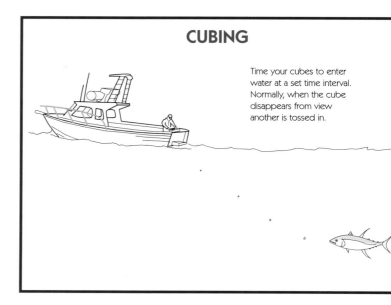

Time your cubes to enter water at a set time interval. Normally, when the cube disappears from view another is tossed in.

preferred by the specialist fin-chaser. But when you run a cube trail and rise to the occasion you can present lures, flies and live baits more effectively.

It is a similar scenario to dogtooth tuna off Tonga, sailfish off Samoa and Spanish mackerel and Wahoo along the Great Barrier Reef in northern Australia. The locations are different and in some cases so too are the fish, but the methods remain the same. And there is nothing so exciting in fishing as bringing fish to you and seeing them before you offer up the bait or lure. Seeing a fish, hunting and stalking that fish and watching it take the bait, lure or fly is what angling is all about.

Cubing or chunking, call it what you will, is about finding an environment likely to hold fish and then value adding to the surroundings. It's not a new technique, but that doesn't make it any less exciting or successful. This method works in tropical and temperate waters, both from the shore and offshore. You can run cubes down deep over offshore reefs, and you can employ similar methods inshore in areas so shallow you can see the bubbles from a crab passing wind. More importantly, cubing attracts quality fish in terms of size.

Like any specialty angling technique, the *modus operandi* is to employ tactics that will produce results. Simply tossing bait into the water relies on luck. Anglers can make their own luck by knowing where and when to cube, and how.

Some people mistake cubing for chumming or what we in Australia call berleying. The difference is marked. When you run a chum trail the object is to create a scent without offering up a feed, which is why fine mist trails, heavily laced with fish oil, are often more productive than those heavy mixes with fish chunks and solid matter. It's a bit like walking past a fast food outlet, it's the smell that attracts you, even if you weren't hungry before you got there. And, whereas a chum mix can be all manner of foodstuffs from chicken pellets to dog food, cube trails are specific in what is offered to the fish.

Allan Greig fished a fly down deep in a berley trail off the north end of Fraser Island and caught this mackerel tuna.

SPECIES

Just about any piscivorous species—preferably fish that hunt other fish—is a prime candidate for a cube session. Most of the mackerels and tunas respond well, as do the likes of sharks, dolphinfish and a host of big reef fish. Even marlin and sailfish will sometimes rise to the occasion of cubes. Ideally, a cubing session should be species specific, which means offering premium bait in an area where conditions are perfect.

But we don't live in an ideal world and sometimes the fish don't play by the same rules as they did the day before. Take sharks for example. Sharks are at their best when they first steam into a cube trail. They are hungry and looking for the source of the trail. When in this aggravated state most sharks will take a cube straight up. Once they settle in the trail though sharks become less aggressive and therefore less willing to attack anything. Something you will notice if you observe sharks in a trail in their own environment is that they rarely feed on small scraps while big chunks of fish flesh are always taken.

The problem with sharks is that when they are in the trail it can sometimes prove a deterrent to other fish. And I can think of nothing more frustrating after spending a few hours drifting to establish a decent trail and being rewarded with a hook-up to have a shark come along and eat my prize.

SUITABLE LOCATIONS

Holding areas for fish are not always reefs and sunken wrecks. Fish are attracted by many different factors including current, water temperature and cover while, when it comes to predators, what attracts them most are other fish, preferably smaller and in good numbers. Reading the water for current lines that signify temperature changes is as important for the game fisher as is finding reefs and drop-offs for the angler hunting fish nearer the bottom. Fish holding areas can be pockets out of the main current, or channels through reefs where water rushing out can bring with it smaller fish.

FINDING FISH

It doesn't matter where you fish, the trick is in knowing how to find the fish. To do so you have to read the water, know the signs and understand what is happening. It is not enough to simply go to the Continental Shelf, find the right water temperature and start fishing.

If you were looking for dogtooth tuna for example then a seamount or reef with plenty of cover would be the first stop. Hook a doggie in that sort of terrain and your chances of landing it are limited. The wonderful thing about running a cube trail is that you can stand up current of such obstacles and bring the fish out to open water.

On the day mentioned earlier, Richard and I were more than 20 nautical miles offshore. We kept motoring until we found the right conditions to get the results. It's a long way in a small boat but given the right weather and seas the extra miles can pay off. Anyway, most

of us probably couldn't swim a couple of miles to shore.

In our instance, we were looking for water temperature of about 18 to 21 degrees Celsius. Temperature gauges in boats give a surface reading but water temperature can be multi-tiered and variable with a patch of cold hiding a warmer layer below it. And temperature is just one piece of the jigsaw, albeit the only piece that can be found through technical means. Good water will also be a deep blue, almost purple, and will have current and birds when the fish are about.

Current on the ocean can be distinguished if you know what to look for. When current is running inshore, you will see the turbulence of water increase as the current runs over shallower grounds such as reefs. Offshore the current can also change the surface appearance of the water. On calm days, the current will be seen as small constant ripples on the surface, a slick or oil patch is a mark of current change.

Feeding birds are a positive sign. You have to know which birds to look out for. On the Australian south coast the important birds are mollymawks (black-browed albatrosses), gannets and shearwaters, either the small fluttering shearwaters or the larger, short-tailed or mutton-birds. Yellowfin push baitfish to the surface and birds like gannets dive from great heights to feast on the unfortunate small fish.

FEEDING OUT CUBES

Like Rubik's Cube, cubing takes thought and application before a pattern becomes apparent. Some never get to see it. Too often we take the outward view—when we should be looking inwards. The secret about cubes lies in the shape and what's on the inside.

Small mackerel, tuna, and other baitfish work well, as do packaged baitfish such as anchovies—a species we call pilchards. I like slimy mackerel best as these can simply be sliced through the body to make oval shaped cubes about one to 1½ inches thick. With larger fish such as small tuna, make a series of vertical and longitudinal incisions to down to the bones and then fillet. The size of the cubes depends on the cuts but two inches square is about as big as you want to go.

Cubes are fed at intervals; the rate of feed dependent on current and drift. As a rule of thumb toss a cube in and just when you think it is about to disappear, drop in another. Always keep at least two cubes in visual range. At the start of the day it can pay to work up some berley in conjunction with the cubes. The key to cubing is to maintain the trail, even when your partner is fighting a fin, as this ensures that any other yellowfin in the trail will hang about.

HOOK-UP

There will be times when yellowfin are running hot to trot through a cube trail taking baits at random. Conversely, there will also be frustrating periods when they will take every cube offered except those with hooks in them. You can bury your hooks in the cubes; use smaller hooks or paint them every colour of the rainbow—it makes no difference.

Notwithstanding any of this, the critical time for anglers is knowing when to set the hook. When a big pelagic speedster takes a bait, you will know about it. These fish don't dally when they're hungry. Most often tuna like yellowfin, big eye and albacore come in from the side and above, inhaling the cube, turning and diving in the same motion. Mackerel and Wahoo hit hard and fast running away, slightly downwards but not quite as steep as the tuna. If you hook a beakie then anything could happen; down, away horizontally or a ballistic manoeuvre straight out of the water. Whichever happens, the take will be one of supersonic proportions.

A good take will be unrelenting. The longer you wait before setting the hook the deeper it is likely to be. When the take is positive and the fish tearing off there is little need to wait more than a few seconds before setting the hook. Cube baits are small and these fish have big mouths and are capable of ingesting food

Richard Carr with a 43 kg yellowfin caught on 14wt fly outfit while fishing a cube trail at the Kink off Bermagui.

Jim Harris with a 35 kg samson fish caught off the Yorke Peninsula in South Australia.

faster than politicians break promises.

When the fish like yellowfin are finicky then setting the hook can be difficult, sometimes it is impossible. What you do is keep the cube trail going and keep feeding out baits until they decide to do the right thing. It can be a frustrating period, and there are no guarantees on any given day. This is fishing and is no different in that regard.

Long deep runs are standard fare and they lug deep, swimming in circles as they are brought towards the surface. It is important to maintain pressure on the fish for the duration of the fight; this is particularly true for yellowfin hooked in the mouth. Because their mouths are hard, the hook barb can wear a large hole and any slackening of pressure can allow a hook to come free.

VALUE ADDING

Cubing can be used as an adjunct to other techniques. If you are into fly-fishing or lure casting for example then cubing is a good way to bring fish within range for a shot with a counterfeit offering. In Australia, I have used cubing techniques to bring tuna and sharks within fly rod range. Off Cairns, some of the local guns practise cubing to have a fly or lure shot at Spanish mackerel and Wahoo. In Samoa I raised a sailfish with a fly after one of the caped crusaders came steaming up a cube trail and in Vanuatu, a similar system has proven itself on dogtooth tuna. All it takes is for someone to have a go.

Fly fishers also find cubing effective for tuna. They set up the trail then work cube flies in similar vein while pilchard flies can be effective with pilchard pieces employed as the attractant.

And cubing works in bays and estuaries for species including snapper, bream, and trevally. Perhaps the prime example of tailoring fish feeding habits to suit your technique can be had with mullet. Bread is ground up and tossed on the surface, sometimes a smidgin of tuna oil helps, and allowed to float about a pier or along an estuary weed bed. If there are any mullet about, they will invariably rise to the occasion. A knowing angler will have a small piece of bread moulded onto a hook and will cast into the trail and allow it to drift to where the fish are feeding. You can work a floater but that's just extra tackle. Fly fishers will work bread flies or alternatively elk hair caddis flies.

LIVE BAIT

It doesn't matter whether you fish offshore or are land based, in fresh or salt water, live baiting is one of the most effective methods an angler can employ. Here are some of the top live baits.

FRESHWATER

Live baits used in freshwater applications are limited. The best are scrubworms, yabbies, shrimp, mudeye, smelt, and minnow. The last five are all caught in similar fashion in a net.

For yabbies, Opera House nets work best, while mudeyes are best found in dams and small swampy areas where there is plenty of vegetation. Shrimp can be found in vegetation either against the bank or in shallow areas of rivers and impoundments. You can catch shrimp and mudeyes using a fine mesh net that is pushed or dragged through the weed and grass in the water. Another method of catching shrimp is to use old paint tins, fill them with gum leaves and twigs, and leave these in the water close to the bank. The shrimp come along and take up residence. It is an effective method at places like Lake

LIVE BAIT CONTAINER

Some times you have to catch your live bait well away from where you intend fishing and that means transporting it. The only way to do this is with a live bait bucket. The larger the bucket the better it will be and a garbage bin is just about right. A lid, aerator, and carrying handles should all be incorporated to ensure an effective unit.

Be careful not to put too many baits into this style of container as this can be fatal for the fish.

FRESHWATER/ESTUARY LIVE BAIT RIG

Fishing with a live yabbie or mudeye under a bubble float is one of the most effective techniques employed. The depth the bait sits at is controlled by a cork stopper positioned on the line below the float. When working weed beds for estuary perch for example you may want to run your bait less than a metre below the surface. In a lake, fishing with mudeye for trout, a full rod length of line from the float to the hook may suit better.

Cork stopper controls depth.

Bubble float. Water pumped in to add weight for casting.

Adjust hook size to suit bait:
Mudeye — No. 12 short shank
Prawn — No. 2–4 long shank
Minnow — No. 4–6 short shank

Mulwala where the shrimp look big enough to take on a medium sized yabbie.

Minnow and smelt are best sought in backwaters away from the main current. Berleying with breadcrumbs will often raise them close enough to allow a net to be used. In some fast running water where the surface has been churned to froth, the minnow often hide under the froth where it lies close to the bank.

SALTWATER

Slimy mackerel: One of the most popular fish used for live baiting is the slimy mackerel, a prolific species that is found right around Australia. This fish grows to about 60 cm in length but the ideal size for bait is about 25 centimetres. Slimy mackerel are blue to blue-green on the back, which sports the distinctive narrow dark bars or mackerel pattern. The body below the lateral line is spotted and they have finlets behind the second dorsal and anal fins. Methods to catch these fish include spinning with small metal lures, or working baitfish jigs or bait in a berley trail.

Yakka: In many east coast areas the yakka or yellowtail scad is the mainstay of live baiting. These fish are basically light brown to yellow above and silver below and grow to a maximum length of about 30 centimetres. Yakkas can be found in Queensland, New South Wales, South Australia, Victoria and as far north as Quobba Station on the Western Australian coast. It is most common in New South Wales and is one of the finest baits available. Berley works well and sometimes, when the bait seems scarce, it is essential to fish for them just before daylight or late in the afternoon.

Baitfish jigs are popular but sometimes you will have your best results by berleying to raise the fish to the surface and then using small

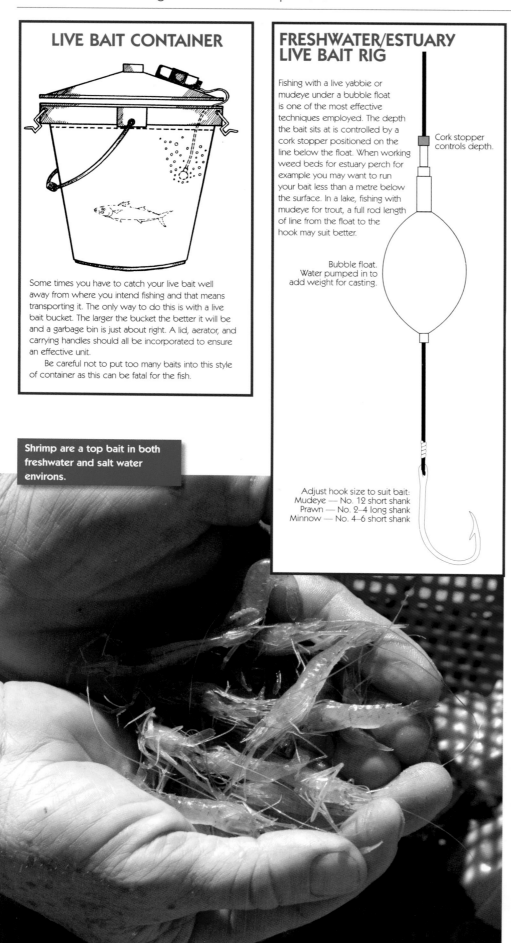

Shrimp are a top bait in both freshwater and salt water environs.

Two of the bluewater anglers' favourite baitfish the slimy mackerel top and the yakka or yellowtail scad below.

FRESHWATER/ESTUARY LIVE BAIT RIG

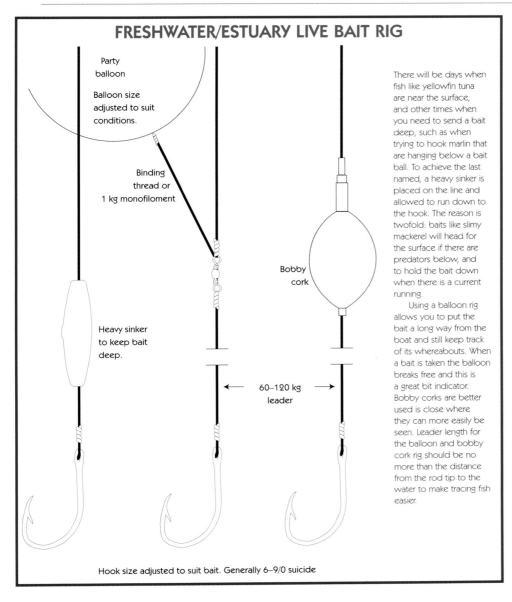

Party balloon

Balloon size adjusted to suit conditions.

Binding thread or 1 kg monofiloment

Heavy sinker to keep bait deep.

Bobby cork

← 60–120 kg leader →

There will be days when fish like yellowfin tuna are near the surface, and other times when you need to send a bait deep, such as when trying to hook marlin that are hanging below a bait ball. To achieve the last named, a heavy sinker is placed on the line and allowed to run down to the hook. The reason is twofold: baits like slimy mackerel will head for the surface if there are predators below, and to hold the bait down when there is a current running.

Using a balloon rig allows you to put the bait a long way from the boat and still keep track of its whereabouts. When a bait is taken the balloon breaks free and this is a great bit indicator. Bobby corks are better used is close where they can more easily be seen. Leader length for the balloon and bobby cork rig should be no more than the distance from the rod tip to the water to make tracing fish easier.

Hook size adjusted to suit bait. Generally 6–9/0 suicide

SALTWATER/RUNNING PATERNOSTER RIG: SURF/BAY/ ESTUARY

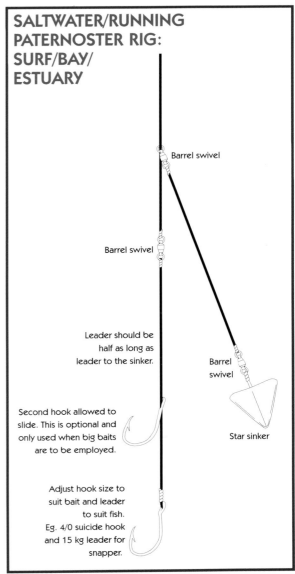

Barrel swivel

Barrel swivel

Leader should be half as long as leader to the sinker.

Barrel swivel

Star sinker

Second hook allowed to slide. This is optional and only used when big baits are to be employed.

Adjust hook size to suit bait and leader to suit fish. Eg. 4/0 suicide hook and 15 kg leader for snapper.

---

bait with no sinker that is dropped into the berley trail while the fish are feeding. Yakkas will eat most fish including small pieces of yakka, sweep, slimy mackerel, and mado.

Cowanyoung: Also known as jack mackerel, cowanyoung are similar in appearance to yakkas and the two are easily confused. Cowanyoung are dark green-blue above and silver below and the lateral line is armed along its length with broad keeled scutes. This fish is distributed from Shark Bay in Western Australia around the southern coastline to southern Queensland.

Silver trevally: While the bulk of this fish is a bright silver the back has a blue tinge, and along the flanks, the fish has a golden stripe, more easily recognised when freshly caught. Silver trevally can be caught in Queensland, New South Wales, Victoria, Tasmania, and New Zealand. Trevally are often caught down deep, beneath feeding schools of yakkas. As live bait, this fish has accounted for most of the

popular sportfish including tuna, kingfish, and marlin. Trevally are particularly effective on bright, sunny days when the big silver flash in the water from the fish's deep flank comes into its own. Trevally can be caught on small lures but bait is the most effective method. The key is to get the bait down near the bottom where they feed.

Sea garfish: Despite the inference in the name this fish also frequents rivers and estuaries. Sea gars can be found in all States and they achieve a respectable 45 cm in length. Bearing a bright green back with three dark brown streaks running along it, they also have a triangular upper jaw, which is longer than it is wide. Garfish generally lurk at the back of the berley trail and to catch them one of the best methods I know of is to allow an unweighted bait to drift out to them. Pieces of fish or dough are effective as bait. Most anglers work garfish in conjunction with small bobby corks. They swim on or near the surface and will last

for hours when properly hooked up. Garfish offer the best alternative for yellowfin when the latter are feeding on sauries or 'no-bill' gars as the professional fishermen call them.

Australian salmon: Also known as bay trout, salmon trout, sambos and kahawai in New Zealand, salmon can be caught in all southern States including Tasmania, where adult fish are referred to as black- backs and the young specimens as newfish. Salmon can be caught just about anywhere there is salt water. They are greenish above and silver below and their pectoral fins are yellow. Young salmon have brown markings on their back and sides, which give them a trout-like appearance. Spinning is the most effective method of hooking salmon, as they do not appear to show any strong preference for schooling and feeding in berley trails, as is the case with yakkas.

Tailor: An extremely popular species on both the east and west coasts of the continent, tailor can grow 15 kilograms. Tailor are successful live bait for sharks and work well as dead bait for Spanish mackerel.

Tailor are silver to white on the belly and the back is grey to blue in colour. The first low dorsal fin can be laid down in a groove on their back while the second dorsal and the anal fin are much higher and appear to balance one another out. The tail is moderately forked and the scales are small and easily removed. Like salmon, these are often caught on lures on the edge of white water, particularly at first and last light.

Nannygai: This species occurs from southern Queensland right around the southern half of Australia, including Tasmania, to West Australia. Not a common capture by shore-based anglers, offshore anglers regard nannygai as hot yellowfin bait. Nannygai are a reddish-pink with tints of gold and purple and bar markings on their sides, the caudal fin is red and they have a white belly. These fish grows to 45 cm but 15 cm is an ideal bait size.

Mullet: Sea mullet grow to a length of 60 cm and attain a weight of up to 8 kilograms. They are also known as the poddy, river and hardgut mullet. The sea mullet is distinctive in that it has a small black spot at the base of the pectoral fin, the colour tone is green above and silver to white below. Yelloweye mullet is also a popular baitfish and their main distinctive features are their bright yellow eyes. Growing to 30 cm in length, yelloweye mullet have brown markings on their fins and are olive brown to green above and silver below.

shopping list

SALTWATER LIVEBAITING:

OUTFIT: Two-kilogram line, small threadline reel, and light rod about 1.6 to 2 m long.
HOOK: No. 6 – 8 for most small baitfish. Ancillary items include: Portable aerator, child's inflatable pool, 10 gallon bucket plus a smaller bucket to change water with and an aquarium net to catch fish in pool. As well, baitfish jigs for yakkas, slimies and salmon and Nymph or tiny White Moth pattern flies for garfish and mullet. Small metal baitfish lures like Lazers, Krome Kritters, or barrel sinkers painted white work well on small tuna, slimies and salmon.

FRESHWATER LIVEBAITING:

Long handled, fine mesh net for mudeyes and minnow and an Opera House net for yabbies, a portable aerator, 10 gallon bucket and an ice cream container for small baits like mudeyes and shrimp.

Most yelloweye mullet are caught in bays and estuaries. Mullet will school and feed in a berley trail and I have found the best method of catching them is to use a pencil float and soft bait such as sandworm.

Snapper: It is hard to imagine someone not knowing what this fish looks like. Snapper are either red or pink, this depends upon where you catch them, their fins have a blue tinge, and running down their back, they have a series of opalescent blue spots along the lateral line. Small snapper of up to 30 cm are excellent live bait, particularly on yellowfin. Snapper can be caught in all States to some extent with the more southern areas yielding the best catches.

Frigate mackerel: The smallest of the tunas, this species is similar to the mackerel tuna in that along its back it displays the same wavy markings. Frigate mackerel range from the southern coast of Western Australia to the south coast of New South Wales and rarely exceed 1.5 kilograms. Due to their small size they are a popular bait for trolling for marlin.

Squid head rigged for a big fish. It isn't necessary to hide the hook in any bait, any fish big enough to take this head will take it in one bite.

Popeye mullet being rounded up by barramundi in Chambers Bay in the Northern Territory.

> If there is anything in angling more exhilarating than being clean spooled by a gamefish hooked from land. I've yet to experience it.

Landbased game fishing is not a discipline for the fainthearted. It requires an almost fanatical dedication and a willingness to endure conditions that would send many normal anglers packing, which probably explains why the numbers of LBG anglers have never been big.

LOCATIONS

Landbased game anglers can be found at various locations right around Australia, fishing for a variety of different species. In South Australia and Victoria, for example the bulk of the effort is aimed at sharks and, to a lesser extent, yellowtail kingfish. Some northern New South Wales locales have established reputations for longtail, cobia, and mackerel while in southern New South Wales, anglers seek yellowfin, marlin and kingfish. Queensland anglers tend to chase big trevally, queenfish and longtail while in Western Australia, Spanish mackerel and queenfish are dominant captures.

In New Zealand the major quarry is yellowtail kingfish and specimens in excess of 50 kg have been taken over there on occasion. The North Island also has mako sharks, whalers, and marlin and yellowfin tuna.

HOT SPOTS

New South Wales: A few of the better known landbased game fishing hot spots on the east coast include Mutton Bird Island at Coffs Harbour, Hat Head, South West Rocks, Seal Rocks and Port Stephens. Closer to Sydney there is Frazer Park, Catherine Hill Bay, Wybung Head, Terrigal, Avoca, Whale Beach, Curra-curang and Kiama. Jervis Bay near Nowra is generally regarded as the choice of the land based game fishing locations and takes in such well known ledges including Devil's Gorge, the Tubes, and Beecroft among others. Pretty Beach, located on the mid-south coast of New South Wales is popular while Tathra, Tura Head, Merimbula, Twofold Bay, and Green Cape complete the New South Wales run-down.

Victoria: Anglers have had success at Cape Conron, Wilson's Promontory, Phillip Island, and Point Lonsdale. Many ledges along the Great Ocean Road have produced the odd yellowtail kingfish, although sharks are the more likely prospects. Port Campbell has deep water and the harbour at Portland regularly produces kingfish in the autumn. Cape Bridgewater probably has the deepest water in Victoria but the rocks are dangerous and seas need to be steady before fishing is contemplated here.

Western Australia: The stretch of coastline which takes in Quobba Station is well known and popular among land based game fishermen, as is Steep Point. Some of these spots require either 4wd vehicles or the ability to walk long distances, clamber around crumbling sandstone goat tracks, climb down ropes, and have no fear of heights—carrying an armful of rods and a backpack.

New Zealand: The North Island offers the land based aficionado excellent fishing for big yellowtail kingfish. Some top spots include Cape Reinga, Spirits Bay, Cape Brett, Hoopers Point, Cape Kari Kari and from man-made platforms such as the wharves at 7Paua, Te Hapua and Manganoui.

TACKLE

On the east coast, live baiting is the most consistent method and there are some specific tackle requirements that apply to most gamefish off the rocks. Serious anglers tend towards 15 kg outfits and look to have between 800 and 1000 m of spool capacity. Whichever line class you choose your outfit must be balanced to suit.

Many ledges are not suited to standard length game rods and LBG anglers developed what are referred to as live baiting sticks. As a rule of thumb, these rods are about 2.4 to 2.7 m in length. Advantages include enabling a bait to be lobbed out to the edge of the wash and keeping the line away from rocky outcrops. More importantly, longer rods contribute to rock fishing safety by allowing the angler to stand back from the edge an extra pace during the fight.

Any reel used for live baiting from the stones needs to be solidly spooled and sturdy in construction. Lever drag models are the most popular and I recommend Penn International wides although most reels of this type are sturdy and reliable enough for the task. If a lever drag reel is out of your price range, opt for a star drag model such as the Penn Senator. At about half the price, it too has proven adequate over a long period with the dual advantages of being lighter and needing less maintenance.

Longtail tuna are one of the most prized captures for landbased game anglers.

Live baits need to be fresh and alert for the best results. To achieve this the angler needs to keep them in an environment where they are not stressed.

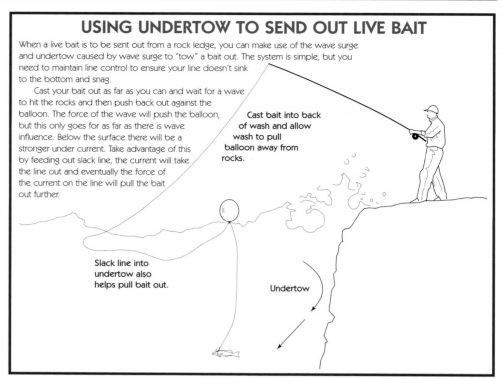

USING UNDERTOW TO SEND OUT LIVE BAIT

When a live bait is to be sent out from a rock ledge, you can make use of the wave surge and undertow caused by wave surge to "tow" a bait out. The system is simple, but you need to maintain line control to ensure your line doesn't sink to the bottom and snag.

Cast your bait out as far as you can and wait for a wave to hit the rocks and then push back out against the balloon. The force of the wave will push the balloon, but this only goes for as far as there is wave influence. Below the surface there will be a stronger under current. Take advantage of this by feeding out slack line, the current will take the line out and eventually the force of the current on the line will pull the bait out further.

Cast bait into back of wash and allow wash to pull balloon away from rocks.

Slack line into undertow also helps pull bait out.

Undertow

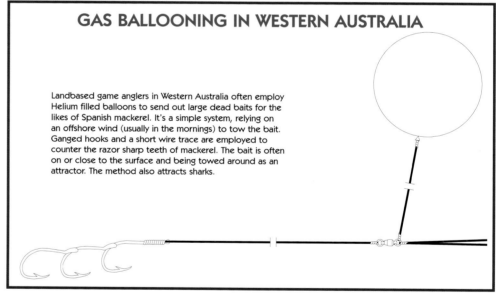

GAS BALLOONING IN WESTERN AUSTRALIA

Landbased game anglers in Western Australia often employ Helium filled balloons to send out large dead baits for the likes of Spanish mackerel. It's a simple system, relying on an offshore wind (usually in the mornings) to tow the bait. Ganged hooks and a short wire trace are employed to counter the razor sharp teeth of mackerel. The bait is often on or close to the surface and being towed around as an attractor. The method also attracts sharks.

A shoulder or back harness and gimbal belt are essential equipment. The harness should be comfortable and the straps detachable to allow it to be fitted without the need for the angler to take his hands off the rod or reel.

In almost every LBG spot a gaff of some sort will be required to secure a large fish. Ideally, the gaff should be a single piece unit that can reach a fish at the bottom of a swell on low tide. Aluminium tubing, 25 mm in diameter with a minimum 3 mm wall thickness is the ideal material.

BAIT FISHING

Live baiting is the preferred method on the east coast and New Zealand for kingfish, tuna, and marlin. Dead baits work well for sharks and in the west, where live baits can be difficult, dead baits such as tailor are more common for the likes of mackerel.

As the name implies, live baiting is a method where a live fish is impaled on a hook in a manner that does not seriously harm the fish or impede its normal swimming functions. The fish is then placed in the water beneath a bobby cork or balloon and allowed to swim out to sea. There is nothing man-made that is better than well-presented live bait in the right place at the right time.

The first thing that needs to be done is to tie a double leader using either the plait or Bimini twist. Both knots are 100 per cent, stay away from quickie knots such as the spider hitch that has been found wanting. Double leaders give an added safety margin in the closing stages of a fight. The length of double used depends on whether or not you are fishing to any standard set of rules, if not then the length is a matter of personal choice. Normally about a rod length and a half is sufficient.

A good average leader from the hook to the double is about three metres and should be a minimum 100 kg breaking strain. I suggest you use leader material rather than monofilament, as most leader materials are about one-third thinner for strength and a lot tougher. Joining

the double to the leader use a ball bearing game swivel.

The rig changes for toothies because wire enters the equation. For sharks, Sevenstrand wire from about 100 kg or more is employed. Mackerel and other members of the razor gang require finer wire and single strand piano wire works best.

The most popular set-up is the balloon rig and it is easy to make up. A partially inflated balloon, approximately 150 mm in diameter, is attached to the leader by a single strand of cotton or A-size binding thread. If you want your bait to swim deeper than your leader length, thread a swivel or a small plastic leader

LIVE BAIT RIG FOR LANDBASED GAME

This is the staple live bait rig set up used for land based game fishing on the East Coast. Leader material is 60 – 120 kg breaking strain and normally about 3 metres long. Hook size varies to suit baits, but 6/0-9/0 Suicide pattern hooks cover most baitfish.

Suicide hooks have an offset and this should be allowed for when setting the hook in a baitfish. With the bait in your hand check that when the hook is inserted the point will be angled towards the head of the baitfish. If the point is angled to the rear it will dig into the bait as it is swimming around. You usually only get one chance to bury the hook and if the point is embedded in the back of the bait there is a good chance you will miss a potential hook-up.

The connection between leader and main line is a good quality ball bearing game swivel, preferably black as shiny swivels have been know to attract bites from small toothies. A double leader is tied on the main line using a Bimini twist knot. Before the double is tied to the swivel, the strands are cut and an Ezi-rig slider threaded on to one of the double strands. A balloon is attached to the Ezi-rig slider either with binding thread or 1 kg monofilament. A stopper knot is then tied over both strands of the double to control bait depth. So, even though your leader is say three metres, you may want to allow the Ezi-rig to run another couple of metres up the line, which subsequently allows the bait to swim 5 metres down the water column.

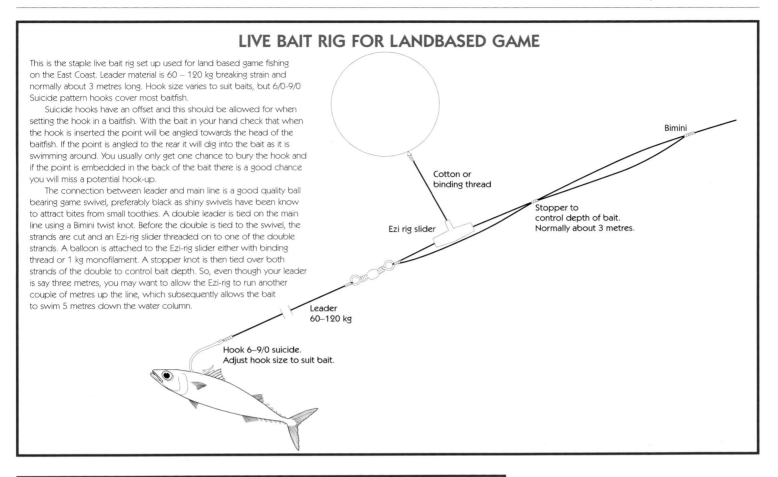

Cotton or binding thread

Bimini

Ezi rig slider

Stopper to control depth of bait. Normally about 3 metres.

Leader 60–120 kg

Hook 6–9/0 suicide. Adjust hook size to suit bait.

TOWING KITE FOR LANDBASED GAME FISHING

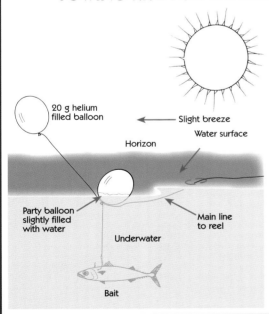

20 g helium filled balloon

Slight breeze

Water surface

Horizon

Party balloon slightly filled with water

Main line to reel

Underwater

Bait

On days when the wind is slight, or when a long drift is required, anglers fishing for land based game can rig up a kite to tow their baits out. Sometimes you can see the wind further out but because of the land behind, there is no influence close to the rocks.

The most efficient system is to inflate a 20-gram balloon with Helium gas. Small gas bottles are available from party hire stores. When filled with Helium the balloon rises immediately and soon finds the wind. This balloon is attached to the top swivel on the trace by 50-100 metres of monofilament about 5 kg breaking strain. Because the Helium balloon continually rises, it will lift the bait near the surface, and sometimes even out of the water. To combat this, the balloon from which the bait is suspended is partially filled with water, the Helium balloon will still lift the bait higher in the water column but it wont pull it from the water.

A disproportionate number of marlin have been hooked when this system was employed. The constant raising and lowering of the live bait fish in the water column acting as an attractor.

ocean. The size of the balloon is dependent upon the circumstances. Given a strong tail wind you can blow the balloon up larger than the recommended size to take advantage of the elements. In a head wind situation, keep the balloon size down to the size of a tennis ball, or less.

Setting the hook into live bait and presenting it is a straightforward process. Hooks are the first consideration and for most live baits a hook size somewhere between 6/0 and 9/0 will usually suffice. The main thing to be alert to is the thickness of the hook shank, particularly if you are working small live baits. Many baitfishes cannot tolerate a thick shank. Slimies in particular have a nervous disposition and are very susceptible. A hook with a shank up to 2 mm thick will not trouble most baitfish. If you use a hook with a 6 mm thick shank on a 15 cm yakka don't expect to be fishing with a live bait longer than a couple of minutes. This is about the amount of time it will take the bait to die. Hook pattern is a matter of personal choice. There is a wide range of live bait patterns to choose from. My preference is for chemically sharpened Suicide pattern hooks.

There are several places on baitfish where a hook can be located without impairing its health or mobility. Just forward of the first dorsal fin is the most common placement. Hooks can also be set through the upper jaw

barrel (I use Ezi-rig running sinker clips, minus the clip) onto one strand of your double line. Then, re-tie the double to the swivel. A stopper knot is tied onto the double to control the depth. An added advantage with this method in that if you are using a game rod you can keep the leader shorter to help casting.

Keep the length of cotton to the balloon as short as possible and never attach it directly on to the line, always tie it to the swivel or whatever clip device you are working. When a tuna hits the bait, it will feel little resistance because the cotton breaks easily. Balloons are also a good strike indicator. It often happens that the first the angler knows of a tuna's appearance is the sight of his balloon freewheeling across the on most bait without causing any problems. On slimy mackerel, there is a fleshy area on the nose that adapts well to hook placement. Garfish are a little different. The hook should be set in the last quarter of the fish's length, either through the back or underneath. When tuna are chasing the so-called no-bill gars or saurys try using a live garfish but first remove the bill.

When placing the hook avoid setting it too deep, about 6 mm is the maximum on most baitfish. If using a Suicide hook which has an offset point ensure the point is leaning forward when the hook is in the vertical position. If you don't, when the baitfish is pulling line out the hook shank will be in the horizontal position and the point, because of the offset, can become embedded in the back of the bait.

The best method of getting a baitfish to swim out is to cast it into a wash where the undertow will assist it to swim out and away from the ledge. Providing all goes well the fish will be on its way in no time at all. One of the tricks of this method is to allow plenty of slack line into the wash. Sometimes the fish will be reluctant to go but the undertow sucking your slack line out will force the issue.

In a situation where there is a limited wash finer line can make a difference. It is noticeable that an angler working a 24 kg line can sometimes have difficulty getting a small baitfish to swim as far as he would like whereas another angler with a finer line, say 10 kg for example will achieve a better result. If there is a strong tail breeze, inflate your balloon to take advantage of the wind or else put out a tow line with a pair of balloons attached. The material

to use for the tow line should be waxed cotton, a little stronger than employed on the balloon to the leader and it can be up to 50 m long.

Knowing where to place the bait comes with experience. As a basic guide stay within 50 m for bonito, longtails, and kingfish but get the bait out 100 m or more for the best results with marlin, yellowfin tuna, mackerel and sharks. If you intend going for the long drift aim at the drift patterns which appear like long semi-calm areas on the surface. Once the fish arrives into one of these drifts he will usually follow it for as far as he is allowed.

Sometimes you will find yourself in a situation where the current is moving in the opposite direction to the wind. In these circumstances your balloon should be inflated to a size you believe will counteract the current and consequently your bait should swim straight out. If you wish to reduce the effect of the current, use polystyrene floats about every 10 m or alternatively, grease your line so that it floats.

THE FIGHT

Knowing when to strike is the all important question that everyone wants to know. Unfortunately, there are no hard and fast rules and a lot depends on the circumstances and judgement that come with experience. Yellowfin and longtail tuna normally take a bait well. The strike is hard and sure, they will take off like rockets, slow down as they turn the bait to swallow it and then scream the reel as they go for the horizon. If this happens, the time to set the hook is on the second run.

Problem is no two fish are the same. Like any other fish, tuna can be finicky and you just never know what you will hook into unless of course you spot the fish first. A big yellowfin is just as likely not to slow down but maintain the speed and when this is obvious, set the hook home. Marlin are also variable. A couple of ticks on the reel can be followed by a couple of metres of muscle and bill charging out of the water to toss bait. If this happens, strike immediately. Even sharks have changeable feeding habits. Most days the take by a shark will be straightforward and followed by a long steady run. But the next day you might watch in frustration as bait after bait is bitten off behind or in front of the hook.

My timing on when to set the hook is worked out on the basis that a bait down the throat of a fish increases the chances of lodging the point of the hook home so I always give them the opportunity to take the bait properly. Even then, you can be wrong. One of the most successful anglers on yellowfin I know insists the hook be set as soon as the fish takes the bait. He has an excellent catch rate, which includes a good number of foul hooked tuna.

Ensure your hook is properly lodged by striking the fish at least twice. The first strike is usually good enough; the second is insurance. If you strike and miss and the bait pulls out wind as fast as you can. Strike and drag the bait and then wind some more, this can induce the fish to come back for seconds.

Finally, if you are into a big fish that has taken off several hundred metres of line keep a close check on the drag system on the reel. A series of tests by Aftco show just how important are reel dynamics. The tests found that as the diameter of line on the spool decreases more force is needed to pull line off the reel. When the diameter of the spool has been reduced by half the true drag setting on the reel will have doubled. To put it another way, when the line diameter on the spool is down to one-quarter its original size the amount of drag setting on your reel will have increased fourfold. Therefore, if you set your strike drag at 25 per cent of the breaking strain of the line, your line will now be at breaking point.

Another series of tests showed how much stress water friction can add to fishing line. A boat simulating a fish took out 220 m of 24 kg monofilament and made a 135 degree turn at 9 knots. Less than 2 kg of pull was felt at the reel, but at the 'fish', the pull registered 10 kg, four and a half times the strain at the reel. The intelligent adjustment of the drag setting to counter these effects comes with experience. Keep it in mind for the day the XXOS gamefish comes along.

Tackle being pushed to land a big fish off the rocks. All tackle and rigs have to be first rate to land big fish off the rocks.

ROCK FISHING SAFETY

The most important factor when fishing from the stones is safety. To ignore this aspect, particularly if you are fishing from rocky headlands, is akin to playing Russian roulette. Eventually, no matter how lucky you think you are, the loaded chamber will come round to

top ledges

Landbased game fishermen can be found at various locations right around Australia fishing for a variety of different species. Here is a list of the top ledges around Australia.

NEW SOUTH WALES
NORTH COAST
Mutton Bird Island - (Coffs Harbour)	South West Rocks
Hat Head	Seal Rocks
Charlotte Head	Port Stephens

SYDNEY
Frazer Park	Avoca
Catherine Hill Bay	Whale Beach
Wybung Head	Curracurang
Terrigal	Kiama

JERVIS BAY
Devil's Gorge	Beecroft
The Tubes	

SOUTH COAST
Pretty Beach	Merimbula (pier)
Tathra (pier)	Green Cape
Tura Head	

VICTORIA
Punchbowl --(San Remo)	Point Lonsdale (pier)
Pyramid Rock --(Phillip Island)	Portland Harbour
	Cape Bridgewater

SOUTH AUSTRALIA
Nundroo	Shark Rock

WESTERN AUSTRALIA
Cape Cuvier	Steep Point
Quobba Station	

NEW ZEALAND
Cape Reinga	Hoopers Point
Spirits Bay	Cape Kari Kari
Cape Brett	

the firing pin when it is your turn to pull the trigger.

Crocodile Heads on Beecroft Peninsula at Jervis Bay is one of a number of top areas that have become notorious for the tragic loss of life. In the same area, Devil's Gorge is reputed to have claimed more than twenty anglers and Eve's Ravine is not for the faint hearted. Tragedies are not restricted to Jervis Bay. In New South Wales waters, anglers have been washed in and drowned, or fallen to their deaths, from ledges as far north as the Queensland border to Green Cape near Victoria.

Nor is it strictly an east coast, or New South Wales event. Victorian anglers have lost their lives after being swept from rocks at places such as the notorious Nobbies at Phillip Island. If you checked the coroner's statistics in the west, you would find an equally gruesome tale of 'death by misadventure' from ledges as far apart as Albany in the south to Quobba, Carnarvon, and parts further north. The stretch of coast that takes in Quobba Station is reputed to have claimed more than thirty lives.

Never fish alone on the rocks and always carry some form of life-line in case you or your fishing friend go for an unscheduled swim. The second thing to avoid is diving into the water after another angler when conditions are rough and dangerous. The result of this sort of bravery can be a double fatality and anyway, if the seas are that bad you probably shouldn't be fishing.

There are three basic types of platforms from which landbased game fishing is carried out; piers, breakwaters and most commonly from rocky headlands. As a rule, piers and breakwaters are less hazardous with most of the threat likely to be from falling or being run over by a truck. Anglers on the rocks on the other hand have to be ever alert and mindful of the waves. This is most important when fishing a ledge low to the sea. Under these circumstances, it can prove fatal to completely

relax and stop being vigilant—you just never know when that bigger-than-average wave might happen to thunder in over the ledge. Some ledges are not a fishable proposition under any circumstances; others are dangerous only when big seas are running.

The first thing any angler should do before venturing down to fish from a rock ledge is to spare fifteen minutes or so to study the pattern of the waves. An idea of the state of the tide is also worthy of comment as it very often happens that at low tide the seas will not wash over the ledge but later on, as the tide rises, the situation can become somewhat different.

safety equipment

SHOES: If you are fishing wet rocks then ensure your shoes have a lot of tread. Some rock fishers attach cleats, but I'm not so sure that this is a good idea for LBG as mobility can be an important factor.

ROPE: A safety rope makes a lot of sense, and doesn't take up much room. Don't make the mistake of using a nylon rope, as a swimmer will have difficulty hanging on. And the rope should have a weighted flotation device at one end to enable it to be thrown. A plastic milk container part filled with water will do this, and there is no need to add water until you are on the ledge so it is light to carry.

STORM VESTS: These vests have been used for a few years now by anglers working baits in areas where a swim isn't unusual. They are light to wear and inflate when they hit the water.

FIRST AID KIT: A first aid kit, similar to those chemists sell for cars, is a sensible investment. Apart from shock, the worst thing about going in off the rocks can be the cuts you receive from the limpets and rocks. But don't go taking a first aid kit along unless you know how to use it, so at the very least you should read the instructions.

MOBILE PHONE: A mobile phone, particularly a CDMA, might prove a lifesaver when you are off the beaten track. Don't leave it in your car or back at camp.

FINALLY: If you are fishing with a buddy who gets washed in, and there is no-one else on the ledge, don't dive in after your friend unless the circumstances are life threatening—and you are certain that you can get out. One dead angler is too many.

shopping list

LANDBASED GAME FISHING:
OUTFIT: 10 – 15 kg, preferably a lever drag game reel and either a game rod or a live bait stick.
HOOKS: 6/0 to 9/0 chemically sharpened Suicide pattern hooks.
LEADER: 60 – 100 kg leader material.
A shoulder or back harness and gimbal belt, and a single piece gaff that can reach a fish at the bottom of a swell on low tide. Safety rope and shoes with good tread.

CHAPTER 8

SPINNING
HIGH SPEED SPINNING

Many people still think high speed spinning is something you do from the rocks. This isn't the case, it is also a highly effective method to use from a boat.

High speed spinning is synonymous with the 1960s pioneering efforts of a radically different style of fishing from the rocks. The method has evolved. Nowadays more anglers work high-speed lures from boats than the shore. There is a major difference, other than the boat, between the two. In a boat scenario, anglers are working their lures to breaking fish, trying to judge the movements of schooling fish, and getting ahead of them to place the lure where

they will come up. Boat anglers only cast when they see fish, which means short bursts of highly charged activity. On land, it is more a matter of keeping a lure in the water all day, and this can mean running a crew to maintain momentum.

Lure development went from thin chrome pencil and hexagonal lures like the WK Arrow, to odd shaped types such as the Irons and Mavericks that relied on action and did not need a super-fast retrieve to produce results. Meanwhile, some anglers preferred to work poppers and bibbed minnows.

In the early days some reels geared at 6:1 were found wanting; fragile pinion gears and modular spool assemblies were a problem while some early attempts at speeding up slower reels bordered on the ridiculous. It was not long before speed gave ground to action and the successful Seascape reel and WK Arrow lure combination was rivalled in popularity by the ABU 9000 reel and Iron lure. ABU reels proved more durable and with a retrieve of 4.7:1 were better suited to the slower lures

that relied on action to attract a response from the fish. Fishing rod technology resulted in faster tapered blanks with more wraps while composite and 100 per cent graphite rods were still in the future along with the Space Shuttle.

The decline in spinning from the rocks can be attributed in part to the dramatic disappearance inshore of surface feeding activity, something very noticeable on the south coast of New South Wales. Professional fishing fleets have taken a heavy toll of the tuna stocks, particularly striped tuna, which were once the mainstay of high speed spinning. One of the ironies of the decline in spinning is that technology has caught up with the specific demands of the sport. By modern standards, the rods and reels used were heavy.

TECHNIQUES

Spinning is not a matter of rigging up a rod and reel with any old lure and casting and retrieving. To fully realise the rewards to be had the angler must first get the basics right, three of which are balanced tackle, lure presentation, and the method of retrieve. Technically speaking there is probably more to spinning than live baiting so, what follows is a generalisation of popular methods.

Whether you spin with light tackle up to 4 kg breaking strain or heavier lines from 6 kg to 10 kg there are two basic techniques employed. The first is high-speed spinning. As its name implies this method relies almost entirely on the speed of the lure through the water. It involves using reels geared at around 6:1 which offer a rapid retrieve rate in combination with thin, low density lures such as the Arrow.

The second technique involves a slightly slower retrieve and lures designed to work when they are being retrieved. A 6:1 gear ratio is not a prerequisite for this technique and you can get away with reels geared around 4:1 depending on the lure. One reason for using slower reels is that 6:1 reels can prove harder to wind when bulkier lures such as Irons are being used.

The speed of the retrieve is governed by the stability of the lure through the water. If you wind the lure in too fast the chances are it will go out of control; wind too slow and you won't get a take—except perhaps for a slow old pike.

Catches taken by anglers using these methods clearly demonstrate how effective they are. Yellowtail kingfish, marlin, Spanish mackerel, and tuna have all been caught. I have always preferred the slower technique in the belief that a pro-active lure that vibrates appears more natural than one which relies solely on speed, a trail of bubbles, or a flash.

High speed spinning requires finely tuned tackle of the highest quality.

In reality, I have achieved good results with both methods.

But tossing a lure weighing 60 g or more over 100 m and then retrieving it as fast as you can takes effort. Making several hundred casts a day, cranking the reel handle and winding on what amounts to kilometres of line will test your stamina. At the end of a daylong session your arms will feel like they are about to drop off and there will be the usual backache. However, time and conditioning will cure these ills as your body becomes attuned. Soreness and tiredness go with the sport.

METHODS

For lines up to about 4 kg, the weight of the lure used would rarely exceed 20 g, for heavier lines you may wish to use up to 60 g although the 40 g to 45 g weight is a good average size.

Leaders help you bring extra pressure to bear on a big fish in the closing stages of a fight, which means you are better able to control it. In the case of smaller fish, which can be difficult to gaff, a shock leader will allow you to lift them inshore. Shock leaders help minimise the chances of throwing a lure off during casting and will withstand more wear and tear if you happen to be hooked into a fish that insists on running through some rugged terrain.

Double leaders tied straight to lures are less effective than single strand shock leaders. Should you opt for a double, don't tie it directly to the lure, instead tie it to a shorter heavy monofilament leader that goes to the lure. If you are looking at the prospect of fish with sharp teeth such as mackerel use a short length of single strand wire to the lure.

Distance and depth are important and if you are working new territory, it can be a worthwhile exercise to cast out a sinker about the same weight as the lure you intend working and allow it to sink to the bottom. As it descends count off the seconds and remember that if you lose the sinker because it snags up in reef you will have saved the dollars that a lure would have cost. Once this experiment with the depth has been undertaken you will know exactly how far you can allow the lure to sink. If the count was 25 for example, then you can allow your lure to sink to various depths and know approximately, where it is by the number of seconds it is allowed to drop.

When you cast your lure, leave the spool out of gear and allow line to run out as the lure sinks. If you have your reel in gear while the lure is sinking, it will be steadily sinking back towards you.

There is a school of opinion which maintains that most fish caught on lures are taken in the

Queenfish like this one are great lure chasers and offer an aerial display when hooked.

first and last three hours of daylight. It is a rule of thumb assessment only. In the heydays of spinning, anglers would work their lures all day and never knew when the next good take would occur. Some days the action would only be morning and late afternoon, but there were also days when the action went right through almost unabated.

When you start retrieving, wind as fast as you can, don't be frightened to vary the speed of retrieve or work the rod from side to side to increase the action of the lure. Common sense is an asset among spin men and those who are the most successful rely heavily upon it. If all the action is on the surface then allowing the lure to sink to the depths can be a wasted exercise. While many anglers prefer to keep their lures under the surface making it skip across the surface can be just as effective. For shore-based anglers, a way of keeping the lure in the water a little longer is to spin with the rod tip pointed at the water. This method is most effective when spinning from high ledges.

The first indication of a strike can be as little as a knock on the line; sometimes it is a hard take. Although most fish hitting a lure that is being retrieved flat out will be hooked by the combined force of the lure and the fish heading in opposite directions at the same time, don't presume the fish will be automatically hooked. Lift your rod and set the hooks home, as you would do with bait.

If you hook up and the fish gets off, increase you speed. The chances are you will get another take almost immediately. Once you have set the hook, it is time to start working the fish. The reel's drag should be set at about one-third the breaking strain of the line being used, in other words a 6 kg line would require a 2 kg drag setting. This should always be set through the rod and not directly off the reel.

Allow the fish to take line at first. The further it runs the easier it will be to subdue. When you turn the fish start to gain line by pumping and then winding on line on the downward stroke. Be careful not to be too severe. Slow strokes are often more effective than quick sharp strokes and lessen the chances of the hook pulling free.

The critical stage in the fight is when a fish has been coaxed in close to the ledge or boat. If it is a king, you have to ensure it is kept well away from reef and bommies. Sometimes this means applying more pressure than you would like to stop them making that last desperate dive for freedom. If you happen to have a big tuna on such as a yellowfin that is heading for rugged territory put your reel out of gear and free spool. Once the pressure is off the tuna will turn away from the reef and head back to clear water.

The aim is to get the fish in close enough to put the double or shock leader onto the spool of the reel for a couple of turns. With the extra strength this gives, you can apply more pressure and hold the fish for the gaff man to finish off the job. Tired fish are much easier to gaff and land than those that come in green and still full of fight.

There will be days when you will not know whether or not there are any fish working the area because you simply cannot see them. On days when you can see fish, when there is surface activity, baitfish are being harassed and birds are diving you have something to work on.

The choice of lure is dependent upon several factors, the most important being the feeding habits of the species sought so it is not a bad idea to check the stomach contents of any fish caught to determine what they are feeding on. For example, there will be times when tuna are feeding on small anchovies such as bluebait, and under these circumstances, they won't look at a large lure. If this is the case, there are several excellent look-alikes that come in a range of sizes and colour schemes to suit most situations.

Sometimes it isn't enough to simply cast out a lure and expect it to entice any piscine predator that happens to be about. Even varying the retrieve speed, depth of retrieve and changing lures—both type and colour— will not bring about that much-desired take. This is understandable on days when there is a distinct lack of action from all quarters, but it can also happen when the ocean is boiling with surface activity. There is nothing more frustrating than being able to witness

your quarry attacking schools of bait fish but refusing to strike any of those fancy 'you beaut' lures you spent last week's rent on.

Variety and change can work wonders in this game. If speed, depth, and action do not produce the desired results then change the colour or style of lure. Should your quarry be a fish that prefers feeding in mid-water then the most suitable lure will be a sinking type. The depth of the retrieve is judged by the time it is allowed to sink and the speed that the reel handle is cranked while the lure is on its return journey.

An alternative would be to use a diver, in this case the size, shape and angle of the bib determines how deep the lure will dive and the angle of descent. The angler can increase this to some degree by cranking more rapidly but there is a point where the lure is at its optimum performance and beyond this, goes out of control and is useless. Learning how to work these lures is very much a matter of trial and error. Conditions often dictate whether or not they are a viable proposition. For example, the divers do not work well in weed-ridden areas and floating minnows perform better in moderate sea conditions where there is little chop. Poppers should be retrieved as fast as possible. On calm days, they can offer up a marvellous spectacle. The commotion they make splashing, skipping and zig-zagging across the ocean can summon a school of kingfish or tuna up from the depths in hot pursuit.

Sometimes all the angler has to do to bring forth a strike is add a little spice to the lure.

Little is involved in this, a fancy tail on the treble hook can be enough, and it is surprising just how effective such a minor addition can prove. There are abundant materials available. Anything from aluminium foil, fly-tying materials, even pieces of rubber thongs have been known to work.

Another ploy, although I have doubts over its effectiveness, is to tie a fly on the line a couple of centimetres above the lure. The idea is to give the lure the appearance of chasing a smaller offering and, hopefully, this in turn will excite a larger fish into striking.

There are many metal lures to choose from. Raiders have become popular; there are several variations on the 'pilchard' style including one produced by JM Gillies. Halco produces the Arrow lure, which has been an industry benchmark since the 1970s, while the Lazer lures are also worth a go.

For my money, it is hard to go past a barrel sinker, painted white and even dressed with a plastic skirt. Cheap and super effective, these are excellent on small tuna and have accounted for a bigger fish as well. In this case, the line is threaded through the hole in the sinker and tied to a set of treble hooks at the rear. Most serious spin men carry a few barrel sinkers in their tackle box. The same goes for poppers. If you don't like the steep price tag that comes with the imported 'name' poppers then make your own. They are easily constructed from 25 mm dowel and homemade varieties work quite well.

shopping list

HIGH SPEED SPINNING:

LINE: Most high speed spinning takes in lines from 4 kg to 10 kg breaking strain.

REELS: Overhead reels that suit lines of 4 kg to 6 kg include the ABU 6500 and 7000, Penn International 975 and Calcutta 400 models. In the heavier line classes, the Penn 525 and 535GS models and the Shimano Speedmaster 3 and 4 are the pick of the overheads. In threadline reels, Okuma, Penn and Shimano have a range of sizes to suit most line classes.

RODS: suited to the heavier 6 to 10 kg line classes and lures should have a fairly fast taper and they need to have a sharp enough action to allow you to 'punch' a lure out and at the same time have good recovery characteristics. Soft rods are not really an option. The sloppy action and lack of recovery restricts your cast and means you cannot apply enough pressure through the rod and onto the fish.

For lines of about 4 kg a threadline rod would be up to about 2.2 m long and have up to seven runners including the tip. An overhead rod for the same class would be the same length, have a butt length of at least 24 centimetres. The main difference in appearance would be the first guide, which on a threadline rod would be a larger stripping guide.

Regardless of brand, the most important factor in all of this is that the outfit is balanced to give optimum casting distance with minimum of effort.

LURES: The problem with the lures mentioned is in deciding which ones are worth buying. The best way to decide is to ask someone who knows. Barring that, I would suggest that to begin with you restrict your buying to those that are established with firm reputations and a reliable manufacturer to back them up. Brand names generally offer a good product manufactured from quality components. More importantly, they will have undergone some testing.

TERMINAL ENDS FOR LURES

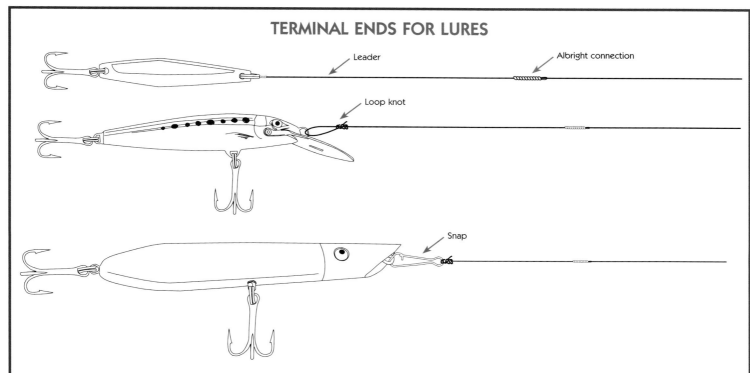

Lures are not all attached to the line in the same way. If the lure is to be trolled at speed, then to eliminate potential line twist problems you should consider employing a swivel instead of an Albright connection at the junction of the shock leader and main line.

For lure casting and slow trolling purposes though a swivel isn't necessary, at most you can use a simple snap if you want to work quick lure changes.

For metal lures the line should be tied directly to the ring, and locked up solidly with a Uni-knot. A shock leader is employed and this is connected with an Albright, locked in with a Rizzuto finish.

Poppers and bibbed minnows offer better presentations when a loop knot or quality snap is used to make the leader to lure connection. If working big lures then forget the loop knot and use a heavy-duty clip swivel as you could suffer line fatigue otherwise.

Wire is attached directly to the lure or a clip to allow for easy lure changes. To improve presentation and eliminate control problems when casting I suggest you attach the main line directly to the wire using the mono to wire connection described elsewhere in the book. The shorter the wire the better, and 20 cm is plenty.

CHASING PELAGIC HUNTERS

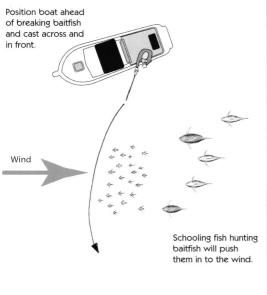

Position boat ahead of breaking baitfish and cast across and in front.

Wind

Schooling fish hunting baitfish will push them in to the wind.

The trick in chasing pelagics in a boat is being able to second guess the hunters and position the boat where they should be. Fish like mackerel tuna and longtails push baitfish into the wind. To make the most of this you should allow for the school's speed of travel and position your boat to cast across and ahead of the school without being so close so as to spook them.

As for lure colour, if you choose white you won't go far wrong. Colour vision through water is different to colour vision on land. West Australian angler Max Garth has done more research on the subject than anyone I know of and he says the attempt to put lure colours into place into the various types of water—oceanic, coastal, and estuarine—gets lost in the process.

A fish under water, looking at another fish or any other object, 'sees' light photons transmitted from the atmosphere, passing through the water surface illuminating, and being reflected by, the object it is viewing. 'Light transmission into the water is not uniform and depends on a lot of things. On bright days of all the light that passes through the water surface at noon in mid summer on the Equator only 40 per cent remains after one metre, 15 per cent after 10 metres and 1 per cent after 100 metres.

In water, white reflects all light photons, black absorbs all light photons, and each colour reflects only it's own colour photons and absorbs the rest. So it stands to reason that anything that reflects light photons massively provides the best visibility.'

Max says white and silver remain visible the longest in normal conditions, and in dirty water

Striped tuna are one of the fastest fish you are ever likely to catch on a lure.

all time best lures

HIGH SPEED
Barrel sinker painted white
WK Arrow
Iron Assassin
Iron Undertaker
Iron Executioner
Stingsildas

JIGS
Halco Trembler
Halco Mulie
Halco Twisty
Krome Kritter

MINNOWS
Rapala Magnum Sinking CD
Rapala Magnum Floating
Halco Laser Pro
Rapala Silver Jointed
Cairn swimmer
Rapala Deep Diver

POPPERS
Cotton Cordell
Tiger plug
25 mm diameter dowel

LIGHT TACKLE SPINNING

Spinning or lure casting has been around for more than 100 years. Working light tackle and lures in the 2–4 kg range is one of the neatest ways there is to fish.

Go into any tackle store these days and the chances are you will see at least one wall almost completely covered in lures. Many of the lures will look strikingly similar in shape, but the colours will vary. Spinning is big business.

I guess one of the incentives for growth in spinning has been the availability of cheaper lures. There was a time when buying a lure was verging on the ridiculous, particularly the brands imported from Europe and North America. Apart from exchange rates and tax, the other problem was the 'tyranny of distance' that has long been a bugbear with both exporters and importers.

These days there are Australian-made lures that are the equal of any of the imported brands. As well, there has been a growth in developing lures here and sending them to Asia for manufacture.

There is a downside though. At a fishing tackle trade show in one Asian country, a lure maker was offering to sell copies of a well-known Australian freshwater lure at less than one-third of our manufacturing costs. And the price fell even further if you wanted to buy in bulk.

Even with the use of cheaper labour in Asia though, I still baulk at the price of many lures, which I believe are sold on their name, not necessarily their ability to attract more strikes.

In the early days, lures were most popular in fresh water and later advanced to the saltwater scene. The first lures were bladed types and these, or their derivatives are still available today. The Celta bladed lures are a prime example, while the Spinnerbaits, which combine a blade and a plastic skirt, are an extension of that development. It was much later that solid metal lures, floating minnow lures and plastic lures came on the market.

Some lures have reached icon status among the converted. The Celtas, Wonder Wobblers, Irons, Arrows, Rapalas, Flopys, and the Mr Twisters are lures of legend. More recently,

gold is best while black provides a black hole in the visual field and dark colours on top of lures absorb photons like mad.

Which explains why gold lures are so popular in estuaries in northern Australia, and why white does so well for anglers spinning from the rocks on sunny days in clear water.

I have always believed that a trout sipping on surface insects sees the outline, not the colour, of the creature it wants to eat. Max says the physical limitations of a fish's vision may explain why a tightly packed school of fish provides better security than single fishes.

'A tight ball of small fish, illuminated from above and seen against the surface space light, would appear as a large blob of contrast rather than a lot of individual fishes. But, single fishes, away from the school, can be identified and are chased and eaten and the main blob remains secure.'

Hunting fish attempt to break up the school to separate the individuals from the blob since the individuals can be identified while the blob is an undefined shape.

'Surviving small live bait fishes, scattered from tuna boats, rush to hide under the boat hull which effectively puts them in the shadow of the hull and part of the large dark shape as seen by the hunting tuna.'

Soft plastic lures have enjoyed enormous popularity growth.

the StumpJumpers and Poltergeists have made serious inroads among native fish specialists.

The only criteria for catching a fish on a lure is that the fish you are after be piscivorous, a predator that eats other fish. Weed eaters such as luderick are not lure takers, at least in my experience. Spinning can be done just about anywhere, from streams and lakes to ocean beaches, rocky headlands and from boats.

The impact of spinning on recreational fishing has been both evolutionary and revolutionary. Back in the late 1960s and early 1970s for example, high speed spinning off the rocks for game fish came into vogue. In recent times, the trend has been towards light tackle. Estuary spinning for fish like bream, flathead and estuary perch has become more popular, while in the fresh water, Murray cod, Australian bass, yellowbelly, and silver perch have developed a bigger following. Spinning for trout of course, has always been popular.

Plastic or rubber lures have also taken a strong hold. Lures like the Mr Twister and derivatives such as the Crystal Creek Wiggletail will catch just about anything. And these days you can buy the rubber bodies and simply insert the hook of your choice if that is what you prefer.

You can use outfits as light as 2 kg to spin. Lures range from Halco chrome slices and Lazers to Rapala surface minnows and deep divers. For the dedicated angler, spinning can develop into a science of presentation where colour and retrieve style, including speed and presentation, are all-important.

The method is simple in concept but requires skill and knowledge to achieve a successful execution. To be successful you must first offer up a lure where the fish are most likely to be. You must also be prepared to vary the retrieve and change lures and alternate lure colours until you hit on the right formula.

TROUT

Trout in streams are one of the easiest species to target with lures. Tackle requirements are a short, light rod capable of casting from one to two ounces and a small spinning reel spooled with line of about 2 kg breaking strain. For

Trout are aggressive fish and often attack to protect their territory.

lures, you can't go past small bladed lures like Celtas. These have been around for a long time, are relatively cheap and best of all consistently produce trout.

In streams, trout will be found in deeper pools, at the head and tail of runs and lying in wait beneath bushy overhangs along the banks. It is necessary to use a bit of stealth when approaching likely areas, work your way upstream, and make long casts wherever possible. Most of the time the water you are fishing will be fairly shallow, about knee deep and it is necessary to wind the lure when it hits the water to avoid snagging up on rocks or branches.

The terrain and their size limit trout in these streams in their ability to fight. They will still jump and run in the classic way and sometimes, in a deeper pool, you will hook into a fish that is much bigger than the average; a fish that is cunning and knows how to test the angler's skills.

NATIVE FISH

It seems hard to believe these days, yet just thirty years ago native Australian freshwater fish struggled for serious recognition among the angling fraternity. There were a few people, like Vic McCristal, who pursued the case for sportfishing recognition of the likes of Murray cod and Australian bass but overall, trout dominated the freshwater scene.

Native fish like bass and yellowbelly require heavier outfits than trout. Many anglers have switched to braid. In heavily wooded country, it is not unusual to come across anglers working braid because it accentuates the feel of the lure.

trout

Most anglers know that trout adopt what are known as feeding lanes in rivers. They conserve energy by sitting where the current will bring food to them. But did you know that these fish are more often found feeding in low-pressure areas in front of rocks rather than behind them?

Using a small boat for estuary spinning allows you to cover more water.

Neil Schultz with a well conditioned average sized barramundi caught on a Predatek Sandviper lure at Lake Awoonga.

Well-known Victorian casting guru Ted Whittam caught this queenfish at Weipa in North Queensland.

Baitcasting and threadline outfits are the norm. Many anglers prefer to run monofilament leaders with braid, or else have adopted Knotted Dog leaders to use in conjunction with braid. The Knotted Dog leaders are an innovation of noted angler Rod Harrison, and are designed to give a tougher terminal end to the line as well as some stretch, both features that all braids lack.

In a boat, the fishing technique is to drift slowly, casting lures into snags, at any bank indentations beneath low-lying, shady overhanging trees or likely lies on weed beds and flats. In some of the most productive areas, snags, in the form of sunken logs, lie hidden just below the surface. When not working floating lures in heavy country, you start the retrieve as soon as the lure starts to disappear. If you let the lure sink too far you will hook on a snag and maybe even lose the lure.

BAY AND ESTUARY

A good average estuary outfit is 3 kg, either threadline or baitcaster. If you intend working light lures, like Halco Scorpions or Legends, then the threadline will give less trouble.

Lures that produce in these waters include pink and silver Galaxia Minnows, black Micro Minnows, Min Min, Rapala CDs and just about any soft plastic lure there is including Wiggletails, Mr Twisters and Sliders.

For flathead, shallow running lures work well on sandflats lined with weed beds. In deeper water, you may want to opt for a lead headed soft plastic like a slider that will get down to the bottom. Bream and perch will be in the snags. On dawn and dusk, or when there is surface feeding activity, surface poppers and lures like the Halco Night Walker can do well on estuary perch. Bream take lures from snags but on cloudy days, these fish often come out and feed over sand flats.

A favourite bay species is the Australian salmon, and just about any lure you can use will gain a strike. A big difference between salmon and the earlier species is presentation. Salmon like a little bit of speed and aren't too fussed with presentation. But for the likes of bream, perch and flathead, twitch, pause, and crank is a standard action designed to imitate a crippled baitfish. In America they call lures worked like this 'jerk baits'. I'm not American. To me this is spinning.

SURF FISHING

Spinning or lure casting has been around for more than 100 years. Working light tackle and lures in the 2–4 kg range is one of the neatest ways there is to fish.

There is no in between in surf fishing, you either love it or hate it. During summer when the water warms and the days are hot, wading in the surf and fishing is not only a pleasure, it also offers some relief. In winter, it can be a cold miserable existence when the fish aren't biting. The only consolation is the knowledge that there are worse things you could be doing, like gardening, painting, and all those other household chores that are generally better left to someone else to do.

There was a long held custom among many southern trout anglers that when the trout season closed they would bring out the surf rods and hit the beaches. Even during those years when there was no closed season for trout, many anglers still followed the tradition, which is probably why so many still fish the surf during the colder months.

Never mind, the rewards are there for anglers who are willing to put in the time and effort. And there is no shortage of beaches to fish. From Queensland to Victoria and across the Great Australian Bight to Western Australia, we are blessed with thousands of surf beaches.

CHAPTER 9

Many of them probably unnamed.

Species that dominate the surf scene are tailor in the north and Australian salmon in the south. There is a cross over. Northern New South Wales and southern Queensland beaches for example are dominated by tailor; southern New South Wales has tailor and salmon while Victoria and South Australia are predominantly salmon. In the west, both species are on the scene. As well as these two fish, there are others including whiting, bream, mullet, flathead, trevally, dart, mulloway and gummy sharks. Whenever there are solid reports of good schools of fish hitting a beach somewhere, you can guarantee the long rods and star sinkers will emerge.

READING A BEACH

Non-fishers look at a beach and see waves and sand. The key to success in the surf is an ability to 'read' a beach. However, if they had donned a pair of polarising sunglasses and taken time out to look more closely in rather than at the water they would be able to see more. Darker shades in the water, where the waves do not break, indicate holes or gutters. A wave breaking offshore is often a shallow point, sandbar, or reef. Where waves change direction and the water flattens or swirls could be a rip.

Big fish like gutters and rips. Larger predators, like mulloway will hole up in gutters waiting for

Dusk and dawn are prime feeding times for predatory fish that hunt in the gutters of surf beaches.

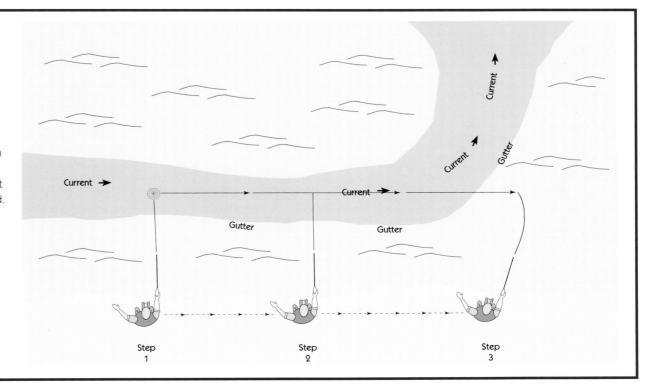

HOW TO FISH

Working a gutter on a beach with light tackle or a fly outfit is about covering ground. The easiest way is to cast and retrieve as you move along the beach with the current.

Current →

Current →   Current →

Current ↑

Current ↑   Gutter

Gutter   Gutter

Step 1   Step 2   Step 3

surf

When fishing the surf don't ignore the white water. The gutters are the places where big fish will wait in search of prey, but often the edges of the white water, where the water is still clean below but froth on top, will produce good catches of fish such as tailor, salmon, mullet and bream. The best way to find holes, gutters, and channels on a beach is to spend a few moments studying the beach from a high vantage point.

shopping list

SURF FISHING:

ROD: Most surf rods are about 3.5 m long and in two-piece configuration. The average surf rod can be used to cast sinkers up to 4-ounces, which is adequate for most fishing situations. When the surf is light and side drift limited it is preferable to come back in sinker weight.

Many off-the-shelf rods are overbuilt and too heavy for the required task. My advice is to go for a rod that you can handle in terms of its weight and power. The 8144 is a popular rod blank for casting weights of 4 – 6 ounces. Rod blank taper and construction determine distance, not the weight of the rod. And how far you cast on a beach depends on where the channels or gutters are. Some days they will be almost at your feet. You must also decide whether you intend using an overhead or threadline reel, as rod runners are different. Threadlines have fewer guides that are mounted higher than those bound on rods for overhead reels.

REEL: If you are new to surf fishing then the easiest way in is to use a threadline reel. Overhead reels can be a problem in terms of getting an overrun when casting. The advantage of an overhead reel is that an experienced angler will cast further and maintain better control in a battle with a big fish. But threadlines are virtually trouble free.

LINE: The rod and reel should be balanced to suit each other and the line weight. An 8 – 10 kg outfit is a good starting point. Braid lines are all the go at present, but I recommend monofilament as the line of first choice. Braid is thinner than monofilament, but it also tangles into impossible birds nests and doesn't have the same degree of abrasion resistance as the thicker monofilament lines.

SINKERS: Star sinkers are the most popular in the surf because they drive into the sand and become buried, making them more difficult to dislodge in the wave action. The best way to attach a star sinker is with a clip swivel as this allows you a fast and easy way of changing sinker weights to suit conditions.

BAIT: Pilchards, bluebait, squid, and pippis are the most commonly used baits in the surf. Anglers wanting to catch bigger fish prefer to work big baits like salmon fillets and squid heads. The advantage of using salmon for bait is that there is less chance of catching more salmon. Some days you spend too much time catching salmon when you are after larger fare, and squid heads are normally too large to be taken by smaller fish anyway. It's all about maximising your chances.

RIGS: Most anglers fish a simple two-dropper paternoster rig. The top dropper has a surf popper or saltwater fly instead of bait, the bottom dropper a 3 – 4/0 long shank, or Suicide pattern hook. If you are chasing larger fish, mulloway for example, then a leader of about 25 – 30 kg breaking strain is used. The rig is a running paternoster and hook size should be about a 6/0 in a Suicide pattern. Ganged hooks work can also be employed on baits like pilchards. These work well for more than just tailor. If crabs are a problem then a small water bomb balloon, blown up to about 15 mm in diameter and hooked on to the top hook of large bait will keep it off the bottom. In case you were wondering, the balloon does not deter big fish.

ROD HOLDERS: These are essential on a beach. No need to buy them, you can make your own simply by purchasing about a metre of 50 mm diameter PVC tubing and cutting a 45 degree angle on one end. As well as holding your rod up while the bait is in the water, the rod holder makes an ideal place to put your rod while baiting up or rigging.

Many off the shelf rods come with wooden sand spikes glued into the butt. Some people think these spikes are to protect the rod when it is pushed into the sand. Think again. The problem with these spikes is that when the varnish wears off, as it does when pushed through sand, the water soaks into the wood, which in turn expands and can split the butt of your rod.

BACK PACK: The best way to carry tackle on a beach is with a backpack. You can put everything in it you need for the outing and that leaves you with two hands free to carry your rods and rod holders, or perhaps a torch when travelling at night.

Finally, don't forget to pack a small nylon bait board. It is one of the handiest items you can take, as it can be difficult filleting a fish or cutting a squid strip on sand.

---

smaller fish to be swept past by the current. Mulloway have large paddle tails that enable them to swim in strong currents. Australian salmon are different. Although fast and just as keen on a feed, salmon schools are most often found hunting along the back of the breakers, or the edges of rips for the same reason. And always, bigger fish are in the clean water, away from the zones where the sand is being stirred up.

TIMES TO FISH

The change of tide is a peak time to fish the surf. Big predators like mulloway and snapper are best sought at night or overcast days. Smaller fish like salmon, tailor, mullet, and whiting will bite best around sunrise and sunset, particularly if a high tide coincides with the changing light conditions.

Some beaches fish better on low tide, others work the opposite way around. I prefer the low tide as this gives easier access to gutters and holes. Gutters and holes on beaches change. One year you may have to wade out into chest high water at low tide to reach a good gutter system, the next year it could be running in close to the beach. It all depends on storms and wave conditions.

ALTERNATIVE METHODS

Many anglers have developed their surf fishing beyond bait and found the joys of spinning and fly-fishing. It's all a matter of the application suiting the beach.

SPINNING

In heavy surf, long rods are best however, on beaches where the surf is not big and the gutters or clean water are close, it is possible to wade and work small lures. For spinning, I like to work a 3 kg outfit as it gives mobility to work different holes along a beach easily. My preference is to cast and retrieve metal lures like the Krazy Kritter, Wonder Wobbler, or Lazers of around 10–20g. A tip is to remove the standard treble hooks and replace them with a single, long shank 3/0 hook. Your hook-up rate will be about the same but fish like salmon have more difficulty throwing the single hook so your catch rate per hook up is better.

FLY-FISHING

Presentation isn't something to be overly concerned about in the surf. The main thing is to first get the fly out to where the fish should be. On some beaches, it simply isn't

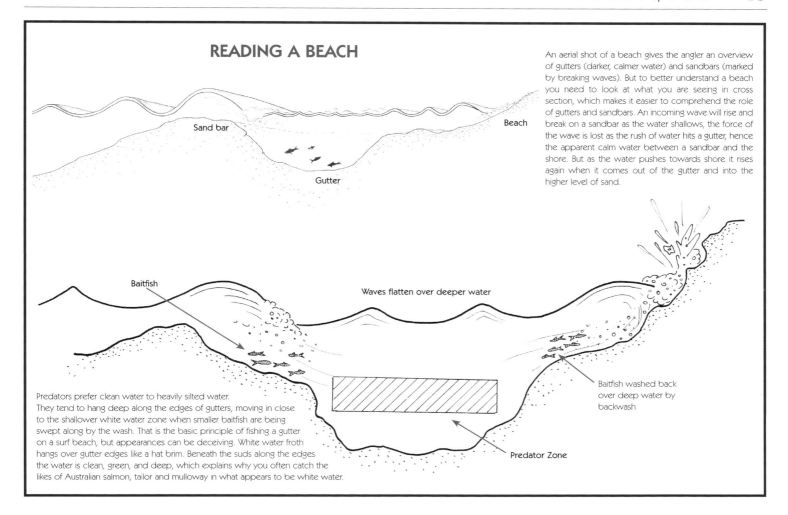

READING A BEACH

Sand bar

Beach

Gutter

An aerial shot of a beach gives the angler an overview of gutters (darker, calmer water) and sandbars (marked by breaking waves). But to better understand a beach you need to look at what you are seeing in cross section, which makes it easier to comprehend the role of gutters and sandbars. An incoming wave will rise and break on a sandbar as the water shallows, the force of the wave is lost as the rush of water hits a gutter, hence the apparent calm water between a sandbar and the shore. But as the water pushes towards shore it rises again when it comes out of the gutter and into the higher level of sand.

Baitfish

Waves flatten over deeper water

Baitfish washed back over deep water by backwash

Predator Zone

Predators prefer clean water to heavily silted water. They tend to hang deep along the edges of gutters, moving in close to the shallower white water zone when smaller baitfish are being swept along by the wash. That is the basic principle of fishing a gutter on a surf beach, but appearances can be deceiving. White water froth hangs over gutter edges like a hat brim. Beneath the suds along the edges the water is clean, green, and deep, which explains why you often catch the likes of Australian salmon, tailor and mulloway in what appears to be white water.

possible to stand in the water and cast. Sometimes the best option is to make use of existing water movement to take the fly to the fish.

Trial and error has proven that a floating line, preferably a 10 wt, weight forward shooting head and a leader of about 1.5 – 2 m will do the job. Stay away from weighted flies, as these will only be dragged along the bottom by wave turbulence. Instead, work heavily dressed baitfish patterns such as the Deceiver. It is a simple method. Find a rip, cast across it and then feed out line as the backwash pulls the fly out. Once you reach what you believe to be the required distance, wait for the line to straighten out and then start to strip. A steady strip works best for me, but others may have a different option. On good days, you will see salmon in the curl of the wave so you know how far your fly needs to be out. If you can't see the fish, just try to ensure the fly is at least in the green water at the back of the breakers.

Gus Storer with a bronze whaler caught at Salt Creek in South Australia.

CHAPTER 10

FLY FISHING
SALTWATER FLY

Saltwater fly-fishing has grown much faster in northern Australia than it has down south. Sadly, too many southern anglers wrongly hold a perception of saltwater fly-fishing being about chasing exotic sportfish in tropical climes. It isn't. It is about the challenge of the species, wherever they are.

From a personal achievement and satisfaction viewpoint, fly fishers need to establish in their minds what they see as the main challenge of this pursuit. For many it is catching different species. Fly-fishing is as much about attitude as it is about results.

Australia has unlimited saltwater flyfishing options in all States. The list of species that can be caught on fly is huge. Offshore they range from game fish like tuna, Wahoo, mackerel, marlin, and kingfish to sharks such as makos, threshers, whalers, and blues. Inshore there are many species of trevally, flathead, bream, queenfish, Australian salmon, luderick, estuary perch, mullet and even whiting. The only limits are those you impose on yourself.

And for those who want to go out in search of something different, check out the weird array of rock dwelling fishes that will take a fly. Because it's called a wrasse, sweep or parrot fish doesn't mean it can't fight, or that the fishing won't be fun. People who think luring a fish to the bogus offering is half the battle have never tried to extract a 2 kg blue throat wrasse from a jungle of bull kelp fronds. Throw in some current and wave surge, the odd hull threatening rock and the challenge is really on. Some of the fish that live in the kelp and reefs feel strong enough to pull a plough.

OUTFIT

Tackle requirements are basic. For most saltwater fishing, 6 – 10 weight outfits are fine. The 8 wt is the best all round choice allowing

When you are swoffing and hook up, you have to be prepared to put your rod down into the water when a fish decides to take off under the boat

you to fish most conditions and scenarios likely to be encountered, either from the beach or boat. And, just in case you were wondering, class tippets as light as 3 kg can be used on 8 wt outfits without fear of breakage.

Bigger fish like pelagics and sharks require a heavier outfit, say, from 12 to 15 wt, depending on the species. The size of the rod is dictated by the size of the fly with firepower a secondary consideration and 150 mm flies will need at least a 12 wt outfit.

Reels are a matter of choice. The important thing is that it is corrosion resistant and has a smooth drag. The choice of direct drive or anti-reverse is an individual thing. There are advantages and disadvantages with both. I have both types in my tackle and have no hesitation using either.

FLY LINES

The ideal fly line has no memory, nor does it require tropical heat to make it supple. Unfortunately, we don't live in an ideal world and most lines need stretching before use. Large arbor reels reduce the size of memory loops in lines, but don't eliminate them.

To improve your presentation the

Golden trevally like this one caught off Hervey Bay by Chris Palastides are great fun on fly.

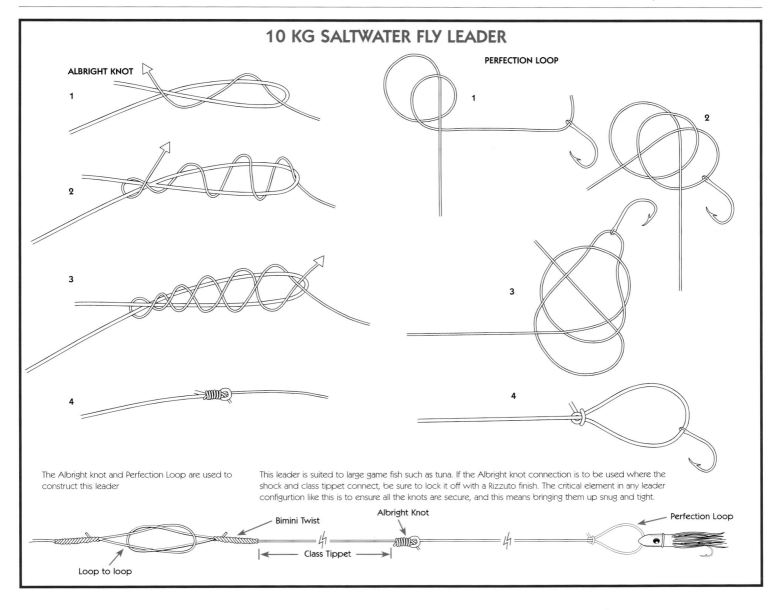

10 KG SALTWATER FLY LEADER

ALBRIGHT KNOT

1

2

3

4

PERFECTION LOOP

1

2

3

4

The Albright knot and Perfection Loop are used to construct this leader

This leader is suited to large game fish such as tuna. If the Albright knot connection is to be used where the shock and class tippet connect, be sure to lock it off with a Rizzuto finish. The critical element in any leader configurtion like this is to ensure all the knots are secure, and this means bringing them up snug and tight.

Bimini Twist

Albright Knot

Perfection Loop

Loop to loop

Class Tippet

combination of sink rate and current need to be calculated to get the fly into position. In most situations, sinking lines will be needed. Slow sink or intermediate lines suit fly rodding off the beach or where the water depth is less than about two metres. Fast sink lines come into their own in deep water or where you need the fly to get down quickly and run it on or close to the bottom. If you want to work deep then lead core lines or LC13 shooting heads are another alternative. Floating lines do well in estuary situations when used in conjunction with long leaders.

In the surf, slow sinking or intermediate lines work best. Most beaches I wade are relatively shallow and a fast sink line puts the fly on the bottom too quickly. If there is a strong rip running on a beach I sometimes change to a floating line, cast to the rip and allow the current to take the fly out. Offshore a fast sink shooting head on one rod and a slower sinking line on the other gives the angler options to

change, just remember to be prepared to vary sink rates depending on the terrain.

RIGGING UP

Thousands of words and diagrams have been used to tell anglers about the need to taper leaders, the knots to use, and a hundred and one other technical points. A lot of it is designed around the need to cast and lay out a straight leader. In practical terms, much of what is written is not necessary in salt water. Leaders can be as short as one metre and still be effective.

For most fishing I use a 25 kg butt to take up one third of the leader length, followed by a single length of class tippet. When working the likes of Clousers and other flies that have lead eyes, the butt section doesn't always help in turning the fly over anyway. Sometimes I do away with the heavy butt section altogether and fish a level leader through to the fly.

A shortened level leader is better suited to sending an unweighted fly to the bottom in

current. The reason is that monofilament has natural buoyancy that will keep the fly above the fly line; shorten the leader and it will more closely follow the line down.

Regardless of the situation being fished or line used, loop connections are used, and I sometimes have the flies pre-tied on tippets for speedy change. The knot used to attach the fly depends on the size of fly. Most flies for bay and estuary fish range from about 20 mm to 50 mm long, and a loop knot, such as the Perfection loop, allows more movement. If smaller flies are employed then tie your line straight to the eye of the hook.

If you want to work big flies and keep them up off the bottom then build in flotation during construction. For small flies a small section of styrene on the line, about 30 cm ahead of the fly, will achieve the same purpose.

For shark fishers not seeking records the terminal end of the leader is snelled to 60 kg, single strand stainless steel wire. A rectangular

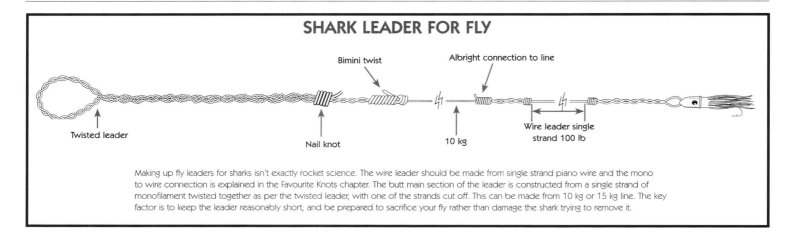

SHARK LEADER FOR FLY

Bimini twist

Albright connection to line

Twisted leader

Nail knot

10 kg

Wire leader single strand 100 lb

Making up fly leaders for sharks isn't exactly rocket science. The wire leader should be made from single strand piano wire and the mono to wire connection is explained in the Favourite Knots chapter. The butt main section of the leader is constructed from a single strand of monofilament twisted together as per the twisted leader, with one of the strands cut off. This can be made from 10 kg or 15 kg line. The key factor is to keep the leader reasonably short, and be prepared to sacrifice your fly rather than damage the shark trying to remove it.

loop, turned up slightly at the end in the style of a hook eye, is made for snelling the leader. To tie wire off, form the loop then make several wraps before turning the tag end of the wire at right angles and finish off with a haywire twist.

PRESENTATION

Delicate presentations to rising trout in gin clear mountain streams are the literary substance of freshwater fly-fishing. The stream is running and the trout sipping. You cast a short arc, a tight loop and the way the line lays and the leader unfolds add up to a presentation that is, hopefully, as faint as a fairy's kiss as your dry fly lands like a windflower on the crystal, effervescent water.

In some saltwater scenarios you might undertake similar practices—bream and estuary perch sipping ants off the surface in a south coast estuary. Or maybe a small patch of wary garfish schooling around pier pilings. You might even want to work similar flies, ant patterns, orange spinners, or even an elk hair caddis.

It's a gentle, pleasant way to fish. It's also a lot of literary humbug; the sorts of 'once upon a time' stuff of dreams. There are those who like to portray an image of fly-fishing as a slow, delicate institution. But they're dreamers, not realists. A hot bite is a hot bite, regardless of where you are. The pace can be frenetic, and lobbing flies so they caress the water isn't always exactly what happens, even if we'd like it to be that way.

A hot bite in the salt can be even more chaotic. There will be situations when you might actually want to make the fly hit the water hard enough to splash. Some days it comes down to speed: how fast you can haul, cast, and strip. Not much science in that. It all depends on the fish, the scenario and, of course, the fly fisher's ability.

In practice, it is not as important in salt water to have the tournament caster's ability to place a fly within a small diameter ring. There is a wider margin for error, unless of course you happen to be working a set of snags. Most of us can put a fly about where we want it to be. Some days we are more accurate than others, and the more we try the better we are.

Many saltwater species tend to move around a fair bit, both because they are hunting and to avoid presenting an easy feed to a larger predator. That is the nature of the marine environment. While a trout might prefer to remain in its feeding lane, marine species are used to hunting and working for their supper.

This isn't to say that you can turn the water into froth and your fly into a missile and still catch fish. Far from it. And, while swoffing is generally more forgiving of us less talented casters, when all the back casts are straightened, piscatorial results still come down to presentation. However, it isn't so much how you cast the fly to fish as the way you retrieve it past them.

BEACH AND SURF

Beach and surf fishing vary, depending on where you are. In a proper surf setting, and I don't mean a half metre shore break, there is no need to be too fussy about presentation. The ideal option in this environment is to make use of conditions to get results. To achieve this you must understand the way surf works, and the feeding patterns of the fish you are after in as much as where they will most likely be found.

The humble Australian salmon is the most common surf species for the fly. Salmon don't like the silted suds and stirred up sand, probably because it plays havoc with their gills. This is the domain of the hunted, not the hunter. You have to go beyond the white water to the clean, green water along the fringe to get to the better fish, and the way to do that is to use the rips and wave surges to put you there.

Even with a shooting head and running line,

Shaun Ash caught this turrum working a system of reefs off the Breaksea Spit in Queensland.

most anglers would have difficulty casting 40 m on a surf beach. But you can send your fly out much further than that if you use the right line to put the line and fly into the current and let the forces of nature go to work for you.

My preferred option is a floating line, preferably a weight forward shooting head, and a leader of about 1.5 – 2 metres. In a surf scenario I prefer to stay away from weighted flies such as Clousers and stick with more conventional baitfish patterns such as the Deceiver. The reason being that I don't want the fly dragging on the bottom; I want it in the water in the current.

The procedure is to find a rip, cast across it and then feed out line as the backwash pulls the fly out. Once you reach what you believe to be the required distance, wait for the line to straighten out and then start to strip. A steady strip works best for me, but others may have a different option. On good days, you will see salmon in the curl of the wave so you know how far your fly needs to be out. If you can't see the fish, just try to ensure the fly is at least in the green water at the back of the breakers.

On beaches where there is minimal wave action you can work whatever you like. I was introduced to blue salmon near Broome by Dan O'Sullivan. It was a matter of spotting the small pods of salmon as they swam towards you and then casting the fly ahead of them, across their path. It didn't seem to matter what sort of fly was used, just so long as it had some pink. The water was relatively shallow and we used intermediate lines and leaders up to three metres long, because the fish were flighty. Distance wasn't a problem as the salmon worked in close to shore, and because the fly was cast ahead of the fish casting presentation wasn't critical either. When the fish came close it was simply a matter of stripping fast; the take was often instant.

ESTUARY AND FLATS

Estuary fishing comes in diverse forms ranging from mud and sand to snags. Each form has its own peculiarities for fly presentation. As well, estuarine waters offer a merger of sight fishing and blind fishing opportunities.

Small baitfish use skinny water to stay out of the way of larger predators. Their problem though is that they are more exposed in the shallows to attack from above, as birds will take advantage of the opportunity. And even then,

in the skinny water, baitfishes are not always safe. Some big, predatory fish are prepared to swim and hunt in the shallows. Mulloway will hunt in a metre of water, and I've seen flathead that I judge would have topped 6 kg take flight in water less than knee deep.

Recently I was drifting over a small, shallow bay in an estuary on the New South Wales south coast. The bay I was covering was no more than a metre deep, and probably averaged about half that. There was no wind; the water calm and relatively clear. I was fishing for duskies, and despite the relative clarity of the water and visibility, the fish were so well camouflaged that they were impossible to spot. It was only when the shadow of the boat passed overhead that a flathead was spooked enough to take off. You didn't always see the fish, just the cloud in the water where it had been lying.

On sandbanks flathead can be just as difficult. When you spook them they will scoot off for about 10 – 15 m before settling down again, but at least you have an advantage in that you know where they have stopped, approximately anyway. Sometimes, because you know where the fish is, you can see it, cast a fly, and retrieve it to pass within the fish's line of vision. In muddy water, the method is more haphazard; you know about where the fish is so you cast in the general area. I prefer to work intermediate lines and an upside down fly like a Clouser for frogs and keep the retrieve slow and steady. Leader length of about two metres is ample, although on overcast days when bream move out to feed over sandbars, a longer leader will work better.

Weed can be a problem, particularly ribbon weed. Some fly-fishers opt for weed guards, or fish guards as some of them are referred to. Most guards are done in a loop of mono that runs from the head of the fly and over the point of the hook. But there is an alternative. Traralgon fly tyer Geoff Skinner employs a different style of guard on his Skinners Shrimp pattern. This consists of a single strand of mono that rises vertically from the eye of the hook to deflect ribbon weed without impeding the hook function, which of course is to impale a fish.

Geoff's fly innovations are all developed through field experience. In the case of Skinners Shrimp and the large Skinners Prawn, he also builds an alternative inverted pattern; that is the fly is designed to swim hook point up. The tie is similar to the Clouser with weighted eyes employed to maintain the inverted ride. However, to ensure the fly doesn't flop on its side when it hits the bottom or a solid object, Geoff ties mono sprigs across the hook shank. Jutting out at right angles to the shank, these act as stabilizers to maintain the fly's attitude.

If you aren't into guards, an alternative is to

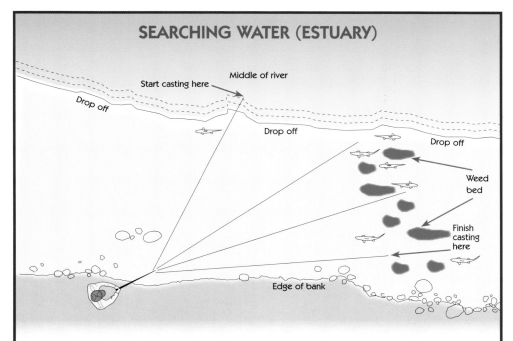

SEARCHING WATER (ESTUARY)

Middle of river
Start casting here
Drop off
Drop off
Drop off
Weed bed
Finish casting here
Edge of bank

As the tide rises in an estuary, fish start moving out of the deep into areas that were previously shallow. To search the water you should start your casts towards the deep water and work the drop-off. As the water rises, progressively start to work structure such as weed beds or yabbie banks.

Presentation in this scenario, whether with fly or lure, is important. Sometimes with a neutral buoyancy fly such as a heavily dressed Lefty Deceiver, the 'do nothing' presentation works best. Just allow the fly to drift and move with the current, giving it a slight twitch at random intervals while closely watching the tip of the fly line for an indication.

Heavy flies such as Clousers should be worked in similar fashion to soft plastics. That is, a strip or lift, and then a pause. It is about creating a shrimp-like action and the take is often as the fly or lure is diving back to the bottom. This erratic approach works well.

For bibbed minnow lures, the retrieve should imitate a stricken baitfish. Speed is the last thing you will need if it is bream or flathead you are seeking. For other predators such as tailor, the same action and just a faster erratic retrieve will work.

Native fish specialists like Rod Harrison have developed specialist techniques for catching barramundi on the fly.

first metre is a 20 kg butt, with a loop-to-loop connection for the 9 kg leader and the Clouser fly attached via a swinging loop.

The idea is that the fly line lies on the bottom, there is no shadow and so the fish aren't spooked. When the trevally arrive you cast the fly about three metres in front of them, allow the fly to sink and when you think the school is on the fly start to strip—fast. The hook-up that follows is hard. Rather than test your tackle to the extreme, the fish is allowed to run on a light drag. Water pressure on the line is counted on to eventually slow the trevally down. Three hundred metres or so later and you can start working the fish back.

BOATS

Fly-fishing in boats offers enormous latitude in the way a fly can be presented. There will be days when you need fast sink lines to get where the fish are. But there are always species that will be caught on or near the surface. And just because you are fly-fishing doesn't mean

tie up a fly that will hold above bottom. Geoff's Baited Breath variation achieves this, and the pattern is tied along the lines of the English Booby flies used in impoundments. In Geoff's version, a closed cell foam cylinder replaces standard weighted eye sets to add buoyancy. The result is a very slow sinking, or even inert fly depending on the amount of flotation added. This prevents the fly from dragging the bottom and weed. Intermediate lines will take the fly down but it is ideal for fishing over ribbon weed beds or when fish are holding at a level in the water column. If full flotation is used the depth at which the fly is required to run is dependent on leader length.

In temperate waters, pelagic species are not common, but in the tropics the situation changes. Fishing at Russell Heads south of Cairns with Kieran Livingstone, we had a hot bite of Queenfish averaging 5 kg to 7 kg, with the odd bigger fish. I was using an intermediate line and tried all the usual flies before using a Rick Keam prototype: a bibbed fly made from some top-secret white material. Purists might say it wasn't a fly, but at least it got the desired result. And to this day, I believe the only reason I caught Queenfish on fly that day was due to the strong action created by the bib. In clear water, I probably would have caught the fish on the usual Clousers, Pink Things, or Deceivers.

Snags are different again. Estuary perch and bream school up in snags, but so too do the likes of mangrove jack and barramundi.

For perch and bream I work a floating line, cast into a snag and, when the fly disappears, watch the end of the fly line for indication of a take. A favourite fly is the Skinner Shrimp. The retrieve is slow, but the take is often sharp and hard. Perch, like their relatives Australian bass, are more aggressive and probably lash out in defence of territory.

In west coast tropical waters I've used intermediate and faster sink lines to fish snags. Fishing for barramundi in a clear West Australian stream with Greg 'Patches' Fiorenza is an example. It was picturesque water. Forest as a backdrop, large sand tracts behind us and the scent of flying fox dung wafting through the air on the zephyr of a breeze. We cast to snags and retrieved the fly with a long sharp strip followed by a pause before stripping again. In one way it is similar to perch and bass, except you get the impression the fish are feeding and not just exerting proprietorial rights.

Flats fishing for the likes of golden trevally has undergone an evolutionary process. Fish may not be smart, but they do seem to be able to associate. In its early days, when the trevally were not so heavily fished, fly fishers used floating lines. Then the methodology changed to intermediate lines, but even these cast enough of a shadow in the gin clear waters to spook the fish. Nowadays, the approach is to fish with a lead core head on a shooting line. The Cortland LC13 is the favourite among anglers I know. Leader length is about three metres. The

saltwater flies

Colour and the ability to get the fly down to the fish are important factors in successful fly-fishing. Sometimes you have to experiment with colour and retrieve methods. Try to match the size, colour, and action of the fly to whatever you believe your quarry is feeding on.

ESTUARY: Deep Clouser Minnow, Lefty Deceiver, Bendback, Crazy Charlie and small baitfish or shrimp patterns offer a good selection. Gold bead head nymphs work well on many estuary species including garfish, mullet and flathead. If you are chasing surface feeders such as poddy mullet, or sometimes even bream, then some dry flies used on trout, such as the Elk Hair Caddis, Royal Wulff and ant patterns will work.

SURF: Lefty Deceiver, Bendback, Pink Thing, Surf Candy, and small, flashy profile baitfish imitations.

BAY: Lefty Deceiver, Deep Clouser Minnow, Crazy Charlie, Pink Thing and flashy profile baitfish patterns.

OFFSHORE: Flashy profile flies are proven on the likes of marlin while Jumbo Pink Things, squid imitations and wide bodied white flies work well on most sharks. Cube flies have proven themselves on yellowfin. Other flies worth having on hand include the Pink Thing, Lefty Deceiver and Deep Clouser minnow.

you shouldn't adopt practices similar to those used by lure and bait anglers. I'm referring to technique of course.

Jigging is popular with the heavyweight lure brigade, and this method can be adapted to fly-fishing. Use a fast sink line, let the fly sink all the way to the bottom and then strip it back as fast as you can. If you aren't fast enough then tuck the rod under your arm and strip with both hands. The technique works on species as different as barracouta, giant trevally, and mackerel.

The best fun in boats is when you are working a school of fish feeding on the surface. Seeing fish and putting a fly to them is sight fishing in its purest form. If you can work poppers and watch the take on the surface, then that's even better. Short, sink tip lines can be deadly when used in conjunction with popper-style flies.

Another presentation that has worked for me in all three scenarios is the do nothing presentation. There are days when you put the fly in the water, and stop and have a think about something or other and then wham! You're on. I can't explain why, but it happens often enough to get me wondering. I guess the answer is a bit like going to a public beach and one reserved for nudists—the 50 mm cloth strips called bikinis hide just enough body to tease and invite speculation, and sometimes that can be a lot more fun.

FLIES

TOP: **Native**
ABOVE LEFT: **Crazy Charlie**
ABOVE RIGHT: **Surf Candy**
LEFT: **Lefty Deceiver**
BOTTOM LEFT: **Pink Thing**
BOTTOM RIGHT: **Bait Fish**
BELOW: **Bend Back**

shopping list
SALTWATER FLY-FISHING:

ESTUARY: Six to 10 wt: Lines—intermediate; sinking, up to Density 4; sink tip and floating.

SURF: Eight to 10 wt: Lines—floating, intermediate and sink tip.

BAY: Eight to 10 wt: Lines—intermediate, fast sink and floating.

OFFSHORE: Eight to 14 wt: Lines—sinking, lead core, and quick decent.

REEL: Reels for these outfits depend on what you are chasing. There is some considerable opinion against the use of anti reverse fly reels, with most noted exponents supporting direct drive. Both have a place. Many swoffers advocate large arbor reels, saying this improves retrieve rate. Again, this is a matter of choice but it is difficult to argue against the merits of this design. The basic requirements for fly reels vary with location and species. If you want to chase heavyweights, like sharks, big tuna or marlin for example, then your reel will need a smooth drag system and have a capacity of at least 600 m of 15 kg braid. Even smaller tuna such as striped tuna or mackerel tuna will peel off 100 m of backing with ease.

In an estuary casting a fly for bream or estuary perch, or working salmon or flathead in a bay, a drag system is not a necessity. Nor is it likely that you will need more than about 50 m of backing. However, if you happen to hook into a good mulloway in the surf then you may need more than 100 m, a golden trevally will run 200 m easily. Make a decision on a reel based on your expectations. There are many different makes and models on the market, ask around to see which are the best value for money.

LEADERS: These should be adjusted to suit the circumstances. In most situations two to three metre long leaders will suffice. However, there will be times when less than a metre of leader is the best option, other times when you might want to run a leader of three or four metres in length. For example, if you want to catch King George whiting on a fly then a short leader will ensure your fly stays on or near the bottom. If you are chasing surface feeders, sipping ants or bugs off the surface, as poddy mullet do, then a long leader offers a better presentation with a dry fly.

MARLIN ON FLY

Saltwater fly rodders are forever expanding their horizons, albeit within the limits of their tackle. Marlin on fly has been regarded as the top end of the sport. It's not a new concept, but that doesn't make it any easier.

I guess what has deterred many fly rodders chasing marlin are the costs involved. Game boats and specialist guides cost big bucks, and are beyond the financial means of most anglers. It doesn't have to be like that. Thirty years ago game fishing was in the same unique position, catering for a small group of people able to pay for the boat, or with enough dollars to buy a big boat. That all changed with the advent of the sportfishing boat. Anglers who had once thought serious game fishing beyond their financial reach were able to do battle with marlin and tuna on the cobalt playing fields offshore.

There are places where marlin are within

Marlin on a fly are uncontrollable in the early stages of the fight and should be allowed to burn off as much energy as they want.

marlin

SAFETY
Before heading out for a day register your vessel, destination, estimated time of return and car registration number with the local Coast Guard and radio in for a weather report.

FLIES: Blue or green backed flashy profile tube flies built by Geoff Skinner. A double hook rig was used with an 8/0-lead hook and a size 10/0 stinger. The hooks were joined on cable wrapped in waxed string.

LEADERS: These were tied to fit in with the new GFAA 15 kg rating. Constructed from Asso leader material, we first created the double Bungie knot that lead to the 15 kg-class tippet material followed by a 35 cm long, 50 kg fluorocarbon tippet. All up, the leaders were just under two metres in length.

OUTFIT: 13 – 15 weight, minimum backing required is about 600 m of braid.

LINES: A sinking shooting taper head, 430 – 575 grain is about ideal to help turn a big fly over and give you control and distance. Suitable lines include Masterline Target ST 14 UFS, Cortland 444 SST or 44SL Quick Decent and Scientific Angler Tarpon, Billfish, Bluewater and Wet Tip Express 575 grain.

relatively close proximity, particularly up the east coast and a trailerboat is fine. The system I have used with success is straightforward, but works best with a crew of three. Teasers are used to raise the marlin. These consist of a Moldcraft bird and squid teaser chain with Skip Smith pusher on the right hand outer, the middle line alternated between a swimming mullet and a Mark Chan Bonito, and a slimy mackerel rigged to skip on the left hand outer. The last rig has proven critical. While the splash and chatter of the bird and squid chain was expected to create the attraction, the best chance of holding a billfish for a fly rod shot ultimately hinges on the ability to tease the marlin into range with the skip bait.

The flies used with most success have been flashy profile, in blue or green. When a marlin comes up it will be lit up like a neon sign and aggressive. The teasers are retrieved first and the fly cast behind the marlin as the skip bait is brought on board. As the marlin turns, it spots the fly and inhales it and you set the hook. At least that's what should happen. Sometimes the marlin takes the fly but because you don't get the hook home properly, it will spit it out. But even then, it is not unknown for a marlin to come back and take the fly again.

FIGHTING TACTICS
Wherever possible the boat is positioned close to the fish and used to change the direction of pull. But even that can be hard as fish like marlin keep doubling back and it's important to keep a tight line straight to the fish. It is disconcerting to be hooked up to a fish with a line heading north only to see it jump 100 m away to the east!

It is difficult, sometimes impossible even, to lift a big gamefish from the depths with a fly rod. In a strong current or slight sea, and once the fish has started to tire, it is important to get ahead of a gamefish, taking the boat overhead and close, and then driving off down current or sea. This has the effect of lifting the fish's head and planing it towards the surface, courtesy of the current and the dynamics of the fish's body shape.

However there are limits. Running down current is a smooth sea exercise; running down with a wind of more than 15 knots or a big swell can be the kiss of death as the influence of wind and sea on the boat is too great and you end up losing line. Wind against current can make conditions too sloppy and wind and current in the same direction can mean too fast a drift. It's all a matter of judgement.

CONTROLLING GAMEFISH

Boat should stay ahead of fish to swim it to the surface.

The difference between hooking a big game fish and landing it often boils down to boat handling ability. No fish likes directional changes as this can disorientate them. But pulling directional changes on a big gamefish isn't usually a practicable application. The way to beat them is to wear them out by working the elements to best suit your situation.

In the early stages of a fight, when the fish is running hard and fast, give chase in the boat but maintain line pressure slightly to one side. This causes the line to pull over the fish's shoulder, and has the effect of restricting its ability to swim. If the line is being pulled from the opposite side of the mouth from which it is hooked, the line will be pulling over the fish's shoulder and be laying hard on the gill plates interrupting its ability to use its gills properly as well as restricting its ability to swim.

The body shape of fish like marlin and tuna means they can sit in the current and seem to still be pulling away from you, even though they are hardly swimming. While the fish is doing this it is resting and gaining a second wind. The best way to put a stop to this and maintain pressure is to work ahead of the fish and stay up sea as fish will swim into the wind or current. Now, every time you pump and wind you are pulling the fish's head up and planing it nearer to the surface, and it has to use energy to fight you. However, when using fly tackle for example and you don't have the lifting power of game tackle, it is necessary to ensure you are ahead of the fish to keep lifting its head up and forcing it to the surface – even when that means being down current.

MARLIN LEADER

Twisted leader or bungie.	15 kg glass tippet.	50 kg tippet	fly with stinger hook
1 metre	1 metre	35 cm	

This is a variation on using the Twisted Leader mentioned earlier in the book. In this case fly fishing for marlin was not about delicate presentations. It was about having the power to work the fish without being overly concerned about the leader breaking under the strain or wear.

Many fish are lost because the hook pulls free when there isn't enough give in the leader. As well, it is difficult to turn a big marlin fly over unless you have a heavy butt section, and then every time you add a joining knot on a tapered leader you have the potential for disaster. In this case there are just two knots: the fly to the tippet, and the tippet to the leader. The 15-kilogram class tippet was based on Game Fishing Association of Australia rules that say the class tippet must be at least 38.10 cm long (measured inside connecting knots). A shock tippet is not allowed to be longer than 30.84 cm. Under GFAA rules for salt water fly, the shock tippet is measured from the eye of the hook to the single strand of class tippet and includes any knots used to connect the shock tippet to the class tippet.

The stinger or second hook on the fly is insurance. Marlin are difficult enough to get a hook into, so why reduce your chances by using just a single hook? In the case of the tandem hook fly, the shock tippet is measured from the eye of the leading hook for GFAA purposes.

TEASING MARLIN ON FLY

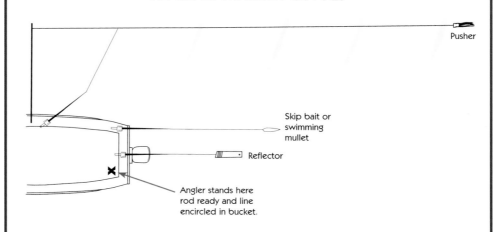

Pusher

Skip bait or swimming mullet

Reflector

Angler stands here rod ready and line encircled in bucket.

The way a sportfishing boat is laid out has a bearing on fly fishing efficiency for marlin. In a perfect system there will be three anglers on board who will share duties of driving, handling the teasers and fishing.

The ideal system is to first establish whether the angler whose turn it is, casts with the rod in the left or right hand. If the angler uses the right hand then all the teasing equipment should be run out of the starboard side of the boat. The opposite applies for left handed casters.

A system that I have found successful is as follows:
Outrigger pole with a Pusher.
Starboard corner, skip bait, or swimming mullet.
Middle stern, a Bonito Flasher or Witch Doctor run short.

When a marlin appears there is no great rush. Pull the outrigger teaser in first, and then the flasher. At this time the angler should be standing in the port corner of the boat. The fly line will be neatly coiled in a large plastic bin alongside, and the angler will be starting to get some line out, and maybe even false cast.

By the time the angler is ready to cast, the boat is put out of gear and the skip bait retrieved and replaced by the fly. One way to be sure of getting the fly to the marlin is to cast across the wake of the slowing boat as the momentum will pull it back through the wake to where the marlin should be hunting for the skip bait. It is better if the fly lands behind the marlin, as these fish often turn and go back looking for the skip bait. With luck it will see the fly and take it. If the marlin disappears, put the skip bait back in the water immediately and start trolling again. I have seen anglers take several shots at marlin before the fish has found the fly.

When a fish is running hard chase it with the boat, pressure from behind or over the fish's shoulder is the best direction as this interrupts the fish's capacity to use its gills properly and restricts its ability to swim forward and down.

Game boats, with twin screws, are able to back up on fish. In a trailerboat, this can be an exercise fraught with danger. The self-draining hull on some small boats makes backing up possible but there is a limit. Don't try backing down too hard; do so slowly and cautiously. The manoeuvrability of trailerboats is such that backing up is often unnecessary.

FRESHWATER FLY FISHING

In its purest form, fly-fishing in freshwater involves trout. Other freshwater species such as redfin, Australian bass, saratoga, Murray cod, and yellowbelly are also sought but barely rate the media coverage given to trout.

Mr Speckles is the ultimate fly rod fish. But he's a contrary creature to the point that on any given day, fly-fishing can range from long periods of exasperating difficulty to sharp encounters of the spectacular kind bordering on the cosmic.

The literary humbug surrounding this method of fishing is immense. As a discipline, fly-fishing has variously been portrayed as art, as a metaphor for life's vagaries and a means of class distinction. Even today, many people still think of fly anglers as the claret and tweed set.

Dreamers like to portray an image of fly-fishing as a slow, delicate institution. But the reality is that a hot bite is a hot bite, regardless of where you are. The pace can be frenetic, and lobbing flies so they caress the water isn't always exactly what happens, even if we'd like it to be that way.

In its purest form, fly-fishing involves trout, preferably brown or rainbow trout. Mr Speckles is the ultimate fly rod fish, but he's a contrary creature to the point that on any given day, fly-fishing can range from long periods of exasperating difficulty to sharp encounters of the spectacular kind bordering on the cosmic.

That the number of fly-fishing participants continues to grow is not surprising given that this discipline suits anybody capable of wielding a rod, regardless of age, sex, creed or colour. And cost is no longer a deterrent factor with a basic, entry-level outfit costing from about $150. The days when fly fishing tackle meant a second mortgage are gone. Mind you, it is still possible to buy tackle in the 'grounds for divorce' price category—but that comes later when the addiction takes hold and you have to make serious decisions. I live alone, by the way.

OUTFIT

It can cost less to get started in fly-fishing than you would pay for a top of the range snapper outfit. Entry-level fly fishing outfits, consisting of rod, reel, line, and leader, start at about $150. Fly fishing rods are rated to suit fly line weights. Most freshwater fly-fishers use six weight outfits (that is a six weight rod and six weight fly line) as a good all round option. In small mountain streams though, I prefer to use a four or five weight while for lake fishing, some anglers work seven or eight weight outfits.

Once you get into fly fishing you might find you are in dire need of a better rod or reel. There is no doubt that the top range rods make casting easier. These rods are generally higher modulus graphite and feature a sharper recovery, which allows the angler to send the line out farther with less effort. When it comes to the reel, this is a matter of personal choice, but you do get what you pay for and you never know when the day might come when you need a good reel that holds a bit more than 50 metres of backing.

FLY LINES

Flies are essentially ultra-light lures, but they are too light to cast. To overcome this fly lines, which are little more than elongated sinkers, were developed. Fly lines come in a variety of configurations but the three most popular are weight forward (heavy taper at the front) in floating, intermediate and sinking. Most

Fly fishing is about attention to detail and presentation.

fly fishing for natives

Rod Harrison used to specialise in fly fishing for native species, particularly in the granite belt of northern New South Wales so these are his recommendations.

Rod says Murray cod can be caught at night on flies. The Dahlberg Diver and Silicon Head Slider are two that work after the sun has gone down. During the day, weighted heavily dressed flies like the Spinster, Barred and Black, Pink Thing and Flash-tail Whistlers have proven effective.

Australian bass, yellowbelly, and silver perch are best fished for around weed beds and two proven flies are the Clouser Minnow and Bead Chain Woolly Bugger.

trout fishers working streams use floating lines, while intermediate (which are slow sinking) and sinking lines are more popular for lakes.

OTHER EQUIPMENT

You will also need to avail yourself of a fly vest. It is no more than a jacket with many different size pockets so you can store fly boxes, line clippers, floatant, forceps (for hook removal), leader material, and other assorted bits of equipment. Waders are essential. For small streams, where plenty of walking is involved thigh waders are more comfortable than chest waders. But in lakes, the chest waders give the angler the opportunity to search deeper water. Add a net to the list, it will come in handy and make landing fish easier.

One thing you should never fish without is a good pair of polarising sunglasses. When fishing heavily shaded streams in valleys, many anglers insist on yellow tinted glasses as these increase light. Where you have constant changes of light and shade, photo-chromic brown or amber lenses also work well. In the case of trout, sometimes it is the wink from the fish's flank as it turns after feeding that gives it away. Even in gin clear water trout, particularly the smaller fish are not always easy to spot. Sometimes you see the shadow of the fish on the bottom before you actually spot the trout. Without polarising glasses though, you won't see anything and will be fishing blind.

RIGGING UP

Unlike saltwater fly, presentation is a critical element when fly fishing in fresh water—particularly in small streams. And while you can get away with a level line in the salt, a tapered leader is better in the fresh. Some anglers prefer to tie their own leaders, but tapered leaders are an inexpensive item. I normally buy a two or three metre leader that tapers down to about six pounds, or just under 3 kilograms breaking strain) and then tie on a tippet or leader to suit the situation.

CASTING

The big hurdle for most would-be fly flickers is learning how to cast and present a fly. This is about understanding the principles of a method where the weight of the line, rather than the weight of a sinker or lure, is used to cast a counterfeit offering to a fish.

Timing and technique are everything. Casting power and therefore distance comes through line speed not physical effort. The faster you can get the line moving, the further it should go.

It used to be that you either joined a fly fishing club or attempted to teach yourself. But fishing clubs don't suit everyone while self-learning, even with the aid of books and

wading

When it comes to fishing rivers and streams many anglers eventually end up wading. It's all about putting yourself in a better position to fish where you believe the fish should be holding.

Before he took a novice in the water, Evan would explain to them why it was important to take it easy, not to rush or panic. The combination of current and an uneven bottom peppered with smooth rocks can make movement difficult, until you get used to it.

Some anglers wear wading boots with felt-like soles believing, rightly, that these offer more grip. I prefer to don waders. My system is to avoid those stretches of very fast flowing water whenever possible, particularly if it is going to be much deeper than just above my knees. In slow water you can easily wade up to your waist and maintain your balance, but add a couple of knots to the water flow and life can become unsteady.

As you wade it is a case of one step at a time. Before taking each step, you should have already placed your front foot firmly and securely. One way to maintain balance is to use a wading stick. It doesn't have to be anything fancy, just so long as it is strong enough to take your weight. By way of insurance, it pays to fish with someone when working fast flowing water. At least then, if you do get into trouble your fishing partner can come to your aid.

videos, can be a drawn out process. When the bug bites you'll want to be fishing yesterday, not still learning how to cast a few weeks or months later. My suggestion is to save many hassles and invest a few dollars in a fly-fishing school. The investment puts the novice ahead in terms of the time it takes to learn to cast and fish flies.

I've walked many streams and lakes with many different trout fishing guides over the years and can vouch for their value. All the good guides have a desire to teach. I picked up plenty of tips on techniques that can take years to learn otherwise through trial and error methods.

MATCHING THE HATCH

Flies are essentially small lures. The difference between a fly and a lure is that fly fishers try to "match the hatch" as closely as possible with their offering. There are two types of fly, a dry, and a wet. A dry fly is one that that floats on the surface as an insects or sits in the surface film (meniscus) to imitate an emerging insect; wet flies include nymphs and streamers and are designed to be used underwater and may imitate the nymphal stage of an insect, or even small fish.

Flies are not expensive and you tie your own. Most flies sold in shops range from about $1.50 for a nymph pattern through to about $3 for more extravagant wet flies. The following flies cover many probabilities, but fall a long way short of covering all eventualities:

An example of matching the hatch was a mayfly dun hatch on a lake in central Victoria. On that October day, I was fishing with Philip Weigall. It was a lake he guided on and he was specific about the duns saying they were actually *Atalophlebia australis*. There are two hatches a year, the first from mid October to early December, and the second in March. In the nymph or mudeye stage these insects crawl about the bottom of the lake and then one day get the urge to move up the water column to the surface. Once at the surface these nymphs force their way through the meniscus or surface film, break free of their eco-skeleton and then sit on the water waiting for their wings to dry.

The lake surface was a floating tent city as the emerged insects drifted across the lake waiting for their wings to dry. But the trout were feeding on the duns as they were coming out of their exoskeletons or emerging. This is when the insects are most vulnerable.

Philip was casting a small Barry Lodge emerger pattern fly. When trout feed on emergers, it is a sip or gulp, whereas when taking the insects off the surface the action is splashier. The only problem was keeping the fly in view. If you lost sight of the fly, the chances

Knowing the best times of day and also where to concentrate your fishing effort in a river or lake will save you wasting time fishing for trout at the wrong time or in unproductive sections of water.

another step forward or upstream, and do it all again. Evan's system works just as well on stillwaters.

There are general rules about fishing that experienced anglers follow for the best results. In rivers, trout often feed best just prior to a change. During early summer for example, it is not unusual for a hot day to be interrupted by an afternoon thunderstorm. When you expect this to happen my advice is to get on the water and start fishing.

Success in small streams comes through knowledge and stealth. Trout lie in deeper pools, at the head and tail of runs, or wait beneath bushy overhangs along the banks. It is necessary to use stealth when approaching likely areas, work your way upstream, and make long casts wherever possible.

Fly fishers find the going a little tougher, particularly where the foliage has overgrown the stream, so roll casts become the order of the day. Invariably, these are the most productive waters as heavy bank-side flora means shade and protection from birds while during summer this growth means cooler water and dark areas suited to ambush.

In lakes, the weed beds around the shoreline are a good place to start. If you have a boat then work the wind lanes as rainbow trout in particular like to feed along these. On hot days the trout may be down deep, if you think this is the case put on a sinking line and get your fly down to where you think the fish are.

If the arc of your cast is the challenge of hunting or stalking fish, and convincing them to take a counterfeit offering that would take flight in a strong breeze, then perhaps this is for you.

were a trout would take it and spit it out before you had time to react and set the hook.

While serious fly fishers are aware of entomology, fly tyers are even more deeply involved. They have to be; their craft requires total perfection. The flies they tie must not only look the same as the bug they are designed to imitate, but have a similar action in the water. If the trout are feeding on size 20 damsel nymphs, then that is what you should be offering.

There will also be days when science goes out the window. Days when you offer up something totally irregular, a fly pattern that matches no known local bug, in a size that is much bigger than the local insect population, and you will suddenly start catching trout. I mean, why do rainbow trout like their nymph flies to have gold bead heads? I can't think of a single bug that has a gold coloured bead on its head.

One of the problems associated with fly fishing trout is conformity. Some anglers have broken off the shackles, adopted a non-conformist approach, and found that it works. Fishing is, after all, not about looking stylish but about getting results. For example, in lakes and big rivers small versions of traditional saltwater flies like Crazy Charlies and Clouser minnows work well on trout. The Woolly Bugger fly tied with small lead eyes is good value for fishing down deep in stillwaters.

WHERE TO FISH

The best advice I ever received on fly fishing a water came from the late Evan Mathews who used to guide fly fishers on rivers like the Buckland and King near Bright. His system was to divide the water up like a draughtboard, and to work his fly through every square metre. You would make several casts, allowing the fly to drift through likely areas and then take

favourite trout flies

WETS:
Brown or black gold bead-head nymph.
Tom Jones.
Hamill's Killer.
Murray Wilson's BMS (Bullen Merri Special).
Woolly Bugger.
Green and black Matuka.
Mudeye patterns and damsel nymph patterns will also come in handy.

DRIES:
Elk Hair Caddis.
Black Beetle (fished wet or dry).
Coch-y-bonddu.
Rusty Dun.
Orange spinner.
Red Tag (wet or dry).

FAVOURITE RIGS

The first thing you need to understand about rigs is that they are not tied, but rather a rig is constructed or built. There is a system for that construction which is little different from any other form of building. You don't put a roof on a house before you put the frames for the walls up, so it is with rigs.

Many rigs employed in different scenarios are similar. It amuses me to see people attach different names to rigs that are, but for slight variations, the same as they have always been.

Make no mistake, the best rig for bait fishing is one that has no lead and consists of a hook to the main line. It sinks at a gentle rate and offers no resistance to a fish that picks the bait up. Unfortunately, circumstances often dictate the need to add lead or swivels or floats. There are times when you need to get a bait to the bottom in current, use a swivel to run a leader from the main line or else suspend a bait below the surface.

Take the running sinker rig, by far the most popular and successful way to fish with bait. There are two variations, the simplest being a ball sinker located directly on top of the hook. There is no better rig for fishing the turbulent waters around ocean rocks. The other employs a stopper that locates the sinker a short distance above the hook. This is a preferred rig for calmer waters. Those differences aside, the running sinker rig is essentially the same for bay, estuary, lake, and rivers.

Hooks, leads, swivels and rings may change to suit the situation but the overall function stays the same. Running sinker rigs afford fish the opportunity to pick up and run with a bait without being alerted by undue resistance.

With that in mind, a shopping list is placed under each species. The rigs come with recommended terminal tackle requirements listed under the species of choice.

The most important thing to do when you have set up a rig is to check the knots

Knowing the best times of day and also where to concentrate your fishing effort in a river or lake will save you wasting time fishing for trout at the wrong time or in unproductive sections of water.

and hooks regularly. Why miss fish because your hooks are blunt or knots have become suspect. In the case of hooks, all hooks regardless of type and that includes chemically sharpened ones, can be improved with a slight touch up on a sharpening stone. I have found that stainless steel and chemically sharpened hooks, in that order, hold their sharpness longer than tinned hooks.

Swivels are commonplace in rigs, with the barrel about the most popular. Barrel swivels are used to join terminal rigs to the main line to avoid line twist when bait is being retrieved. Many serious anglers prefer black believing they are less likely to reflect light that could scare away fish. A swivel will stop line twist only when placed above the object that spins. Always choose a swivel with a wire diameter similar to the line diameter. If the line is thicker than the wire, the wire can cut the line.

My advice is to avoid three-way or cross-line swivels whenever possible. Apart from being weak in their design, they don't work in

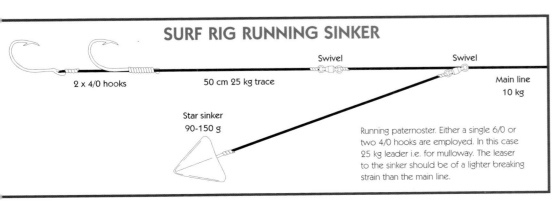

SURF RIG RUNNING SINKER

2 x 4/0 hooks

50 cm 25 kg trace

Swivel

Swivel

Star sinker
90-150 g

Main line
10 kg

Running paternoster. Either a single 6/0 or two 4/0 hooks are employed. In this case 25 kg leader i.e. for mulloway. The leaser to the sinker should be of a lighter breaking strain than the main line.

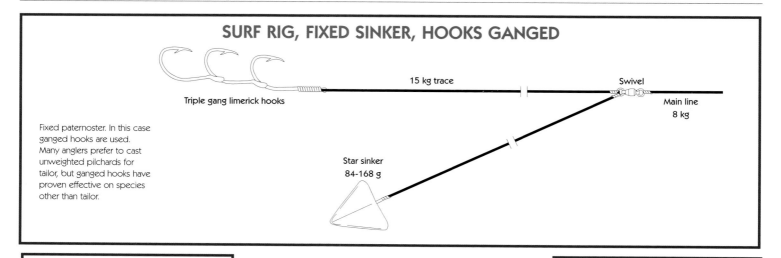

SURF RIG, FIXED SINKER, HOOKS GANGED

Triple gang limerick hooks

15 kg trace

Swivel

Main line
8 kg

Fixed paternoster. In this case ganged hooks are used. Many anglers prefer to cast unweighted pilchards for tailor, but ganged hooks have proven effective on species other than tailor.

Star sinker
84-168 g

BAIT RIG (ONE HOOK)

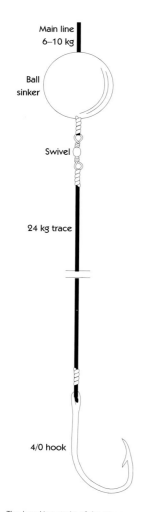

Main line
6–10 kg

Ball
sinker

Swivel

24 kg trace

4/0 hook

The breaking strain of the trace depends on the species. This rig is typical for snapper.

For the likes of whiting the trace would be 4 kg, the same for trevally.

Hook sizes are also changed to suit the species. Instead of a 4/0, this would be replaced with a No. 4 or No. 6 for whiting.

running water for even though the terminal rig will spin on the axis of the barrel this can still result in leaders to the sinker and the bait becoming entwined.

Snap swivels can be handy for a quick change of lures or even some terminal rigs, although I prefer the simple snap minus the swivel for this—except when trolling.

Ball bearing swivels used in salt water have a surface that is greater than that of normal barrel swivels so they won't lock or jam even with erratic lures trolled or spun at high speeds. Ball bearing snap swivels are popular with game fishers for eliminating line twist when trolling at high speed or for quick changing leaders when live baiting. Ball bearing snaps have also become popular among freshwater and estuary lure fishers working tough species such as mangrove jacks. The heavy-duty snap device, which locks securely, plus the large bearing surface of these swivels enhance their performance under intense loads.

Rolling swivels are midway between ball bearing and barrel swivels in terms of strength and efficiency. The major advantage of these swivels is that they are more streamlined to offer a finer entry through the water, which is why they have become so popular among freshwater anglers who prefer to troll. Choose the black ones if you can as there is less likelihood of a flash scaring away timid fish, or attracting a bite-off from a voracious predator.

A crucial factor in rig construction is in the knots. A well-constructed rig starts with securely drawn knots that won't slip. When you read the section on knots, you will see my strong preference for the Uni Knot for most attachments. The only time I prefer to use a different knot for attaching hooks is when using Circle hooks, as these are best suited to being snelled. That is, instead of passing the line through the hook eye and tying it off with a Uni Knot, the line is passed through the eye of the hook and tied to the hook shank. This gives a more direct pull to the hook and, I believe, helps the turned-in point penetrate better.

There is a simple rule of thumb with any rig being made up and that is to create the least amount of resistance possible. If you can fish with a 28 g sinker, you would do so in preference to one that is 56 grams. Some anglers will tell you that this doesn't matter if

BAIT RIG (TWO HOOKS)

Main line
6–10 kg

Ball
sinker

Swivel

24 kg trace

2 x 4/0 hooks

The second hook is allowed to slide on the leader and act as a keeper. This helps in making fillet baits more presentable for species such as snapper and mulloway.

FIXED SINKER RIG

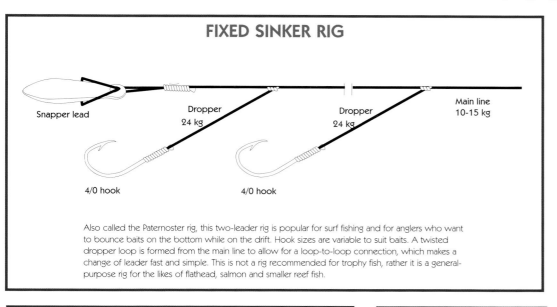

Snapper lead

Dropper
24 kg

Dropper
24 kg

Main line
10-15 kg

4/0 hook

4/0 hook

Also called the Paternoster rig, this two-leader rig is popular for surf fishing and for anglers who want to bounce baits on the bottom while on the drift. Hook sizes are variable to suit baits. A twisted dropper loop is formed from the main line to allow for a loop-to-loop connection, which makes a change of leader fast and simple. This is not a rig recommended for trophy fish, rather it is a general-purpose rig for the likes of flathead, salmon and smaller reef fish.

ESTUARY RIG 2

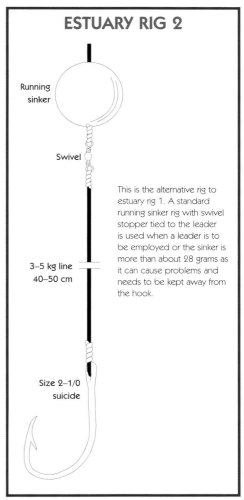

Running sinker

Swivel

3–5 kg line
40–50 cm

Size 2–1/0
suicide

This is the alternative rig to estuary rig 1. A standard running sinker rig with swivel stopper tied to the leader is used when a leader is to be employed or the sinker is more than about 28 grams as it can cause problems and needs to be kept away from the hook.

BAY RIG

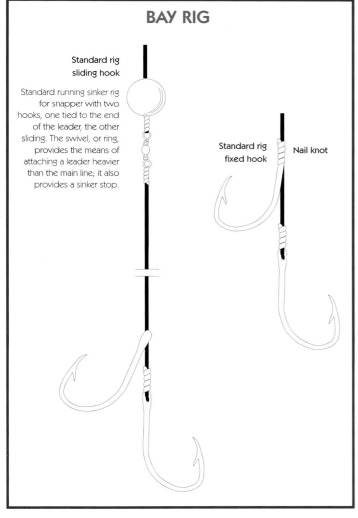

Standard rig sliding hook

Standard running sinker rig for snapper with two hooks, one tied to the end of the leader, the other sliding. The swivel, or ring, provides the means of attaching a leader heavier than the main line; it also provides a sinker stop.

Standard rig fixed hook

Nail knot

ESTUARY RIG 1

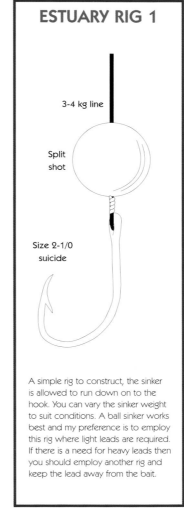

3-4 kg line

Split shot

Size 2-1/0 suicide

A simple rig to construct, the sinker is allowed to run down on to the hook. You can vary the sinker weight to suit conditions. A ball sinker works best and my preference is to employ this rig where light leads are required. If there is a need for heavy leads then you should employ another rig and keep the lead away from the bait.

you are working a standard running sinker rig. But this is a fallacy; it does matter and it can make a difference, even when fishing in gear, as I do most of the time, for snapper.

When fishing shallow water with current, such as a river or estuary, you can improve your catch rate by simply ignoring sinkers and being prepared to work your baits. When I fish the bream in a boat, the technique is to cast an unweighted bait to a snag or rockwall and allow it to slowly sink. The boat will be on the drift so eventually the bait has to be retrieved and cast to another snag. As the bait sinks, the small bream nearer the surface will attack it; this probably excites the bigger fish below to strike the bait. It is an effective way to fish, but one that requires the angler to be prepared to work and not just sit there waiting for a bite. If you find a productive snag then you simply

ESTUARY RIG 3

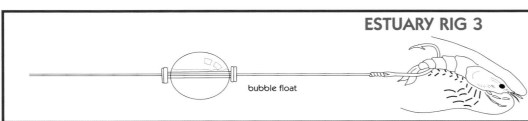

bubble float

This is a common rig employed using nippers of yabbies for estuary perch. The bubble float is transparent and weighted with water to enable casting. The hook should be a medium to long shank and the size varies to suit the bait. Most anglers will find a hook about No. 2 to No. 4 will cover most situations, although larger hooks can be used.

ESTUARY RIG 4

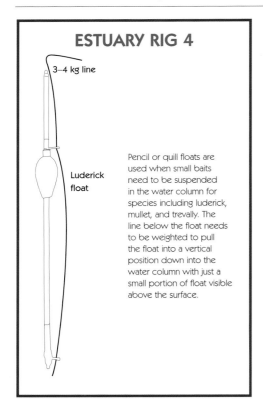

3–4 kg line

Luderick float

Pencil or quill floats are used when small baits need to be suspended in the water column for species including luderick, mullet, and trevally. The line below the float needs to be weighted to pull the float into a vertical position down into the water column with just a small portion of float visible above the surface.

FRESHWATER LIVEBAIT RIG

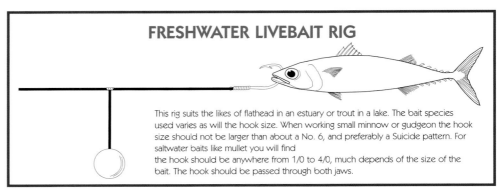

This rig suits the likes of flathead in an estuary or trout in a lake. The bait species used varies as will the hook size. When working small minnow or gudgeon the hook size should not be larger than about a No. 6, and preferably a Suicide pattern. For saltwater baits like mullet you will find the hook should be anywhere from 1/0 to 4/0, much depends of the size of the bait. The hook should be passed through both jaws.

RUNNING SINKER RIG

Swivel stop for hook trace.

Ezy rig allows bomb style sinkers to be run along line.

take the boat around and follow the same drift. If you were using sinkers in this scenario, the bait would shoot straight to the bottom and your chances of success would be much reduced.

Having said that, the situation changes for flathead. Sometimes a sinker on the line when drifting, can entice a strike. The action of the sinker bouncing off the bottom and stirring up little puffs of sand may be just the eye catcher a flathead requires.

Other fish like whiting need to be fished with a sinker as well, and the important point

Cam Whittam caught this fish in the Genoa River.

Murray cod will attack lures with a vengeance, provided you push the lure right into the cod's home turf.

to remember is that the bait should be below the sinker for best results. If you are fishing a whiting ground, have a nibble, and miss the take, change the bait immediately. Whiting prefer to chew on bait that hasn't already been nibbled.

Live baiting requires a different approach. In lakes or rivers, when fishing for trout with mudeyes for example, the effective method is to employ a bubble float. These floats have a pumping device that allows you to suck water into the float and add weight to enable casting. When it is half or three quarters full, the float is difficult to discern on a ruffled surface. Whether the same applies to a hawk-eyed trout, I am unsure. For anglers working live baits in salt water the bait can be suspended beneath a balloon or alternatively sent down deep with a sinker. The idea of the balloon is to keep the bait off the bottom and hold it in the water column at a set depth, usually about three metres. But in some circumstances, such as dropping live baits into bait balls, you want the baitfish to swim down and not up, so you run a sinker down the line.

Such is often the case on the 12 mile reef off Bermagui. It is an area where large balls of baitfish, mainly slimy mackerel and yellowtail scad, congregate. Many anglers will back up to a baitball and drop a live bait down and then slowly move it out of the ball. The movement of the fish away from the ball represents a straggler. When predators are working, this fish can be taken almost immediately.

Trolling rigs are different again. In fresh water, lures are worked near the surface by flat line trolling and the depth can be adjusted on some lures by raising or lowering the rod. Where lures need to be trolled deeper, lures with diving bibs are used, and the same lures will run deeper again if you use braid instead of monofilament. The ultimate in deepwater trolling is with downriggers, where the bomb is sent down to the depth of water to be covered and this holds the lure at that level. And to add

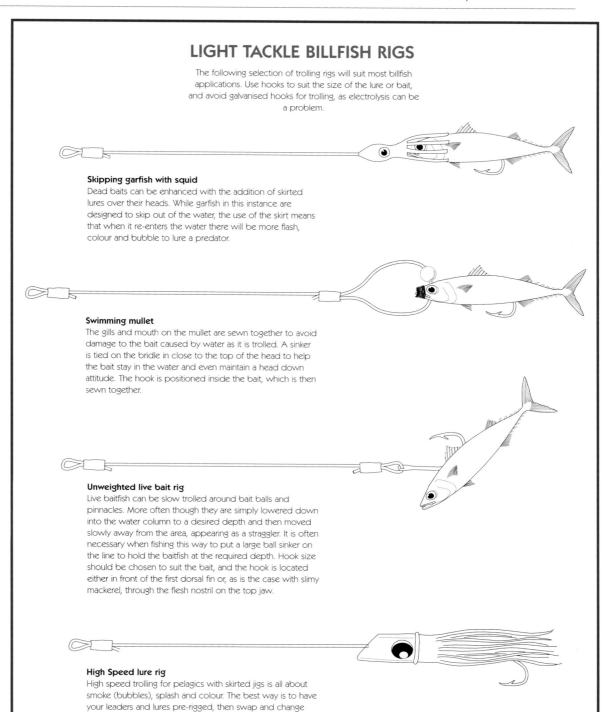

LIGHT TACKLE BILLFISH RIGS

The following selection of trolling rigs will suit most billfish applications. Use hooks to suit the size of the lure or bait, and avoid galvanised hooks for trolling, as electrolysis can be a problem.

Skipping garfish with squid
Dead baits can be enhanced with the addition of skirted lures over their heads. While garfish in this instance are designed to skip out of the water, the use of the skirt means that when it re-enters the water there will be more flash, colour and bubble to lure a predator.

Swimming mullet
The gills and mouth on the mullet are sewn together to avoid damage to the bait caused by water as it is trolled. A sinker is tied on the bridle in close to the top of the head to help the bait stay in the water and even maintain a head down attitude. The hook is positioned inside the bait, which is then sewn together.

Unweighted live bait rig
Live baitfish can be slow trolled around bait balls and pinnacles. More often though they are simply lowered down into the water column to a desired depth and then moved slowly away from the area, appearing as a straggler. It is often necessary when fishing this way to put a large ball sinker on the line to hold the baitfish at the required depth. Hook size should be chosen to suit the bait, and the hook is located either in front of the first dorsal fin or, as is the case with slimy mackerel, through the flesh nostril on the top jaw.

High Speed lure rig
High speed trolling for pelagics with skirted jigs is all about smoke (bubbles), splash and colour. The best way is to have your leaders and lures pre-rigged, then swap and change during the day via a ball bearing snap tied to the main line.

spice to the lures, attractors such as Cowbells or Ford Fenders can be employed.

In salt water, trolling is generally a much faster exercise in terms of boat speeds. You jump from what can be walking pace in a lake to 7, 10, or even 12 knots. Bluewater trolling for marlin involves running skirted lures in conjunction with teasers and a large mirror attractor, which is run short just at the back of the propeller wash. Most anglers will be trolling lures out of 5.5 to 7 metre runabouts. Most boats only have two or three anglers on

board so it pays to limit yourself to four lures and one or two teasers. Outboard motors have higher noise levels than inboards, so it can pay to run the lures further back than you would if you were fishing on a game boat.

In salt water and saline lakes, electrolysis is a problem for hooks. It causes rapid corrosion on non-stainless hooks, and any hooks moving at speed through saline waters are more prone to electrolysis than stationary hooks. Serious lure trollers prefer stainless hooks with either knife-edge points, or standard points.

PART 4

Favourite Saltwater Sportfish

CHAPTER 12

MIXED SPECIES

Defining a sportfish is about how individual anglers think of different fish. The following list is not complete. Many excellent fighting fish have been omitted. I make no apologies for this, but this is my list and these are my favourites

Australian salmon rate as one of the most spectacular southern sportfish.

AUSTRALIAN SALMON

You can say what you like about Australian salmon—just don't call them dull. Whether you catch them on bait, fly or lure, no other fish in southern climes is so consistently willing to put on a feisty display of acrobatics. Dull is not an adjective that fits this fish.

The sight of one of these green-backed powerhouses rocketing out of a wave, arching its back in a head-shaking attempt to dislodge a hook stirs the adrenalin of even the most hard-nosed angler. And, even with an aerobatics display, the same fish is likely to have enough stamina to strip line from your reel and make sudden, sharp dives that test your reflexes.

I've also chased these battlers in Victoria, South Australia, New South Wales and even across the Tasman in New Zealand. The single common denominator, regardless of whichever state or country you catch these fish, is that they always give a good account of themselves. Salmon may not rank among the top 10 on the Epicurean list of fine seafoods but in southern waters at least, they sit comfortably in the top two or three for spectacular fighting performances.

You will find salmon in the clean water around rocky headlands, offshore, break-waters and in the surf. Without salmon, many southern beaches would be hardly worth fishing. Salmon will take most lures and surface poppers, a variety of live and strip baits, whitebait, and bluebait. Forget the wire traces, salmon don't have teeth. As well as their fighting ability, salmon are reasonably plentiful and are a year-round proposition.

Salmon will most often hit a beach or rocky headland around the top of the tide, preferably when this event coincides with dawn or dusk. On a beach, those slight gutters can become deep holes at high tide and the salmon are sure to be nearby. One place you won't find them though is where the water is sullied by sand. Salmon like clean water and the biggest salmon will most often be found along the edge or just outside of the white water zone in the surf. This can be different on rock ledges. The water here is generally deeper, sand is usually not a problem, and the white water zone is on the surface while down below the environment is clear and clean.

TACKLE

Salmon will readily take baits but I don't advocate using baits in conjunction with sinkers wherever possible. In the surf, this is unavoidable. However, in a boat with a berley trail running, or sometimes even off a pier or breakwater, it is possible to fish for them without any lead on the line. Anglers who opt to use unweighted baits, lures or a fly will enjoy their salmon fishing much more.

Salmon are a treat to catch on light tackle spin gear. My preference is for a 3 kg outfit, or lighter. Heavier gear takes a lot of the fun out of the equation as it limits a fish's ability to perform out of the water. Metal lures of 10 to 15 grams, poppers, and surface minnows are best. Even in the surf, it is not always necessary to throw that far. Pick the gutter or water you want to fish and work it constantly. Remember, salmon don't just sit around waiting for a feed. They are hunters and, eventually, a school is bound to pass your way. Of course, you can encourage them along by using berley to attract and hold the fish in the vicinity. Recommended lures include Wonder Wobblers, Halco Chrome slices and the Intruder Krome Kritters in the metal varieties and Rapala CD5s and similar minnow patterns in the floating lures.

When trolling, plastic octopuses in white or pink are deadly. So, too, is a short piece of white plastic tube about 10 cm long. A ball sinker in the head of a plastic lure will keep it down under the surface. Treble hooks can be a nuisance, particularly if you are into catch and release, and single hooks such as Gamakatsu Octopus patterns are highly effective. To ensure the fish suffers minimal damage, flatten the barb on the hook.

Speed of the troll should be about six to eight knots, it is really a matter of trial and error until you get the revs right on the motor.

species tip

AUSTRALIAN SALMON

Salmon will work along the edges of deep-water channels and through channels in weed where baitfish might be hiding. These fish prefer clean water. Match the lure or fly to suit baitfish, vary the retrieve speed, and use a countdown method to bring your lure in at different depths until you strike the right one.

I know that many years ago I used to troll for salmon using small chrome Wonder Wobblers towed behind a dinghy I was rowing. The dinghy never got up to six knots but I still caught plenty of salmon.

shopping list
AUSTRALIAN SALMON
BAIT FISHING & SPINNING:
OUTFIT: Two to 3 kg line, threadline or small baitcaster with a rod suited to line class and capable of casting up to 20 grams. Off the rocks or surf the outfit should be boosted to about 5 kg, be able to cast lures up to 40 grams.
HOOKS: Size 2/0 to 4/0, Suicide or Octopus pattern, preferably chemically sharpened.
BAIT: Squid, pilchards, fish fillets
LURES: 10 – 15 g, Halco Twisty or chrome slices, Krome Kritters, Wonder Wobblers.

FLY FISHING:
OUTFIT: 8 – 10 wt, intermediate or sinking line up to Density 4.
Tippet about 3 kilograms.
FLIES: Lefty Deceiver, Deep Clouser Minnow, Surf Candy, and baitfish patterns suited to hooks from No. 4 to about 3/0. Colour combinations that are proven include chartreuse and white, yellow and white, blue and white or plain white.

BARRAMUNDI

Barramundi have been promoted as northern Australia's premier sportfish. I have no argument with this tag. However, this wasn't always the case. In the late 1960s and 1970s barramundi stocks were so low in parts of the country that there was a serious move made to introduce Nile perch from North Africa. This is no longer the case. In the Northern Territory, to ensure the stocks of barra are maintained at a level to continue to encourage visitors, the government reduced commercial fishing effort and introduced strict guidelines for amateur anglers. In Queensland, where impoundment fishing has enjoyed enormous growth, barra have been successfully stocked in waters such as Lake Tinaroo near Cairns. All of which is very good news for the fishery.

Barra have all the attributes of a classic sportfish. Visually pleasing, they are hard fighting fish that often leap clear of the water in spectacular fashion and have the added bonus of providing top table fare. Barra will attack lures and live baits with equal ferocity—when they are feeding. Like any fish though, certain conditions encourage them into aggression. I recall spending a day drifting down the Mossman River north of Cairns when the barra weren't so co-operative. Along with Ross Finlayson, we cast lures and flies at every snag we came across for limited success. On another trip to the opposite side of the

Ever opportunistic, barramundi often do a double dip when it comes to tides. Good observers might sometimes sight barra hitch-hiking an incoming tide - head down, tail up and stiff as a board to present a maximum body area to the flow.

country, near Broome, I was introduced to a small creek and told that when the tide turned to flood the barra would come on big time. Along with another angler, we caught more than a dozen fish to about 4 kg in just over an hour on fly.

This species lives in a range of inshore waters from salt to fresh, ranging into estuaries and brackish waters. Barra inhabit both estuaries and fresh water areas. Most are found not far from river mouths, harbours and inlets, as they need access to salt water for breeding purposes. However, these fish can survive for years in billabongs and lagoons blocked off from the sea. Barramundi caught in salt water are usually silver to bronze in colour while the landlocked fish are darker and not rated as highly for their fighting characteristics by anglers.

A unique characteristic of this species is its ability to change sex from male to female as it matures with few male fish caught over 4 kg and few females caught below this weight.

A word of warning to the uninitiated is to be aware of the razor edge of the outer gill casing that can easily sever line or leave a nasty cut on unwary fingers.

METHODS
Barramundi are predators and can be caught on bait, lure or fly either from the shore or a boat. March to December is the best time to fish for the barra with the end and onset of the wet season the peak times.

Live prawns or popeye mullet set out under a float make excellent baits although the banning of throw nets in the Territory has made sourcing live bait more difficult and consequently reduced the popularity of this method. Barra will sometimes crush and kill bait without taking it in so it pays to be alert. If this is happening it may be the fish felt line

Barramundi are the most sought after sportfish in our northern waters. Dean MacFarlane caught this fish in Tommycut Creek in the Northern Territory.

Kay Allan with a barramundi she caught at Lake Awoonga. Impoundment fishing for barramundi has taken off in a big way in Queensland.

shopping list
BARRAMUNDI

BAIT FISHING & SPINNING:

OUTFIT: tackle needs to be tough and 6 kg to 8 kg breaking strain line is about standard, and many anglers prefer to work braid on their baitcasters. Because of the sharp gill cover, a 20 kg monofilament trace is used and the lure is attached with a Perfection Loop to allow it to swim properly.

HOOKS: When using prawns a long shanked hook about Size 2 – 4 is fine. For live baiting, hook size is governed by the bait size and a 3/0 to 4/0 Suicide would cover most situations.

LURES: Diving minnows and rattlers do well. Barramundi are not put off by size.

BAIT: Live mullet and prawns.

FLY FISHING:

OUTFIT: should be 8 – 10 weight. Intermediate, sinking, and sink tip lines work in most applications.

FLIES: Dahlberg Divers, 10 cm green and white Lefty Deceivers and Gold Bombers work in most waters. In muddy drains, heavily weighted Clouser Minnow flies are effective and these should be allowed to skip through the mud. Hook size on the flies should be from 4/0 to 6/0, use a 6 kg to 8 kg tippet.

pressure too early and should have been given longer to take the bait properly.

Most anglers seeking barramundi prefer to work lures up to 15 cm long, mainly poppers and diving minnows. Surface lures are always preferred in areas where snags are a problem as they have less chance of becoming fouled and lost in this environment. Many anglers remove their treble hooks and replace them with single hooks for the same reason.

BREAM

If you want a serious light tackle challenge then try bream fishing. It isn't like any other form of angling, just ask a bream specialist. Cunning, finicky, contrary and great battlers, it is for all of these attributes that bream rate so highly among southern anglers.

Southern black bream is the mainstay of estuary fishing in Victoria. In New South Wales, yellowfin bream is the popular species, and as you work up the coast, you find other members of the bream family like pikey bream. All the bream are similar but different. For example, even though both black and yellowfin bream fight well, the black bream is more difficult to catch and less likely to be caught on lure or fly.

The Victorian bream are strictly a bay and estuary fish while the New South Wales variety

Fishing for bread and butter species like bream has made a significant comeback with the soft plastic lure revolution.

can also be caught in the surf. I had a bit of luck on the bream fishing with a couple of anglers who not only knew their bream pretty well but, more importantly, knew where to find them in co-operative numbers. What both episodes showed was how different bream can be.

In case you're not up with bream, it is necessary to understand that many anglers specialise in nothing else. To some, bream are almost a way of life. Diaries are kept with all the tide, barometer and moon phases noted, baits have to be fresh and, depending on the time of year, they need to be soft or hard.

In Victoria, bream stocks have been in a bit of trouble. Over-fishing and poor spawning success has been blamed for what is seen as a dramatic decline in fish numbers. For East Gippsland towns, like Lakes Entrance and Bairnsdale, the decline in the bream fishery has had an impact on tourism. Large bags of bream caught over so many years by thousands of anglers haven't helped the cause. Nor has commercial netting of the Gippsland Lakes system.

On a trip to Lakes Entrance I caught up with local angler Greg Jerkins who organised a couple of canoes, some fresh shrimp and a trip up a secret backwater he assured me was 'producing heaps of good bream'.

Some of the arms off the Gippsland Lakes system are like overgrown ravines. Melaleucas grow right down to the water's edge, behind them are stands of Blackwood and then eucalypts. Trying to find your way in on foot would require a good compass, a big axe, and plenty of snake repellent. This particular backwater was about four kilometres upstream from where we launched the canoes. Once I got the hang of the canoe and found some balance, the paddling was easy and, as it turned out, well worth the effort. Just a few locals knew the bream were in the area so the fish were relatively untouched and not at all hook-shy.

I had brought along a small Penn Spinfisher reel spooled up with 3 kg breaking strain line and one of those fold out rods that break down to about 56 cm and easily fit in a suitcase. Some anglers like to work a running sinker rig with a leader from a swivel or ring stopping the sinker. I use a No. 6 hook and as small a lead as possible, allowing the lead to run to the eye of the hook. Shrimp are put on in criss-cross fashion. About half a dozen at a time with the hook set through the centre of the shrimps' bodies.

On this trip it was a matter of paddle the canoe to a likely looking snag, park the back end of the canoe hard against the shore and start fishing. Every snag produced fish, but not every fish was landed. The terrain took its toll on tackle and bream, a fish capable of sucking six carefully threaded shrimp off a hook in the twinkling of an eye, are past masters at snag tactics. You know that old line about 'you should have been here yesterday' well, the fishing was so good I thought it was yesterday.

Sometimes bream are in the most unlikely places, like an old shell grit mine at the back of Queenscliff. The area is a backwater off Swan Bay in Victoria, a former creek before the shell grit mining dug out a large rectangular shaped bay. It's okay to publicise the place because by the time you read this it will probably already be a marine park.

No snags, relatively shallow water and hook-ups normally preceded by long, fast runs. Bream move into the old creek on a rising tide at night, seeking out the brackish water to spawn. The bay is so shallow that on calm, moonlight nights the tail and back of a running fish will sometimes break the surface as it runs.

Unlike Greg's secret location, this one is well known. Nevertheless, success here still only comes to those anglers who have prepared themselves properly, and that means fresh bait. Now, it may come as a surprise to some anglers to learn that fresh bait does not come out of a freezer. We source spew worms and yabbies and keep them alive and there-fore fresh. The bream are definitely finicky in this backwater and we never expect to catch heaps. Even then, unless a fish is hooked too deep and bleeding, it is always liberated. On

shopping list
BREAM
BAIT FISHING & SPINNING:
OUTFIT: Two to 3 kg line, threadline reel balanced with a light rod about 2.3 m long.
HOOKS: No. 4 to No. 8 Baitholder patterns cover most situations but some anglers swear by Suicide pattern hooks of about 1/0.
Selection of small ball sinkers.
BAIT: Nippers (Bass yabbies), freshwater yabbies, prawns, pippis, spider crabs, and shrimp, beach worms and mussels.
LURES: Small sinking bibbed minnows, soft plastics.

FLY FISHING:
OUTFIT: 8 wt, floating or intermediate line. Minimum three metre long leader and a 3 kg tippet.
FLIES: Crazy Charlie, Skinners Shrimp.

the upside, anglers willing to put in the effort and source fresh bait generally do best.

Now that was the same lesson that came out of the Lakes Entrance trip. It wasn't so much that the fish were co-operative, it was more that they were being offered fresh bait that was to their liking. And therein lies one of the keys to successful bream fishing.

ELEPHANT FISH

When is a fish not a fish? When it's an elephant fish. Like the names of many marine creatures, elephant fish is a misnomer. They would have been better-named elephant sharks because that is what they are, sharks. Belonging to the family of ghost sharks, these creatures have become more common and popular catches in recent years.

They are odd looking sharks, with a proboscis that protrudes like an elephant's trunk from the head. Even the way they swim is

Elephant fish numbers have increased dramatically in Victoria in recent years. They make excellent sport on light tackle. Many anglers prefer to release any of these sharks they catch.

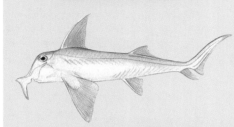
strange. Sharks swim by moving their tails from side to side; rays achieve the same by rippling their wings. Elephant fish look like sharks but swim using their pectoral fins.

Despite the weird contradictions, the good news for anglers is that these sharks fight well and are delicious into the bargain. They are found over the same sort of terrain that you would expect to catch gummy sharks, mud flats, sand, and rubble ground. Many are caught by anglers while fishing for snapper with the late summer and autumn the top time of year.

Western Port and places further east were the most common haunts of these sharks, but in recent years they have become more regular captures in Port Phillip Bay and the Barwon River estuary. The emergence of these sharks in good numbers has only occurred in recent years and there is a train of thought, unproved, that the decimation of school and gummy sharks in Bass Strait by commercial fishers has allowed these fish to increase in numbers.

The only drawback with elephant fish is the poisonous spike located in front of the first dorsal fin. When this weapon meets your

line, it spells the end of the battle so, as a precaution, put on a tough monofilament trace such as Jinkai or Asso. For a rig choose a running sinker, as light as the current will allow, and use size 4/0 hooks. Best baits are fresh fish fillets, pilchards, and squid.

Elephant fish will confuse you when you hook one. The big question will be is it a snapper or a ray? These sharks run well but often fight near the surface like eagle rays and if you haven't caught one yet, you will be pleasantly surprised when you do.

FLATHEAD

Flathead are one of Australia's top sportfish in the sense that they have to be hunted in a way similar to a fly fisher seeking trout. There are several types of flathead but the dusky is undoubtedly the most prized. This is the trophy fish of the flathead family, a fish that can grow to more than 14 kilograms. Distinguishing features of this basically estuarine fish are the large dark blotches on the tail, a dark, olive brown body, and a series of white spots about the head.

A similar flathead to look at, the Yank or southern blue spotted flathead, is keenly sought after in shallow, protected bays in Victoria, South Australia, Western Australia and northern Tasmania. Both fish have similar habits and what is written about the dusky flathead, with the exception of its liking for estuaries, also applies to the Yank flathead.

What makes both flathead so special is that they can be caught in shallow water, will take a live bait, lure or fly and are among a limited number of inshore saltwater species that offers the sportfisher the chance to polaroid. The dusky is a keen inhabitant of estuaries, moving in from late spring until autumn to spawn and hunt. During this migratory period, these fish will also move outside the estuary to hunt in gutters and holes on adjacent beaches. Big specimens put up a tough, head shaking fight and can thoroughly test anglers working light lines.

METHODS

Flathead rely on camouflage and ambush to capture their prey. Lying partially buried in sand or mud, often along the edge of a weed line, flathead face into the current. So complete is their ability to blend in with the surrounds that often only their eyes are distinguishable. When a small fish or prawn sweeps past in the tide the flathead uses a brilliant turn of speed to spring from its lair and snatches the offering.

These fish also have an acute sense of

Clint Logan shows how to cradle lift a dusky flathead. A prime sportfish, the dusky flathead is one of the few salt water species that can be caught on bait, lure or fly.

smell that can be used to advantage. A fine mist berley trail will bring them right up to the berley bucket at times. Boat fishers can use two simple methods to achieve good results. The first is to simply drift and allow the bait to drag and bounce along the bottom. The movement of the sinker stirring up the sand seems to encourage flathead to strike.

The second option is to drop the anchor and start up a berley trail. This method works best in estuaries and bays. A berley mix consisting of fish, tuna oil and feedstock such as chicken pellets is popular. Grind the mix into a fine mist so that the fish get a scent and taste, but not a meal. For anglers working lures and flies, berleying in this manner in shallow water offers the opportunity of polarising the flathead as they move into the trail.

In bay areas, these fish congregate in along the edges of channels. Along beaches, they prefer to lurk in channels and gutters, relying on the surge of the waves to sweep small fish within striking range. In estuarine areas large flathead lurk along the edges of drop-offs or lie in ambush on the shallow flats among the weed. On low tide these lairs often become visible as flathead sometimes leave a teardrop shaped indentation in the sand. Large flathead can leave a spectacular signature and surveying an area on low tide gives you the opportunity of picking some likely areas to fish.

For bait exponents a running sinker rig works well. Hook size should be about 1/0 to 3/0 with a thin wire leader. Big flathead have a good dental setup and their head shaking antics in a fight can work through monofilament. If working moving bait in an estuary or the surf then use a running sinker rig, preferably a ball or bean sinker and allow it to run down to the hook. Best baits include mullet, pilchard, prawn, and squid. Live baits such as small mullet can be set in a channel and allowed to sit there until a roving flathead decides there is a good chance of a meal.

If spinning or working a fly the key to success is often to put the lure on or just above the bottom. Dark coloured lures are best as the flathead will be looking upwards and darker lures offer a better silhouette against the surface light. Freddy Bayes, better known as Flathead Fred, has made flathead a specialty and he catches all of his big flathead on black coloured plastic jigs about 10 cm long. Fred prefers first and last light, or overcast days with some ripple on the water. Anglers of Fred's calibre don't just go out and catch big flathead. They work long and hard for their rewards.

species tip

FLATHEAD

When flathead are in predator mode, they often extend their pectoral fins like arms and raise themselves off the bottom and remain motionless and poised to strike. In clear water, they will swim a long way to take a lure, fly or bait.

---

shopping list
FLATHEAD
BAIT FISHING & SPINNING:
OUTFIT: Two to 3 kg line, threadline reel, and rod balanced to suit and capable of casting unweighted baits or small lures.
HOOKS: For live or dead bait fishing, 1/0 to 3/0, Suicide or Octopus patterns.
LURES: Rubber tailed lures such as Mr Twister or Vibratails work well. Small chrome slices and Wonder Wobblers will also attract a strike when worked deep.
BAIT: Pilchards, pippis, squid, and fish fillets.
BERLEY: A fine mist or bran, chook pellets and fish mixed together with tuna oil works well. Always fish along a slight drop off, even if it is only 10 cm, and use current to disperse the berley.

FLY FISHING:
OUTFIT: Eight to 10 wt outfit rigged with sinking line up to Density Four, depending on depth and rate of sink required. Use intermediate or sink tip lines over shallow flats and fast sink lines in deeper channels and along drop-offs.
Use a tippet minimum of 3 kg breaking strain. Fluorocarbon material works well and this can be used up to 10 kg if you are concerned at a big frog wearing your leader, although this doesn't happen often as most hook-ups are in the side of the jaw.
FLIES: Deep Clouser Minnow—white and red, chartreuse and white or plain white; Crazy Charlie—blue and white, light blue or gold; Lefty Deceivers—blue and white, pink and white, chartreuse and white and Woolly Buggers—brown, black or olive.

Fly fishers will find flathead will take a range of offerings with the Clouser Minnow probably the most effective. Other flies that have taken flathead include the Crazy Charlie and Deceiver patterns in blue and white and dark Woolly Buggers.

Landbased anglers do well wading and casting baits, lures or flies along the edges of gutters, weed lines and across open sand patches surrounded by weed, and then retrieving slowly. If the area being fished is relatively weed free then allowing a bait or lure kick along the bottom can sometimes initiate a strike. As prolific as flathead may be, the trophy fish won't come along and bite you on the big toe. You have to seek them out and this is what makes them such a challenge to the sports minded angler.

GUMMY SHARKS

While gummy sharks are spread right across southern Australia, the species has developed a following of serious proportions among southern anglers. There are those anglers who specialise in chasing gummies in the surf, others who work inshore reefs. In recent years, a new breed of gummy shark angler has emerged, individuals specialising in chasing these toothless tasties in shallow water at night.

Gus Storer with a nice surf caught gummy shark. Something of an obsession among some Victorian anglers, gummies give a solid account of themselves.

Anglers fishing snapper grounds consistently come across these sharks. Most of the gummy sharks caught by anglers, average about 5 kg but can grow to more than 30 kilograms. I have seen them to about 25 kg but know of specimens in excess of 32 kilograms.

My most recent encounter with gummy sharks was at Flinders Island on board Jim Luddington's charter boat, Strait Lady. We were drifting and bottom bouncing a notorious stretch of water known as the Pot Boil, just out from Lady Barron on Flinders Island. Using basic snapper gear, I latched onto a neat 6 kg shark that gave a good account. The fight was prolonged by the rough conditions and strong tide.

Gummy sharks are not difficult to land once hooked, although they do try hard and the bigger sharks can test your skill and tackle. A large gummy will sometimes fight like a big black stingray and hug the seabed, at other times they will run like a snapper attempting to roll and twist up the line. The way to tell the difference between a snapper and a gummy is that when you have a good snapper on you can feel the tail beat through the line, but with a gummy shark this is missing and you can feel when they are rolling in the line.

Most anglers catch gummies while fishing over whiting or snapper ground. These sharks do not have teeth, instead they have bony plates in their mouth similar to those found in stingrays and feed on much the same type of food as snapper and rays, food such as crabs and molluscs that are found over mudflats and reef.

Fishing techniques are the same as for snapper, although gummy sharks are more partial to a solid berley trail and can be consistently fished for in shallower water than snapper. The best time is at night, and I rate moonlight nights the best. In the surf, I prefer the high tide and subsequent runoff. Like any large fish, gummy sharks make use of water depth to seek out new areas to feed over. And these sharks know how to make full use of the rips and eddies that go with a surf beach. If you had to rate a bay-caught gummy against one of the same size hooked in the surf you would most likely rate the surf-caught shark at least twice as hard to land on the difficulty scale.

In shallow bays, anglers have taken to fishing for gummy sharks under floats. The idea is to have the bait just off the bottom so that the dense crab population can't feed on it. It is a method I haven't used but have been assured that it does work. A method that has come into vogue in recent times is to use a spotlight in shallow water to spot feeding gummies. When you find them, drop the pick and start fishing. Although easily spooked the sharks will come back to the area where they were feeding.

MANGROVE JACK

Tough and uncompromising, mangrove jacks are one of those sportfish that are the topic of legends. Most of the jacks you are likely to catch will be under 1.5 kilograms. A 2 kg jack caught in a snag-riddled estuary is a good fish and the chances are that when you hook into bigger specimens they will do you cold.

Mangrove jacks spend the early years of their lives in estuaries of northern Australia and can be caught consistently as far south as the Queensland/New South Wales border. The canals at Surfers Paradise for example hold solid populations of jacks.

These fish are attracted to snags where they lie in ambush under the cover of branches of submerged trees or mangrove roots. You often find a pod of jacks around bridges and beneath jetties. When they mature, jacks move offshore and live among the reefs and fish of 5 kg and more are not uncommon and plenty of jacks are caught bottom bouncing.

They are well endowed with teeth and will make a mess of lures and flies so be prepared to repair or lose a fair amount of tackle if you decide to specifically target them.

METHODS

Spinning, fly-fishing and especially livebaiting techniques will produce jacks. For live baiting, a small mullet or prawn is allowed to drift back to a snag. Some Queenslanders I've fished with use a float, others prefer to cast their baits and allow them to drift or sink down naturally. The

Mangrove jacks are tough battlers, using any opportunity to take lure and line through snags.

Persistence pays off. I saw Ross Finlayson pull a half dozen cod from the same snag one day before pulling a 2 kg jack. Many would have given up on the snag and moved on. Jacks are territorial and swipe at lures because they have entered their space. Allow the lure to sit, or sink before retrieving as this annoys the fish. A proven method for bait fishers is to rig up a live prawn and allow it to float near a fallen tree or sunken log.

strike when it comes can be hard and fast so be prepared to apply the brakes instantly, or risk being dragged into the snag and done.

For spinning, diving minnows up to about 100 mm long are effective. Because you don't pull a fish from a snag on the first cast doesn't mean there isn't one there. Some days you

may need to cast a dozen or so times at the same snag, allowing the lure to sink to different depths and even alternate the retrieve before a result is forthcoming. Fly-fishing is less effective than both methods. You will get the hook-ups but fly rods don't have the same amount of stopping power as spin or bait rods.

MULLOWAY

Mulloway, or jewies as they are called, are one of the enigmas of Australian fishing. Some anglers who specialise seem to be able to produce jewies almost at will, but a great many other anglers are still waiting in hope. Despite this, the range of this fish is extensive. Jewies are found right around southern Australia, except Tasmania, and as far north as southern Queensland on the east coast and Exmouth Gulf in the west.

Jewies are closely related to the teraglin and belong to a small group of fishes known as croakers in America. They can be caught during the day or night and will take live bait, strip baits, lures and even flies. While they can grow to 70 kg, most of the jewies caught by anglers would weigh less than 15 kilograms.

There are three basic areas where jewies are caught: estuaries, surf and over reefs in bays and offshore.

In estuaries, these fish enter in search of small bait fish and will work their way up river as far as the tidal influence or water depth allows. When the estuary has had a good flush of fresh water, and the flood tide is strong, you can often distinguish a demarcation where the fresh and salt meet. It is common to find jewies close behind this demarcation, or even swimming through it. After a flood, the first tide that brings the river salinity back into equilibrium is regarded as worth fishing. Even though the salinity of the water is getting back into balance, the water may still be dirty—conditions many anglers believe jewies thrive in.

The most productive surf beaches are those close to an estuary. In South Australia, the beaches adjacent to the mouth of the Murray River are legendary for their jewies fishing. Ocean Grove beach near the Barwon River estuary is similarly productive. A pattern that can be followed right up the east coast.

Anglers differ on the best time or tide to fish. Many favour low tides when gutters are more easily reached by casting. Others prefer to work the high tides. Either way, anglers would do well to remember that jewies have a tail shaped like a broad paddle and are designed to swim in water that many other

fishes would probably find too difficult.

In bays and offshore, anglers fishing for snapper have made many jewie captures. In South Australia, it is not unusual, when working the wider reefs for the big snapper, to come across big schools of jewies. South Australian angler Greg Brown is a past master of mulloway fishing. He says hooking the two species (snapper and mulloway) together is not unusual.

METHODS

Jewies might be predators that hunt their prey but they are no suckers for a bait with a hook in it. The problem when live baiting is to get them to do more than simply mouth a bait. Having been witness to captures of this fish when a live bait was used, I find myself persevering with this method and, like many other enthusiasts, hoping for that XOS monster with a ravenous appetite and carefree attitude to happen along.

Rigs for live baiting are similar for all species including jewies. Rather than go over ground covered elsewhere, I would prefer to make mention of a method I first heard of being used by locals who fish the Glenelg River system at Nelson, near the Victorian/South Australian border.

A mullet is hooked through the back and allowed to trail several metres behind a small dinghy. The angler then uses the oars and takes several wraps of line around his hand. As he lifts the oars in the normal procedure of rowing the bait swims up nearer the surface, the angler feeds out a few feet of line and the bait swims down deep once more. The procedure is then repeated. This method is very popular in the area that I mentioned and has brought forth some very good results. Jewies tactician Geoff Wilson employed a similar method in the Barwon River with excellent results.

Among the more choice live baits are salmon

Mulloway are a prized catch anywhere and Rod Mackenzie is justifiably proud of this fish caught on a baitcaster outfit.

action as well as pulse on the horizontal plane. 'If you're fishing at night use black or dark coloured flies. During the day grey to silver, colours that resemble mullet, and hook size should be 4/0 to 5/0.'

Harro recommends short to medium strips with a brief pause in between. 'Vary the retrieve. When beginning the strip, trap the line between two fingers in the rod hand, retrieve the fly so there is no slack line at the end of each strip, and keep rod tip low. As the fly departs the strike zone, strip in metre long glides. Anglers have to remember that in this game presentation is the critical point, especially when blind fishing.'

The size of the rod is dictated by the size of the fly with firepower a secondary consideration. 'Six inch (15 cm) flies will need at least a 12 wt outfit and I would combine this with a sinking line, the sink rate depending on the terrain. To improve your presentation the combination of sink rate and current need to be calculated to get the fly in to position,' he explains.

Anyone contemplating jewies on the fly should ensure they are working a shock tippet of at least 30 kg and super sharp hooks. Once hooked in open water jewies are no sweat but, get them near rocks and structure, and you can't get a worse scenario. They are a powerful fish over short distances and you have to stick it up them to try to stop them.

and mullet that abound in estuaries around the south-east and southern coastline. Do not be too worried about the size of the bait you choose either, for jewies have a cavernous mouth, even the smaller specimens.

The key factor in the bait selection is that it is fresh. Jewies are as finicky as bream and anything less than fresh will often be ignored. Choice baits are squid, pilchards (especially when used in conjunction with a pilchard berley trail) and fish fillets. Some South Australian anglers prefer salmon guts, claiming mulloway are unhesitating in their willingness to take this offering. A problem though is keeping the salmon guts on long enough as the crabs and pickers make short work of soft baits. Prawns can yield good results and another bait, similar to prawns, are the delectable bass yabbies that smaller school jewies find delectable.

Back in the mid-1960s and early 1970s, feather jigs became well regarded along the east coast as a formidable jewie lure. Another popular lure at the time was the so-called 'chairleg', a home-made variety that, as its

name implied, was made from a wooden chairleg—at least it probably was at first. These days big poppers such as the Rapala Magnums have established themselves as jewie producers and according to people like Geoff Wilson the key factor is that the water be discoloured.

Rod Harrison has caught jewies on the fly, black jewies of the tropical north. He has also caught southern jewies and says the two fish, although different, are not so far apart in approach and attitude. 'The thing about jewies is that presentation is critical; you've got to put the fly right on their nose and the ideal scenario is to find them when they are feeding or holed up. Forget about prospecting, jewies have to be in a feeding mode,' he says. 'I prefer shallow water so I can be sure of getting a presentation. Surf gutters and river mouths are the best for jewies and a boat is a definite advantage.'

Harro says any fly for jewies should be substantial, in the order of 150 mm or six inches on the old scale. His preference is for flies with lead eyes to give an undulating

shopping list
MULLOWAY
BAIT FISHING & SPINNING:
OUTFIT: 10 kg suited to surf or boat. Overhead or quality threadline reel with minimum 250 m capacity and smooth drag system.
HOOKS: Size 4/0 to 6/0, Suicide or Octopus pattern, preferably chemically sharpened.
LEADER: Asso or Jinkai, 15 – 24 kg trace material.
DEAD BAIT: Squid, fish fillets, prawns, and bass yabbies.
LIVE BAIT: Salmon, mullet, tailor, or garfish.
LURES: Rapala Magnums and Halco Laser Pros.

FLY FISHING:
OUTFIT: should be a 10 – 12 wt, intermediate or sinking line up to Density 4.
Use a 30 kg shock tippet, preferably fluorocarbon.
FLIES: Wide-bodied flies, about 150 mm long and use 6/0 hook size. Employ a stinger hook one size smaller than first hook.

SNAPPER

Big Red is one of those cosmic species most anglers put on their '10 most wanted to catch' lists. How high up this ranking snapper rate is in inverse proportion to how far south you are.

As with any popular sportfish, there is always room to improve. Tackle and tactics are forever subject to advances. Even habits and movements of snapper need to be monitored because fish can change and you have to keep up. Over many years of fishing for snapper, both in Australia and New Zealand, I have come across many different approaches. The only constant, when all else such as tackle and baits are equal, are time and effort. You cannot catch snapper consistently without doing the hard yards.

WATER TEMPERATURE

Water temperature may influence whether snapper are on the bite. According to some marine research, snapper feed best between 12 and 18 degrees Celsius, with about 14 to 16 degrees regarded by most serious snapper aficionados as being about as good as it gets. How you establish the temperature of the water being fished is up to you. Just remember that even in bays there are thermal layers so the temperature at the surface may vary to what exists 10 m further down in the water column.

HOOK STYLES

The first point to remember about hook choice is that bait size controls hook size. Don't use big hooks with small baits or vice versa. Beak hook patterns are about the best hooks available, accounting for thousands of snapper. For many years the Mustad 92554, 4/0 Suicide hook was just about everybody's favourite. Times have changed and there is more variety in the market.

Some of the best snapper hooks include: Dynatec Suicide, Gamakatsu Octopus and SL 12S and Mustad's Big Red, a chemically sharpened and heavy duty version of 92554 Suicide.

The next development in hook technology may be taking place right now. Researchers at the Marine and Freshwater Research Institute at Queenscliff are testing a New Zealand snapper hook concept that is claimed to increase the chances of the fish being hooked in the mouth. If successful it will benefit snapper, as a gut-hooked fish has little chance of survival compared to one hooked in the mouth that hasn't sustained any internal organ damage.

The hook being used is not new, a 5/0 Eagle Claw Circle pattern. There is however a major structural difference in that a 20 mm long piece of wire comes off the back of the hook near the eye, at a right angle to the hook shank.

In trials in New Zealand, 10,000 snapper were caught and released and it was claimed this system reduced mortality rates of undersized snapper by 95 per cent. The trial hooks came with leaders that were snelled, that is tied on

Big snapper, as distinct from pinkies, are now a serious proposition on soft plastics as Jim Harris shows.

the shank rather than the eye, as it was found this method of connection improved the hook-up rate by 20 per cent.

The theory of a Circle hook is that it is swallowed and then, because there is no exposed point, it should pull back out of a fish's gullet without snagging any internal organs. It is when the hook turns the corner, so to speak, that the hook point goes home–right into the corner of the fish's mouth.

What happens is that when the hook shank begins leaving the corner of a fish's mouth the pull on the line against the pull of the

Big soft plastics—like big baits—catch big reds.

species tip

SNAPPER

Not enough anglers pay heed to water temperature. Snapper rarely feed when the temperature falls below 12 degrees Celsius, with 16 degrees the optimum.

fish causes the hook to rotate. As the shank no longer shields the point, it penetrates the mouth. Test this by tying line on a Circle hook, putting the point against your thumb and pulling. The hook shank will tip downward so the point of the hook will be angled to penetrate at an angle parallel to that at which you are pulling the line.

By adding the short strip of wire, the Kiwis have taken this concept one step further. When a snapper eats bait rigged with one of these hooks, the wire prevents it from swallowing the hook. However, as the fish moves off with the bait, the hook will still snag in the corner of the fish's mouth as it is supposed to. And because the hook never gets past the snapper's mouth, the chances of inflicting any serious damage are negligible.

RIG STRATEGIES

The least resistance is always best, regardless of where you are fishing. If you can eliminate the sinker or perhaps cut it down to pea-size and allow it to run along the line up to the bait, do so.

A running sinker rig is the most popular rig used by snapper enthusiasts. Variations come

in leader lengths that can be from about 35 cm to one metre. Shorter leaders are more suited to casting and as for sinkers, these are adjusted to suit tidal flow.

Wire trace isn't necessary unless you have problems with the likes of couta. The teeth in a snapper's mouth, particularly those in the centre of the top of the mouth, are sharp on the tips while the rest of the teeth are molar-like and rounded. And because leaders of 10 kg or less would sit between a snapper's molars, these were preferred. Experience showed that most bite-offs were occurring when leaders of 15 kg or more were used, and it was blamed on the thicker line snagging on top of the teeth.

While heavy leaders reduce the chances of a snapper taking a bait, fishing for reds is a learning experience. Sometimes you just have to get back and use heavy leaders, whether you want to or not. In recent years, there have simply been too many bite-offs to take the chance. This is particularly so with fresh summer fish. Fresh from wintering offshore, these fish seem to be better dentured than fish that have been in the bay for long periods.

As scenarios change so to do rig strategies. In strong current, it can sometimes be necessary to use a lead of 1 kg, or even more. An adaptation of the paternoster rig, where the sinker is on a leader and allowed to run, is often employed here. It is a useful technique in areas of long, heavy weed where you need to keep the bait above the fronds. With this rig, it is best to ensure that the breaking strain of the leader to the sinker is less than that of the main line as it is preferable to part with a sinker than a snapper.

And some anglers use braid in preference to monofilament to fish fast water. As well as offering a sharper bite indicator, braid lines are thinner and consequently have less water drag so it is possible to reduce sinker weights by up to two-thirds. But the main benefit of braid in these conditions, its fine diameter, is also its Achilles Heel. Braid has little abrasion resistance and in areas of reef can prove disastrous. To overcome this, many anglers have adopted the practice of extending their terminal tackle and starting the braid to monofilament connection further up the line than would be normal practice.

TAILOR

Tailor are one of the finest sportfish available to anglers. Greedy and willing, these fish are not frightened off when one of their clan is hooked, which is a bonus for anglers. This fish runs in schools and when they are on the bite the action will come hot and fast.

Tailor can grow to more than 10 kg but most of those taken would be from about 0.5 to 2 kilograms. The tailor is a voracious predator that hunts in schools and are most often found in areas where baitfish are likely to congregate. White water locations along rocky headlands, estuary mouths and in the surf. Often the first sign of their appearance in an area will be birds circling and diving to feed on the scraps.

More tailor are caught from surf beaches than any other species. Along beaches, these fish tend to work the region inside of the main outer gutters. Tailor can often be found working in white water zones off beaches and around headlands. Early morning and late afternoon are the peak times, regardless of the state of tide.

This tailor weighed in at 3.15 kilograms. A light tackle sportfish, tailor have a set of sharp teeth and this sometimes necessitates fine wire on lures and flies, or ganged hooks on bait.

---

shopping list

SNAPPER
BAIT FISHING:

OUTFIT: About 7 kg the optimum size. The rod needs to suit the occasion, boat or land base. It needs low down grunt or lifting power but a light enough tip to enable an unweighted bait to be cast out. However, if using an overhead reel, and these offer better fish fighting capabilities, then the rod butt on the shop-bought item may need to be extended to give more advantage when throwing. Most shop bought snapper rods are designed for use with threadline reels. These reels make casting unweighted baits easier than overheads, and the Freespool facility most have works well when fish are finicky.

HOOKS: 3/0 to 6/0, preferably Suicide or Octopus pattern and chemically sharpened.

BAIT: Squid, cuttlefish, garfish, silver whiting, mullet, flathead (skinned), octopus, salmon, pilchards and fish heads off whiting, salmon, flathead etc. If you want to concentrate solely on big snapper then use fish heads. Small snapper have difficulty with heads but a big snapper will crush and swallow a couta or whiting head like you or I will chomp a jelly baby.

TAILOR

Always use a thin wire trace, preferably single strand piano wire as tailor have sharp teeth and can easily cut through monofilament line. Whole pilchards are ideal and should be rigged using ganged hooks. Tailor disable baitfish by snipping off their tails so ensure the bottom hook is close to the tail of the bait.

A major variation to this rule is estuaries where these fish will often run at night on the flood tide. In bays and estuaries look for channels and reefs. Tailor will hunt baitfish into shallow water so it pays to be observant and keep an eye out for the tell-tale flash.

METHODS

Whole baitfish such as garfish or pilchards are held on with three or four ganged hooks and fuse wire. The size and number of hooks used is dependent on the size of the bait. Wind the fuse wire around the bait to keep it on.

It is important to present the bait as naturally as possible so don't remove the head or the tail. A running sinker allowed to run down the line to a swivel is used. Ball sinkers are best. These allow the bait to move around with the action of the waves and this movement will often attract tailor to the bait.

The bait is cast out and then retrieved at a slow to medium speed although this can vary. Sometimes fast retrieves are the most productive so it pays to vary the retrieve rate until you arrive at the correct speed.

Lures are not as effective as bait but still account for plenty of tailor in the right circumstances, particularly in bays or where there is plenty of white water such as around rocky headlands. The retrieve is not super fast and should once again be varied to find the best pace.

These fish are armed with a set of razor-sharp teeth and a short wire trace about 45 cm long is best practice to avoid being bitten off. This applies particularly to situations where a single hook or a lure is being used. It is not so vital when ganged hooks are being employed.

A tailor's teeth are also dangerous to anglers so be wary of removing hooks with your fingers. If a bait is swallowed give some thought to using a hook disgorger or a pair of

pliers rather than put your fingers at risk.

To improve their table qualities tailor should always be bled on capture and this will slow the deterioration of the fish's flesh.

shopping list
TAILOR
BAIT FISHING & SPINNING:
OUTFIT: For lures, a spinning outfit should be the same as for salmon, that is 2–3 kg coupled with a threadline reel and a rod suited to line class and capable of casting up to 20 grams. Off the rocks or surf, the outfit should be boosted to about 5 kg and either an overhead or threadline reel. Both outfits can also be used for casting and retrieving whole pilchards.

HOOKS: Size 2/0 to 4/0, long shanked and capable of being gang rigged if fishing with pilchards.

BAIT: Whole pilchards or small fish, rigged on ganged hooks is the popular bait method.

LURES: 10 – 15 g, Halco Twisty or chrome slices, Krome Kritters, Wonder Wobblers.

FLY FISHING:
OUTFIT: Seven to 10 wt, intermediate or sinking line up to Density 4. Tippet needs to be light wire, preferably wire that can be knotted, as tailor have plenty of fine, sharp teeth.

FLIES: Lefty Deceiver, Deep Clouser Minnow, Surf Candy, Bendback, and baitfish patterns. Flies should suit hooks from No. 4 to about 3/0. Red and white, blue and white and chartreuse and white colour combinations have proven successful.

WHITING

Many anglers probably remember whiting as being among the first fish they caught. King George whiting is one of the most sought after fish in southern inshore waters, especially during the warmer months of the year. And sand whiting, which range down the east coast from Cape York to as far south as Lakes Entrance in Victoria, are just as popular. Both fish are relatively easy to catch, are good table fare, and will give a good account of themselves.

KING GEORGE WHITING

Everywhere you fish for King George whiting there seems to be a locally sourced bait and adaptations to methods that work better. The most common rigs are variations of the

When it comes to a feed, many anglers are reluctant to return whiting.

paternoster style. Either one or two leaders are used and these are about 20 cm long with No. 6 or No. 8 long shank hooks such as the Gamakatsu Oceania or Mustad 540S, 34007 or 8260 patterns. Sinker weight used depends on the amount of current, the less lead the better. Most experienced anglers prefer to have their baits below the sinker, even if is only a couple of centimetres.

An alternative rig is the running sinker; hook size is the same, leader length is stretched to 30 cm and again the amount of lead is governed by conditions. In strong tidal areas, a paternoster/running sinker variation rig with a single leader of up to one metre in length is sometimes the most effective method. The sinker is set on a short leader and the leader is tied to a swivel above the sinker swivel and allowed to run.

These rigs work in most areas. In some places though, a pyramid sinker is preferred in the deeper areas where the current is very strong. And instead of casting out and leaving the bait to sit on the seabed, anglers have developed a more productive technique. What they do is drop their bait to the bottom and then lift it and allow it to drop a little further behind the boat. This is done several times before the bait is retrieved and checked. When the strike comes it will be at the top of the lift, the whiting having followed the bait up to take it.

A popular ploy has been to place red tubing on the line where it joins the hook, the theory is that this resembles a worm and attracts whiting. Baits vary with locality: The first rule of whiting fishing is to remember that fresh bait does not come out of a packet. Fresh baits are those that you source yourself, either the same day or the evening before your outing. Sandworms, pippis, squid, mussels, and yabbies are among the more popular.

There is rarely any need to use an outfit heavier than 3 kg, if you go down to lighter outfits—terrain and conditions permitting—you will have a lot more fun. But to catch a fish you must first find it. King George whiting like to forage in areas where there are weed beds broken up by intermittent patches of sand. A top whiting fisher can be distinguished from the rest by his ability to lob his bait in a sand clearing, which is where the fish will be found feeding. In deeper water, the same rule applies. However, there are exceptions and one of these is along the edges of channels where larger whiting can sometimes be found feeding on ledge formations. Nevertheless, they will never be far from rubble, reef or weed.

Berley is also essential. As well as finding the fish, you also have to keep them in the locality and the only way of achieving this is to use a berley mix. Some anglers simply throw their empty mussel shells over the side, the thin hard sinew that lines the edge of the shell being enough to keep the fish around. Crushed mussels, bread, and chicken pellets in combination work well while pilchards are an excellent additive to a berley, albeit

shopping list
WHITING
BAIT FISHING:

OUTFIT: About 2 – 3 kg will suit most areas. Balance it out with a small threadline reel, and choose a rod capable of lifting up to 1 kg in weight but with a reasonably light tip.
HOOKS: No. 6 to No. 8 long shank in a Baitholder pattern works well.
BAIT: Beach worms, mussels, pippis, squid, pilchard strips, nippers/Bass yabbies, prawns, and shrimp. Bait pump for sourcing worms and yabbies.

FLY FISHING:

OUTFIT: Six to 8 wt with a fast sink line as the fly needs to be on the bottom.
Tippet can be as light as 2 kg, but overall leader length is important, not more than a metre at the maximum to ensure the fly stays on or near the bottom.
FLIES: Crazy Charlies and sparingly tied Deep Clouser Minnows no bigger than No. 4 hook size. Fawn, yellow and gold all proven colours.

one that introduces interesting ramifications. Whiting will not normally feed on pilchard if it is used as a bait but when used in conjunction with berley small strips of pilchard on the hook will sometimes out-fish all else.

SAND WHITING

For sand whiting, light tackle and fresh bait combined with good presentation are the keys to success. Sand whiting are shallow water feeders, sometimes timid but always alert because of their vulnerability in the areas they are feeding over. They grub in the sand for food such as worms and nippers. As a rule, these fish feed best when the tide is on the make. At this time they often move over the flats in search of worms and yabbies that were denied to them when the tide was low.

Beach worms and cockles are top baits and they prefer the bait to be moving. If fishing still water then it pays to move the bait, winding it in slowly before recasting. In the surf, the action of the waves usually achieves the same bait movement.

While sand whiting will be caught after sunset in some locations, generally the best fishing is had for them during the daylight hours. Most are caught close to shore, in estuaries, bays and in the surf within easy casting distance. Sand bars and shallow gutters are preferred haunts. In the surf, anglers should be careful not to cast too far out.

TREVALLIES

There are many different species among the trevally family, none of which are easy when it comes to the fight. There are many worthy sportfish among the trevally family, including the likes of silver trevally, dolphinfish, bluefin trevally, dart and others that I haven't mentioned.

SILVER TREVALLY

If golden trevally have one of the toughest mouths among the trevallies, then silver trevally have the softest. Silvers are one of the most commonly caught trevallies due to the large numbers that school inshore in bays and estuaries. These fish range as far north as North-west Cape in Western Australia, across the southern states and up the east coast to southern Queensland.

Tough and tenacious, pound for pound this fish is one of the toughest scrappers in our waters. It will hit bait, lure or fly and can be worked into a feeding mood with the sensible application of berley. Most anglers catch silver trevally from piers or near reefs and most fish are from 0.3 kg to about 1.5 kilograms. However, a new awareness of silvers has opened up with bluewater anglers jigging over deep reefs off Perth in Western Australia and catching specimens of more than 5 kilograms.

Silver trevally will test most anglers on light

species tip
WHITING

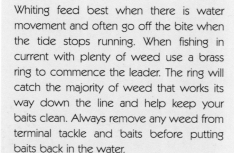

Whiting feed best when there is water movement and often go off the bite when the tide stops running. When fishing in current with plenty of weed use a brass ring to commence the leader. The ring will catch the majority of weed that works its way down the line and help keep your baits clean. Always remove any weed from terminal tackle and baits before putting baits back in the water.

species tip
SILVER TREVALLY

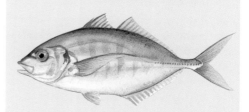

Silver trevally have a soft mouth and should be played out with a light drag when possible. The species is susceptible to a fine mist berley and will rise to the occasion, coming near the surface from deep holes.

Silver trevally do not attain the large size of some members of the trevally family, but pound for pound, they rate as highly as their bigger relatives.

YELLOWTAIL KINGFISH

They are called kings, hoodlums and bandits. Whatever vernacular you want to apply to yellowtail kingfish, there is no denying they are one tough opponent. A few years ago in a feature on kings, I adopted a line from the Yakka work clothing advertisement—'any tougher they'd rust'—to describe these fish. My opinion hasn't changed.

An inhabitant of temperate and sub-tropical waters, yellowtail kingfish can be caught in New South Wales, Victoria, Tasmania, South Australia, and Western Australia. Although a member of the trevally family, kings don't have the thin body and deep flank normally distinctive of the species. As their name implies this species has a yellow tail. The colouration of the upper part of their body is an almost opaque sea-green with a bluish tinge, the colour fades slightly down the flanks, and there is a dividing yellow stripe running along the flank separating the green from the milky white belly. On freshly landed fish a thin, black stripe is sometimes visible running across the eyes, almost mask like—hence the vernacular name hoodlum.

lines, particularly in areas where there are obstacles such as pier pilings; and that's where you find them. On a good run with fish of 1 kg or more, it can be hook up and hang on, as the fish dives for the pilings and the angler hopes his line isn't snagged or the hook pulled free from the soft mouth.

These fish are often found schooling in good numbers where there are deeper holes, always where there is current, in estuaries and bays. In these circumstances, and when the water is clear of obstacles such as sunken logs or pilings, you can adopt ultra-light outfits and give the fish their head during the fight.

Berleying is important. A fine mist berley will bring the fish higher in the water column and encourage them to feed. Baits such as sandworm, prawn, bass yabbie, bluebait and pilchard strips work well. Use light lines, hooks from No 4 to 1/0 and as small an amount of lead as conditions will allow.

My preference for a rig is to use a paternoster with the hook leader set to hold the bait about a metre off the bottom. Many anglers prefer to fish under a float and will run their baits down 2 – 3 metres, keeping it there by crimping split shot onto their leader.

Silver trevally can also be caught on flies, particularly small baitfish imitations, Crazy Charlies and Clousers. A good trick with flies is to add a soft plastic tail. Flies should be fished on a sinking line and retrieved erratically, that is fast strip and pause, then a slow strip and a pause.

The take often happens during the pause between strips. In the case of lures, my best results have come from small metal jigs worked near the bottom with a slow to medium retrieve, making the lure act erratically by moving the rod tip about.

---

shopping list
SILVER TREVALLY
BAIT FISHING:

OUTFIT: About 2 – 3 kg will suit most areas; balance it out with a small threadline reel, and choose a rod capable of lifting up to 1kg but with a reasonably light tip.

HOOKS: No 4 to 1/0 in a Baitholder or Suicide pattern work well.

BAIT: Baits such as sandworm, prawn, bass yabbie, bluebait and pilchard strips work well. Use light lines, hooks from No 4 to 1/0.

LURES: Small soft plastics; shads and curly tails both work.

FLY FISHING:

OUTFIT: Six to 8 wt with a sinking line as the fly needs to be able to sink down through the water column.

Tippet can be as light as 2 kg, but overall leader length is important, not more than a metre at the maximum to ensure fly stays on or near the bottom.

FLIES: Jelly Tails or Crazy Charlies and sparingly tied Deep Clouser Minnows with rubber tails. Hook size about No. 4. Colours that produce include white and chartreuse, fawn, yellow and gold.

Yellowtail kingfish have suffered due to commercial fishing in many areas. Fish of the size pictured have been more common in recent years, with the kingfish population showing signs of making a comeback.

species tip

YELLOWTAIL KINGFISH

Kingfish have an insatiable curiosity. When you hook a fish, such as a small tuna, let it thresh around in the water and make a commotion. Chances are if there are kings in the area, they will converge on the scene to investigate the disturbance.

Even though kings can grow to 70 kg, I rate a 10 kg king as a job well done. The largest I know of caught from a landbased situation went a cool 50 kg, or 110 lb on the old imperial scale—caught by a young woman on her honeymoon, would you believe! Plenty of 30 kg kings have been caught from boats, but a lot more have been lost than have ever been landed.

Kingfish normally lurk near reefs and rocky headlands where just about any small fish that happens by is fair game. One of the features of kingfish is that they will take lures, live bait and strip baits, particularly squid. The choice of live bait is wide but garfish, mullet, salmon, trevally, pike, yakkas and slimy mackerel all work. Attracting kingfish is a bit like Rice Bubbles, all about snap, crackle and pop. The three lure styles mentioned offer a throb (deep diver), rattle, and splash (popper). And the more din you make the better your chances. Winding fast and keeping the rod tip pointed down while moving the rod tip from left to right is a hot way to attract kings.

Golden trevally caught near the pier at Wiepa by Ted Whittam.

species tip

GOLDEN TREVALLY

When fly fishing the flats for golden trevally use a lead core head on a shooting line a leader of about three metres. The first metre is a 20-kilogram butt, with a loop-to-loop connection for the 9 kg leader and the Clouser fly attached via a swinging loop. The idea is that the fly line lays on the bottom, there is no shadow and so the fish aren't spooked. When the trevally arrive you cast the fly about three metres in front of them, allow the fly to sink and when you think the school is on the fly start to strip – fast.

GOLDEN TREVALLY

A flats fisher's dream, golden trevally feature a striking golden pectoral fin and a huge rubber mouth that is as tough as tyre rubber. Goldens are keenly sought after on the shallow tropical flats where they can often be seen with their tails waving about out of the water as they suck nippers and crabs from the sand.

This fish will take small live baits, flies and lures—preferably soft plastics. In shallow water where these fish can be easily spooked, it is necessary to work a sinking fly line that lies on the bottom and consequently doesn't cast a shadow. In deep water, they can be jigged with both lures and flies, and live baits are best used in the deeper water. The hook-up that follows is hard. On light tackle, you can expect to lose a couple of hundred metres of line in a first blistering run.

GIANT TREVALLY

This fish is the granddaddy of the trevally family. A big giant trevally is often seen hunting alone across flats and reefs, and these fish are often found hanging about coral bommies. In Fiji, I found some bucket-mouthed monsters running with schools of smaller fish to about 4 kg in coral lagoons.

Giant trevally are very receptive to surface poppers. Toss the lure ahead of the fish, or around an area where you reckon they should be, and wind like mad. The more splash and noise you make the better.

If I had to rate the fight, I would say it is more predictable than is the case for yellowtail kingfish, and certainly on a kilo for kilo basis, nowhere near as hard or prolonged as that offered up by a golden trevally. Nevertheless, the bulk and size of some of the giant trevally make them tough opponents and difficult to land. A word of warning, the tail scutes are large and sharp, so wear gloves when you lift them out of the water.

species tip

GIANT TREVALLY

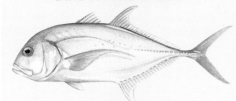

These fish love speed, and lures can be run deep or else made to splash and bounce across the surface. The best places to look are around reefs and rocky headlands, particularly where there is current or wash to push the smaller fish around. Sometimes a lure that is dropped to the bottom, allowed to sit there for a few seconds, and then jigged to the surface will produce results when nothing else does.

Rod Harrison with a GT caugh trolling a Halco Laser Pro.

Queenfish are fast and furious, an angelr's dream when hooked.

QUEENFISH

Queenfish are also commonly caught on lures in tropical areas, particularly Western Australia and Queensland. Bright silver with a greenish hue on its back, the queenfish is an elongate fish, the lower jaw protrudes beyond the upper, and the eyes are well forward on its snout. Its most distinctive feature is a single row of five to seven dark blotches along the flanks above the lateral line.

A clean honest battler that offers spectacular displays, the queenfish is one of the most sought after sportfish by spin and fly anglers. Poppers are generally regarded as offering the most exciting sport while high-speed metal lures will also entice spectacular strikes. My favourite lures are the fizzer type.

species tip

QUEENFISH

On big tides in estuaries, where the water mix is more salt than fresh, queenfish will invade in hot pursuit of whitebait and hardiheads. The action those line-burners provide can extend through a six hour cycle, half tide in to half tide out. Small Fizzer lures and surface poppers work a treat.

COBIA

Cobia or black kingfish is a tropical pelagic, a relative of the trevallies, they are usually caught in more northern climes with odd fish taken south of Sydney. Its range is from Cape Naturaliste in Western Australia across the top and as far south as Jervis Bay in New South Wales.

Dark brown on top these fish have a creamy horizontal band but are sometimes mistaken for sharks at first sight due to their prominent dorsal fin and flat, round head.

Mark Griffin has his hands full with this cobia he caught off Southwest Rocks in New South Wales.

shopping list
COBIA

LIVE BAITING:

OUTFIT: 10 – 15 kg outfit, either full game rod or live baiting stick (cut down spin rod). Use a game reel, preferably lever drag.

LIVE BAIT: Whatever live baitfish are about in the area should be the first option. In southern waters, this could be yakkas or slimy mackerel, with mullet and other small baitfish the option in tropical areas.

HOOKS: Chemically sharpened Suicide or Octopus patterns or Tuna Circles. Hook size is governed by bait size, but anywhere from 4/0 to 8/0 might be used.

FLOATS: Balloons or bobby corks.

SPINNING:

OUTFIT: A 7 – 10 kg outfit suited to throwing up to 50 grams is about right for the bigger fish like GTs and kings. The rod needs a heap of power in the butt section. There are few threadline reels on the market that will take the wear and abuse of a big trevally on the rampage. For the likes of kingfish and giant trevally you need some serious stopping power as they head towards the nearest outcrop. For smaller trevally, you can reduce the outfit down to about 5 – 7 kilograms.

LURES: Poppers, Fizzer-styles, Rapala Magnum, Halco Lazer Pros, Halco Arrows, Irons and Raiders.

FLY FISHING:

OUTFIT: In estuary situations 8 to 10 wt: Lines - intermediate; sinking, up to Density 4; sink tip and floating. Offshore outfits should be 10 – 13 wt, intermediate and sinking lines doing well when working deep, and floating lines for surface action and drifting over shallow reefs.

FLIES: Deep Clouser Minnow, Surf Candy, Left Deceiver and Pink Thing.

LEADER: Use a leader or trace material of about 24 kg minimum in reefy areas.

species tip
COBIA

Will follow a cube or berley trail in to a boat and often hang around berley for lengthy periods. Live baits work well as do fresh fillets. Poppers and high-speed metal lures will produce results.

Cobia can turn on a searing initial run of more than 100 m or they may choose to fight like the traditional kings and go non-stop for the bottom. The difficulty is often having them about the place long enough to have a shot with lure or bait. Lures including high-speed poppers and big minnows are a good option.

TUNAS

There are eleven species of tuna in Australian waters and several species of mackerel, all of them closely related. Not all of them are listed, but that doesn't make them any less of a sportfish.

In the case of tuna, each one is a perfect missile. Every external feature of a tuna's body is designed to lessen resistance as the fish cuts through the water; in fact even the dorsal and pectoral fins fold neatly into grooves along the body. Scientists have estimated that tuna can attain speeds in excess of 60 km/h without even trying. These fish are balls of muscle, torpedo-shaped speed machines that constantly burn energy and consequently require large amounts of fuel in the form of food.

Most fishes are cold blooded in that the temperature of their blood is the same as that of the water they are swimming in. The tunas on the other hand are warm blooded; their body temperature is usually several degrees warmer than the water temperature. Biologists put the reason for this down to the smallness of the viscera—the interior organs in the body cavities. The stomach and intestines of tuna are tucked away in a comparatively small space. Because tuna have to consume a great amount of food to furnish the energy necessary for their swift propulsion, and remembering they have only a small stomach capacity, the food has to be passed through the digestive organs rapidly. In other words, the fuel must be burned quickly with the result being a high body temperature.

One of the real joys of fighting a big tuna is that they do not like reef. If you have a good-sized tuna on and he wants to head off over dangerous territory back the drag off and free-spool the fish. The sudden relaxation in the pressure encourages the fish to turn away from reefs and head back towards safer ground. Never try to bring a green fish to the gaff. Always allow your fish to fight it out and if this is done properly, the gaff shot will be the easiest part of the exercise, as the tuna will just lie there.

LONGTAIL TUNA

Also known as northern bluefin, longtail tuna are tropical and sub-tropical fish that can be caught as far south as the Victorian border on the east coast and Fremantle on the west coast and are prolific around the northern coastline of Australia. Longtails move into bays and are regularly caught at places such as Moreton Bay in Queensland, Port Stephens in New South Wales and Shark Bay in the west.

The best times are from December through to late May with February and March peak months. In many areas, longtails are the mainstay of landbased game fishing. They love to run down the coast hugging the rocks and can even be caught in the surf.

Longtails are different from other tuna in that they lack a swim bladder. In so far as the difference between this species and the southern bluefin is concerned, the longtails are not as solid in their build, especially in the tail portion, being a much longer looking fish with the bulk of their weight in the front half of the body.

When still alive and fresh the longtail have a dark blue back with a tinge of green along the fringes of the blue, the belly is often

Longtail are a serious challenge on a fly rod.

Spinning is the best method to use and the retrieve rate should be rapid. It doesn't do any harm to make the lure work in an erratic manner either although this is not essential. Both high speed and action lures will work and there doesn't seem to be any real difference in terms of results when it comes to colour or chrome varieties. Stripeys are clean fighting fish and light lines are practicable although much of the real thrill of the fight—feeling the full-on power of a stripey—can be lost by going down to too light a line. With this in mind, I suggest lines between 6 and 10 kg breaking strain.

> Few fish have the turn of speed of striped tuna and they are the epitome of a true sportfish and ideal light tackle candidates for anyone who understands the true meaning of fight.

species tip

LONGTAIL TUNA

Longtails are well known for hugging the rocks as they feed. They are also caught at the back of the breakers in the surf and in bays. Baitfish is the lure that attracts them. For best results, keep your lure size down to something of similar size to the baitfish the tuna are feeding on.

STRIPED TUNA

Also known as skipjack tuna and stripeys, these fish are extremely fast over a short distance. Lightning strikes followed by sizzling runs, never seeming to have any route or set direction of travel once hooked are a trademark.

Striped tuna are uniformly dark blue on the upper part of the body and have longitudinal stripes on the belly portion. This fish is encountered in large schools in coastal waters of New South Wales, Tasmania, Victoria, South Australia, and Western Australia. Stripeys hunt in schools mainly on or about the surface and can often be spotted a long way off as they move along the coast.

species tip

STRIPED TUNA

Speed is everything when it comes to spinning for striped tuna. Remember to allow your lure time to sink, varying the depths of retrieve by doing a countdown after each cast. When you get a strike and recast your lure count to the same number so that the lure will come back at the same depth as the last fish was caught.

blotchy and the finlets are yellow. Longtails are a landbased angler's dream fish in that when they migrate along the coast they hug the rocks. So close do they run that there is no need to send out live bait any more than about 20 metres. Many anglers sitting on a high vantage point often see a longtail before it actually strikes.

Longtails don't seem to grow much past the 30 kg mark and most fish caught seem to range between 6 and 10 kilograms. The first run from a longtail is usually made at a blistering pace after which it will tend to fight in a long arc as the angler continues to regain line.

Golden snapper rate a prized catch in the tropics.

Mackerel tuna have an exhilarating first run and are one of the most popular tuna species sought by light tackle enthusiasts.

MACKEREL TUNA

Commonly referred to as 'mack tuna', this tropical species is one of the most exotic looking tunas. It has a dark green back, light, and dark green markings, which run horizontally around the top of the body in a wavy pattern, the belly portion is silver, and there are two to five dark spots located above the ventral fin.

Mackerel tuna have been known to attain weights of more than 15 kg but most of those taken would average about half this size. This species has a wide distribution, can be caught as far south as Green Cape on the east coast and Cape Leeuwin in the west, and are widely distributed across the Northern Territory and Queensland.

While not caught as regularly as bonito, striped tuna and frigate mackerel in south coast waters, this fish is a common capture further north at places such as Hervey Bay, Port Stephens, and Coffs Harbour. Mackerel tuna hug the rocks as they migrate along the coast in the same fashion as the longtail. When hooked, mackerel tuna will put on an initial burst of steam, which takes most of the fight out of them. Spinning, fly-fishing and live baiting techniques will achieve results.

species tip

MACKEREL TUNA

Like all of the small tunas, mackerel tuna tend to be fast and frenzied and if you don't handle them efficiently you can spend longer fighting them than you should. Saltwater fly rodders and light tackle enthusiasts shave fighting times when the fight gets to close quarters by using sideways and downwards pressure from the rod. These low blows have a disorientating effect on stubborn fish. To be effective however, the fish needs to be either in shallow water or high in the water column.

BONITO

Australian bonito are often confused with striped tuna by inexperienced anglers. The differences between the two species are quite marked and obvious when a bonito is put alongside a stripey for comparison. Bonito have a green back and the longitudinal stripes running along the bonito's back stop about midway down the flank (except in the case of oriental bonito which are restricted to Western Australia). On a striped tuna, the bars are distinctive on the belly portion and this fish is much darker in colouring.

Bonito also possess a more formidable array of teeth, which stand out noticeably, and their shape is more elongated whereas the stripey is more rotund and there is a sharp dip rather than a gradual slope to the tail.

If you are still in doubt, the final test is in the eating. Bonito have a white flesh that is an epicurean delight. Striped tuna are full of oil and blood and best used as live bait or for berley.

Bonito are an excellent fighting fish and great fun on both lures and live bait. In recent years, this species has replaced striped tuna on the south coast of New South Wales as the mainstay of spinning.

And while bonito are not as fast as striped tuna, they are dogged and powerful in their actions and in some ways more cunning. For example, when first hooked a bonito will run deep and is not averse to diving under ledges and through reef. This species will keep the pressure on all the time and rely more on power and tactics to defeat the angler rather

species tip

BONITO

Bonito are an inshore tuna and because you are fishing from shore does not mean you have to cast out 100 metres to catch fish. Many anglers make the simple mistake of not looking at the environment around them. In a boat, motor up to rocky headlands and cast into the wash, the bonito will be working the fringe of the aerated water.

Bonito are one of the smaller tunas available to anglers. They are good value on light spin gear and flyfishing gear.

than speed, as is the case of striped tuna and frigate mackerel.

Bonito run along the coast hugging the rocks and most average about 3 kg to 4 kilograms. Outfits up to 6 kg breaking strain will suffice. Bonito will take all the commonly used live baits, most lures and flies.

YELLOWFIN TUNA

One of the glamour fish of game fishing, yellowfin tuna range along both the east and west coasts of Australia and can grow to more than 200 kilograms. Yellowfin are a beautifully coloured fish with their dark blue back, iridescent golden band running along the body as a dividing line between the silver belly and blue back. All the fins of this species are yellow, smaller specimens have white bars along the lower side and belly region. The most distinctive feature of this species are the second dorsal and anal fins, which lengthen noticeably in fish in excess of 35 kilograms. On 50 kg plus yellowfin, these fins become long and sabre-like and instead of sloping back towards the tail protrude almost at right angles before curving back to the tail.

Ideal conditions for yellowfin would read something like this: crystal clear water with a deep blue hue and a little sparkle about it, plus a water temperature reading of at least 20 degrees Celsius. And while the above is the ideal it seems someone forget to tell the

When it comes to catching yellowfin, it is not enough to simply go to the Continental Shelf, find water temperature and start fishing. Water temperature of about 18 to 21 degrees Celsius is ideal. Good yellowfin water will also be a deep blue, almost purple, and will have current and feeding birds when the fish are about. Offshore the current can change the surface appearance of the water. On calm days, the current will be seen as small constant ripples on the surface, a slick or oil patch is a mark of current change.

fish for yellowfin tuna can be caught in water turned the colour of mud by floodwaters. Sunny days also seem to be the best and it is a combination of these factors, which appear to be synonymous with productivity.

Yellowfin can be caught on both lures and live bait and what it really seems to depend on is whether you are after big fish or little fish. The largest confirmed fish on a lure that I know of went about 35 kg and the angler was using 8

kg line and a chromed Iron Assassin lure. Small yellowfin of up to 10 kg are most commonly caught on lures.

For bluewater anglers, cubing and live baiting are productive. When a yellowfin takes a bait the strike is often hard and fast and the fish will run a long way at a fast rate of knots but the speed will not vary. Don't try to halt the run; the faster and further the fish runs the easier it will be to defeat. Yellowfin adopt a deep lugging action during a fight and tend to fight in a long series of arcs. A major problem with big fish is working them too easily and having them die on you. If you think this is the case (that your fish is close to death or dead and starting to sink) keep it moving. Even drive off if in a boat, as once it sinks to the bottom it can be an almost impossible task sometimes to raise the fish again.

SOUTHERN BLUEFIN

This species has been described as the perfect projectile due to its rotund shape, short body, and fast taper to the tail. Southern bluefin are dark blue above and have a silver belly, all their finlets are yellow, and occasionally the fish will have a yellow hue about the fins and can grow to more than 200 kilograms.

The fish range from Port Macquarie in New South Wales around the southern coastline and as far north as Shark Bay in Western Australia. This species follows a well-chartered migration route commencing in the spawning grounds

Yellowfin tuna will test both angler and tackle.

Bluefin are barrels of power. Most are caught trolling skirted lures at high speed. And while they can be hard to find, their inherent power can make them difficult to land. It is vital your tackle is up to scratch and the drag tension set correctly. The correct fighting tension for a reel is about one quarter the line breaking strain on lines about 6 kg or less, and a maximum of one third the line breaking strain for heavier lines. For example, the drag setting on a 4 kg line should be about 1 kg; on 10 kg, line set your drag at about 3 kilograms.

off north-western Western Australia, down the coast and across the Great Australian Bight, down around Tasmania and up the New South Wales central coast. From here, the fish move back to Tasmania and then across to New Zealand.

Both live baiting and spinning will prove successful although the majority of fish caught are less than 10 kg and taken on lures. The most consistent catches are taken trolling, with places such as Port MacDonnell in South Australia, Portland in Victoria and the St Helens in Tasmania among the better places.

MACKEREL

SPANISH MACKEREL

Narrow-barred Spanish mackerel are a tropical species and the further north you head up either the east or west coasts the more likely

species tip

SPANISH MACKEREL

Spaniards are attracted to structure, will hang about them on the lee side of the current, and linger in a berley trails. Fishing a deep coral bommie along the Great Barrier Reef one day, we managed to hold mackerel for several hours by cubing. Wire leader should be employed and hook size should suit bait, but about 4/0 to 6/0 will cover most situations. Occasionally anglers have the opportunity to cast lures and flies when these fish move high in the water column.

are your chances of success. Odd fish have been caught as far south as Jervis Bay while anglers working off Bermagui regularly take a few fish when the water gets really warm.

This fish is highly regarded for its incredible burst of sustained speed when it first strikes a lure or takes a bait. In Spanish mackerel the upper jaw is longer than the lower, the fish sports a dark blue back, silvery flanks and belly and irregular dark bars along the flanks.

Lures such as poppers, or else metal types retrieved at high speed across the surface will induce a strike from these super fast pelagics. When spinning, a short length of single strand or piano wire should be used as Spaniards are well endowed with teeth.

Spanish mackerel will take live and dead baits, and react well to cubing techniques. This fish is a member of the so-called 'razor gang' due to its mouthful of sharp teeth. With that in mind, single strand wire leader is commonplace.

SHARK MACKEREL

Smaller than Spanish mackerel, shark mackerel grow to about 15 kilograms. Bearing a light green back, the fish is washed with a golden hue over the flanks. The most clearly distinguishable feature of shark mackerel is a double lateral line; the fish also sports an array of black spots and has scales.

Rob Zynevych with his 120.8 kg southern bluefin tuna caught off Portland.

Lindsay Mutimer with a Spanish mackerel.

At about 10 kg, this shark mackerel held by Geoff Taylor gave a good account of itself on the 14 wt fly outfit. The fly was dead drifted over some reefy terrain, and the mackerel came out of the blue and took the offereing.

These fish are keenly sought on lures and also by exponents of saltwater fly. Landbased game exponents in Western Australia and Queensland have also taken shark mackerel on lures.

species tip

SHARK MACKEREL

One of the best methods I have seen for catching shark mackerel was on the Breaksea Spit off the northeast corner of Fraser Island. We were drifting over reef and allow our flies to trail behind the boat. You don't do anything, just allow the action of the boat in the waves and current to do it all for you. Shark mackerel will also take fish strips the same way. Don't forget to use wire leader.

shopping list

TUNA AND MACKEREL
LIVE BAITING & CUBING:

OUTFIT: 10 to 24 kg game rod or (if fishing the stones) a 10 – 15 kg livebait stick. Reel should be a lever drag with a minimum spool capacity of 600 metres.

HOOKS: Chemically sharpened Suicide or Octopus patterns about 6/0 to 9/0 depending on bait size. Tuna Circle patterns are becoming more popular due to their ability to grab hold in the corner of a fish's mouth, so reducing the chances of gut hooking fish and enabling a higher chance of survival in a catch and release scenario.

LEADER: For tuna, use a leader or trace material 37 – 70 kilograms. Lighter, thinner traces increase the chances of a hook-up. But abrasion caused by rubbing on the body or fins of the fish can be a problem and diameter is what gives you wear resistance. Mackerel need wire, preferably single strand piano wire about 50 kilograms.

FLOATS: Balloons are the most effective but bobby cork can be okay.

BAIT: Yakkas, slimy mackerel, and frigate mackerel. Cube baits can be anything from pilchard pieces to slimy or yakka strips.

SPINNING:

OUTFIT: Three to 10 kg depending on the size of the species. For example, spinning for small frigates, bonito or striped tuna then a 3 to 6 kg outfit would do the job. It's more a matter of balancing out the outfit to suit the lures. Threadline reels will cover most light line scenarios, but when you start working heavier lines give some thought to an overhead reel with a 6:1 gear ratio.

LEADER: Use a minimum 10 kg leader for spinning with 15 kg about the optimum size for heavier tackle. Add a short wire leader for mackerel.

LURES: Size ranges from 10 – 60 g depending on the spin outfit. Some lures with a proven record include Halco's Arrows, Twistys and chrome slices; Wonder Pilchards, Juro Slim Jim and Lazers; Tailor Made from 10 g to 70 g, Bumper Bars, Irons and the many generic baitfish patterns now available.

MARLIN

There are three species of marlin caught by anglers; these are the black, blue, and striped. It is difficult to imagine anyone not knowing what a marlin looks like. The three fish can appear similar to look at in the water, although striped marlin are generally obvious as the name implies. But the main physical feature that separates black marlin from the others is that the curved pectoral fins, while they may be moveable in fish up to 60 kg, will not sit flat along the body.

Fast and spectacular, a marlin can be the most difficult of opponents. Landbased game anglers often get the first indication of a marlin take with the sight of a marlin shimmering in the sunlight as it soared vertically out of the water shaking its head in an effort to toss the bait. At other times the first indication of a take is a very slow run, little more than a few ticks of the ratchet—followed by a screaming run as line pours off the spool.

Bluewater anglers generally troll. Switch baiting is one method used. In this case skirted lures are run as teasers on the outriggers, and a large attractor like a Witchdoctor is run close to the boat in the wake. The Witchdoctor, basically a mirror that swims, emits a huge intermittent flash in the wake while the skirted

Black marlin are called the stallion of the seas with good reason. Super fast and acrobatic, they can put both angler and crew to the test. PHOTO:CRAIG SMITH

species tip

MARLIN

Bait balls are natural fish attractors that can hold several billfish below. One method of fishing bait balls is to drop a couple of baitfish into the school and slowly move them out of the ball. This exposes the baits as stragglers. An alternative is to use a sinker on your leader to ensure the baitfish will go down deep and right through the balled up to where the predators are likely to waiting below. Either way, the live baits are offered up as stragglers, alone and exposed and that makes a quick and easy meal for a predator.

Current fronts can turn on some hot action for striped marlin particularly if the water temperature is to their liking on one side of it. These current fronts create the right food chain reaction that in turn attracts bigger predators, so it is a wise move to run your lures or baits along the edge of the front and also to troll a zigzag pattern though water temperature overlap.

lures simply leave a trail of bubbles, or 'smoke' as the game gurus say. As well as this array, there are often two lines of plastic squid on outriggers that also act as teasers.

When a marlin comes up and looks at a lure or teaser a live bait, such as a frigate mackerel or a slimy mackerel that has been bridle rigged with a tuna circle hook, is slipped back and the lures pulled from the water. Hopefully, the marlin takes the bait.

A more traditional method is to simply bridle rig a couple of small tuna or slimy mackerel, towing one short to skip, the second further back and running deeper. In this case a couple of skirted lures are also run to act as teasers and again a mirror attractor is put in the wake.

Marlin have a bony mouth and setting the hook can be difficult so the angler should always strike more than once to ensure the hook is sent home.

FIGHTING TACTICS

Once the line is cleared and the fish 'settled' it is easier to take the boat to the fish. This eliminates fighting the fish on the backing. Save that effort for when the fly line comes onto the reel. To maintain the angler in the

best possible position to apply telling rod angles, take into account that if the boat is upwind/upcurrent from the marlin, the fish will tend to position high in the water column where better pressure angles are to be gained. Conversely, if the situation reverses—which it will do many times in a long fight—the fish tends to lug deep leaving the angler with little option than to knuckle down to a gruelling pump and wind routine from the overhead quadrant. Not the best position from which to undertake a lengthy fight.

It is difficult, sometimes impossible even, to lift a big gamefish from the depths with a fly rod. Once the fish has started to tire, it is especially maintain an upwind or upcurrent position. This has the affect of lifting the fish's head and planing it towards the surface, courtesy of the current and the dynamics of the fish's body shape. Through much of the fight it will be a matter of judgement but there will come a stage over the final rounds when the fish is within view thus providing angler and helmsman the opportunity to counter its every move.

When a fish is running hard chase it with the boat, pressure from behind or over the fish's shoulder is the best direction as this interrupts the fish's capacity to use its gills properly and restricts its ability to swim forward and down.

Game boats, with twin screws, are able to back up on fish. In a trailerboat, this can be an exercise fraught with danger. The self-draining hull on some small boats makes backing up possible but there is a limit. Don't try backing down too hard; do so slowly and cautiously. The manoeuvrability of trailerboats is such that backing up is often unnecessary.

Good numbers of marlin are caught by anglers fishing from sportfishing boats.

SHARKS

Shark fishing has a dedicated following, both shore-based and offshore. The most common captures include whalers, blues, makos, hammerheads, and tigers.

Unfortunately, not every shark is a fighter. Where one shark might offer little resistance and appear to do little more than swim in with the bait, another will challenge the line capacity of your reel. Black whalers are estimated to grow to 4.5 m in length and attain a weight of up to 500 kilograms. Bronze whalers can weigh up to 350 kg but rarely exceed 3.5 m in length.

A distinctive feature of the whalers is their pectoral fins, which are long, wide, and used to plane down deep in currents. Bronze whalers are the colour of a shiny copper coin while black whalers are normally darker ranging from dark grey to black. In all whalers, the upper lobe of the tail is longer than the lower lobe and there are no keels at the tail junction.

Another shark often encountered is the odd-looking hammerhead that is easily identified by its unique, mallet-shaped flat head. These sharks are found along both the east and west coasts and the majority of those taken by anglers will generally have a dark grey back although some sport an almost tan coloured back. Hammerheads will often be spotted a long way off cruising close to the surface due to the height and shape of the slightly rounded dorsal fin protruding above the surface.

Great whites and grey nurse sharks are protected so these are off limits. Blue pointers or mako sharks are common and can really test the angler and put on a display to rival that of a marlin. Makos will take live baits and are often caught on bridle rigged live baits such as frigate mackerel being trolled for marlin. The colouration of the back is cobalt blue, they also have large dark eyes and are magnificently proportioned tapering sharply back from the shoulder region to the keels at the tail junction. The upper and lower lobes of a mako shark's tail are almost equal; it has long thin teeth in both jaws and short pectoral fins.

Because of their colouration, blue sharks are sometimes mistaken for makos. However, blue sharks have long pectoral fins, the upper lobe of the tail is longer than the lower lobe and there are no keels at the junction of the tail and body. Blue sharks do not have the same turn of speed and power as the mako.

Seven gill sharks are common captures, particularly in Victoria while they also frequent Tasmanian and South Australian waters. The easiest way of identification is by the seven gill slits—most sharks have five—and the single dorsal fin that is situated almost three-quarters of the way back from the head towards the tail.

Tiger sharks are not commonly encountered and these are best identified by the distinct bar pattern on the back, which may not be present on larger specimens. This shark sports a blunt head and a wedge shaped body with low keels at the tail junction.

As well as the sharks already mentioned, snapper or school sharks and thresher sharks are sometimes caught. These sharks follow large fish migrations. School sharks are more common in bays when snapper have moved in while thresher sharks will be caught in deeper coastal areas, often near reefs.

There are no set rules for sharks as far as the fight is concerned as no two will necessarily take a bait or fight the same way. Sharks take bait on the horizontal and the strike is normally steady and slower than that of pelagic fish such as yellowfin. Having said that there will be times when the first the angler knows of the strike is a mighty splash and the scream of the reel's ratchet as line pours off the spool in one super fast, unstoppable run.

Sharks can be caught from shore and boat; the only common denominator controlling their actions is their unrelenting search for food. Successful shark anglers understand this and work up tuna oil based berley trails to bring the sharks to them.

Sharks move with large schools of fish as they migrate along the coast. For example, if there is a beach nearby which is having a good run of salmon or tailor then sharks will not be far away. If the snapper have moved

Mako sharks like this one caught by Nathan Jackson are dangerous, noted for their habit of jumping into boats.

Mark Rushton with a 100 kg thresher shark that took more than an hour to land on 24 kg tackle.

This wahoo had an unfortunate encounter with an oceanic whaler off Gladstone.

Trolling for tuna or marlin sometimes produces other species, like whalers.

in on a particular reef then it won't be long before anglers are hauling in heads as sharks can generally be counted on to arrive at this sort of fishing utopia before too long. Areas that have resident seal colonies always have resident sharks lurking in the neighbourhood while bays that consistently produce are bound to be frequented by sharks.

It has been my experience that sharks are to be found just about anywhere that they can get a feed, the larger the food source the more plentiful the sharks. It is noticeable in southern waters that the numbers of shark sightings increase after long spells of hot weather. Three or four days of temperatures in the high thirties seems to bring the sharks out of the depths and into the shallower areas.

BAIT

The popular method of shark fishing is to suspend a bait beneath a balloon. Landbased anglers do this to drift baits offshore, and the system works just as well when fishing from a boat. The method is simple. A balloon is attached to the trace about three metres or so above the bait.

If fishing from shore you will find it better to blow up a couple of 10 or 20 g balloons to act as a tow. These are tied to about

SHARK

Sharks are at their best when they first steam into a berley trail. They are hungry and looking for the source of the trail. When in this aggravated state most sharks will take bait straight up. Once they settle in the trail though sharks become less aggressive and therefore less willing to attack anything. Something you will notice if you observe sharks in a trail in their own environment is that they rarely feed on small scraps while big chunks of fish flesh are always taken.

30m of line and allowed to blow offshore to gain momentum before the bait, which is suspended under a single balloon, is tossed in to be towed out.

HOOK UP

Contrary to popular belief not all sharks charge a bait and engulf it in one hit. Live baits struggling on a hook send out the sort of 'vibes' that can induce the instant savage strike that usually results in a hook-up. Dead baits do not appear to induce this type of strike. During the daylight hours, in particular sharks will often be more wary, even hesitant.

The actual hook-up can vary but it is important to strike several times to be sure of setting the hooks firmly. Judging when to strike is up to you. If the shark is ripping line off the spool then wait a couple of seconds before sinking the hooks home. On the other hand, if the shark is tentative and taking matters very slowly then wait until he turns on a sudden burst of speed before setting the hooks. If you don't achieve a hook-up, leave the bait in the water for a while, as there is always a chance the shark could come back for another go.

The tactics that sharks employ are as varied and different as are their distribution and much can depend upon the area being fished. For example, if you are fishing near reefs or gutters then you will probably find that the first shark you hook will head immediately towards these obstacles in no uncertain manner. If the shark is not turned before he makes this ground then it is normal for him to dive down a gutter or ledge and this has the potential to sever your line.

In shallow areas sharks tend to do the obvious and head for the relative safety of deeper water.

In a strong current, many sharks use their large pectoral fins to advantage by planing in the current. Another ploy you probably won't expect is for sharks to sit on the bottom, something usually associated with tactics of a big stingray.

When fighting a shark, or any big fish for that matter, the best tactic of applying pressure is to use a mobile pump and wind technique. Instead of being stationary the angler should pump his fish by walking back a few paces with full pressure on, and retrieve line as he walks forward keeping the rod tip slightly dipped. On hot days always keep a wet rag handy to keep your line moist and pliable, this will lessen the chances of it parting or weakening under pressure.

Finally, don't rush the action during the fight. Set out to control the pace from the outset and keep it moving along steadily. If you do try to hurry matters along you may find yourself running out of stamina before the shark does

or, even worse, making errors of judgement. By maintaining self control, you will also be able to dictate the fight and once this has been achieved much of the battle is already over.

When it comes to setting the gaff, the two best places are either in the gill slits or the mouth.

Three is an ideal number when it comes to landing a big shark, one angler, wearing gloves of course, can grab the wire trace, another locate the flying gaff and a third pull on the rope to set the gaff hook.

OUTFIT: 10 – 24 kg, lever drag game reel, and game rod.

GAFF: Flying or rope gaff is best as sharks twist around and can break a fixed head gaff.

TRACE: Seven strand stainless steel minimum 100 kg breaking strain. Do not compromise when it comes to quality. Always use the manufacturers specified crimps and crimping pliers and cut the wire as close to the end of the crimp as possible as this will prevent any loose ends of wire protruding from the crimp.

HOOKS: Shark hooks are most commonly from about 8/0 to 12/0, but that can vary with patterns. Many anglers prefer to run two hooks on their wire trace and fly fishers do likewise for best results.

Mustad have the largest range of hooks and Mustad consultant Dave Harrigan says the pattern most commonly used for shark fishing with conventional baits, such as a fish fillet, in this part of the world is the Mustad Sea Master, ref. 7699. This comes in sizes 20/0 down to 4/0 and is a forged offset hook (kirbed) with a knife-edge point and special tin finish. There is also a Needle Eye version of the Sea Master. This is the 7690, available in sizes 20/0 to 4/0.

If you wanted a straight (non-offset) shark hook, the choice would be the 7698B, which is similar in shape and characteristics to the 7699, but straight, and available 12/0 to 6/0. There is also the 7691, which is also a forged straight hook; it is the non-stainless version of the 7691S and available 14/0 to 1/0. All these three patterns have a turned-in style point and special tin finish. None of the hooks referred to has a 'chemically sharpened' point. When you get to hooks of this size and type, the advantages of a needlepoint with chemical sharpening are doubtful.

Favourite Freshwater Sportfish

sports 4.75

REDFIN

Also known as English perch, redfin are a favourite of many freshwater anglers. The average size is about 0.25 kg to 1 kg but fish in excess of 3.5 kg have been caught. This fish is a light line speciality. Redfin hit a bait, lure or fly well and the fight is more dogged than most introduced species.

Big redfin tend to hole up among logs, tree roots and shady overhangs. They can be caught in most of the lakes and rivers of southern Australia as well as quite a few farm dams. The methods of catching them are straightforward. Redfin will take worm, gudgeon and minnow on the bottom or fished under a quill float as well as most small lures including spoons, minnows and flies. When working lures, the best results are had by casting along the river and retrieving in close to the bank.

Jock and Kenna Mackenzie are pleased with their redfin.

species tip
REDFIN

When fishing for redfin look for structures, particularly trees where they will lurk under the dark or shady areas. When casting from a riverbank the take is often at your feet. And redfin are often at their best near sunset after a hot day.

shopping list
REDFIN

BAIT FISHING & SPINNING:
OUTFIT: 3 kg, small threadline reel balanced to suit a rod about 1.6 m long.
HOOKS: No. 10 hook for smelt or minnow, and a No. 6 to 8 hook for worms.
LURES: Most bladed lures and small minnows—floating and mid-water—will work and Baltic Bobbers.

FLY FISHING:
OUTFIT: Four to 6 wt rod, weight forward floating or sinking line.
TIPPET: 1 kg to 2 kilograms.
FLIES: Gold bead head nymphs, Tom Jones, Woolly Bugger and Matuka.

TROUT

Trout are Australia's most popular freshwater fish. Despite the publicity given to native fishes such as yellowbelly and Murray cod, the trout still reigns supreme among southern anglers who have the option.

There are two main species introduced into Australian waters, the brown and rainbow. Both have their supporters and detractors, I'm just happy to catch either. Small concentrations of Atlantic salmon, brook trout, and Chinook salmon also exist and what follows can be applied to these in varying degrees.

LAKES

Trout have thrived in lakes and impoundments. In some waterways such as Lake Eucumbene in New South Wales and Lake Eildon in Victoria, access to feeder streams with suitable gravel beds have resulted in self sustaining populations. In other waters the trout live only to eat; lack of feeder streams or suitable gravel beds means many become egg bound and die.

Perhaps the most significant benefit for anglers working lakes is that barring specific fisheries' regulations to the contrary, all methods produce fish. A boat is a bonus, not a necessity. You can catch lake trout spinning, trolling, working a fly or by the more traditional bait under a float technique. Sometimes, such as when the fish are inshore feeding along the margins, a boat can be a disadvantage.

Most boat anglers concentrate along the weed beds for the trout. On hot, sunny days, the deeper cooler water is generally more productive. In exceptionally wet winters, some lakes will spill into paddocks, when this happens the trout move over the grass to mop up the snails and other insect life flushed out by the water.

Many lakes fire up better after dark. At Lake Eucumbene, the water is fished by two shifts: daylight anglers and those who prefer to be on the water after sunset, usually before the moon rises or after it has gone down. The reason for this is that the bigger trout, particularly browns, move inshore to hunt along the lake margins for gudgeon, minnow, and smelt.

METHODS

The techniques used include bait fishing with mudeyes, glassies, worms, or live minnow, spinning, trolling, and fly-fishing.

Whether in a boat or land based, bait fishing is still the most popular method and for most anglers it involves the use of bubble floats. These floats differ from quill floats in that they are not solely designed to keep a bait suspended off the bottom at a set depth and act as a bite indicator. Rather, the main purpose of a bubble float is to assist the angler to cast his bait out.

Bubble floats have a tube that passes through the centre, acting as a pump to fill them with the required amount of water. The more water, the heavier the float, and the further the angler can cast. The line is passed through this tube and a small piece of cork is threaded on the line below the float, but above the bait to regulate the depth of the bait. To enable casting hold this length to the length of your rod or less.

After the bait has been cast out the bail arm

A nice haul of rainbow trout from Eildon Pondage.

popular wet fly. The aquatic life is so diverse that nymph patterns ranging from black and brown through to chartreuse colours can work well at different times. Smelt patterns can be productive, particularly during spring while a hot northerly and an ensuing insect hatch will see Elk Hair Caddis and Adams patterns in vogue.

RIVERS

For me, the best trout fishing is in running water surrounded by a pristine environment. No litter, no boats, and best of all, isolation. Most small southern streams, particularly in mountainous regions, host reasonable populations of brown trout. Some streams hold lesser numbers of rainbow trout. In most cases, the browns are part of a self-sustaining population.

For the most part small streams mean small trout. In many cases fish size is not reflective of age. They are often adult fish in miniature, their growth limited by the environment and feed. Stunted they may be but these trout can test an angler's skills far more than the farm grown variety bred on liver pellets for put-and-take fisheries.

If you are looking for a grassroots, primordial

Fly fishing for trout is more about the hunt than the size.

on the reel is left open and line is taken off the spool at right angles. Some anglers place a small coin on the line; others prefer to hook the line around an empty aluminium drink can. When the can topples, line runs out freely and the angler knows he has a fish at the bait.

The only variation in terminal tackle between the baits is hook size. Mudeye, which are dragonfly nymph, are delicate and require a small hook that is passed gently through the wing casing. A No. 14 to 12 Gamakatsu Octopus pattern hook works well. If glassy is to be used, then the hook size and pattern can be altered. A No. 8 to No. 10 Gamakatsu hook in the same pattern, or a Mustad Viking pattern will suffice. The hook should be threaded through the bait from the tail and the point exposed in the region of the head. A half-hitch is placed around the tail to keep the bait straight.

Minnow and gudgeon are popular live baits and when they are used, a No. 8 or No. 10 hook is employed. The hook is passed through the upper jaw of the fish, but not so deep as to do the bait fish any harm.

Another bait fishing method is to use a small running sinker and fish on the bottom. It can be very successful, especially when worms are used for bait.

Often the first indication that a bait is taken is the fish jumping about the surface. They do not always wander far and so line is not always removed from the spool at first.

If bait fishing from a boat use a small sinker on your line and allow your bait to sink to the depth you think the fish will be feeding at. An echo sounder can be a good guide in this regard. Berley works well and don't be backward in using standard saltwater baits such as bluebait or pilchard for trout—they will take it quite readily.

Tassie Devil style lures and rainbow pattern Rapalas are popular for trolling. Some anglers run downriggers to control the running depth of their lures. If this isn't so in your case then set your rods horizontal to the boat, and vary the length the lures are trolled behind the boat, as this will put them at different depths.

These lures work equally well for spinning. The best results on lures come by varying depths and retrieve rates. Concentrate in areas where trout are most likely to be hunting, that is along drop offs and weed beds where there is cover for small fish.

Fly fishers work many variations of patterns. Woolly Buggers, in dark or bright colours, work well along with the ever-reliable Red Tag (wet and dry). The Tom Jones is probably the most

wading safety

Avoid wading in very fast flowing water; keep the water level around the knee line and in still water, avoid wading in areas that would be over your waist. Place your foot firmly and securely before taking the next step. If you are insecure with your footing, always use a wading staff or a dead branch; either will save you from a lot of slipping and sliding.

challenge, have a yearning to hunt and stalk a quarry in a quality environment, then look no further than small mountain streams. Finicky, frustrating, and downright contrary, these fish are survivors in difficult, even hostile conditions. Caution is the key to survival. Transfer that into fishing scenarios and you begin to understand why they are a challenge.

One of the wonderful things about small stream trout is that tackle requirements are minimal. A short spinning rod with line of about 2 kg breaking strain and a small bladed lure is a deadly combination. In hip pocket terms, your initial outlay is probably not much more than the cost of a good Thermos.

The small bladed lures, No.1 Celtas or Crystal Creek models, are relatively cheap to buy, best of all they consistently produce trout. Small thumbnail sized minnow patterns also produce but don't cast as well. You can afford to lose a lot more bladed lures than some of the more expensive minnow patterns.

If you aren't into spinning then alternatively,

species tip

TROUT

Small bladed lures consistently produce trout but surface and shallow running minnows are often more successful. In streams, trout will be found in deeper pools, at the head and tail of runs and lying in wait beneath bushy overhangs along the banks. It is necessary to use a bit of stealth when approaching likely areas, work your way upstream, and make long casts wherever possible. I prefer to fish lures across and against the current.

the same outfit with a No. 8 hook, a small piece of shot on the leader and worm or grub for bait can work wonders. Even putting a small wet fly on the end of your line and running a couple of split shot about 50 cm up the line is effective.

Fly fishers find the going a little tougher, particularly where the foliage has overgrown the stream. Invariably, these are the most productive waters. Heavy bank-side flora means shade and protection from birds. During summer, this growth also means cooler water and dark areas suited to ambush. Roll casts become the order of the day. Those state-of-the-art, U-beaut fly rods built out of space age materials suddenly find they lose their value as the terrain becomes more difficult.

Success in small streams comes through knowledge and stealth, and the angler has to understand what constitutes a likely lie, the sort of food trout will seek and how best to

camouflage

Many anglers pay attention to camouflaged clothing. But it can all be to no avail if you don't wear a hat with a brim to shade your face. Anglers fishing small streams will often crouch when they are near the water as the higher you are above the water the easier it is for the fish to see you.

present lure, fly or bait. Trout lie in deeper pools, at the head and tail of runs, or wait beneath bushy overhangs along the banks. It is necessary to use stealth when approaching likely areas, work your way upstream, and make long casts wherever possible.

It is worthwhile considering the end of the day when you start out. Walking several kilometres of stream and finishing with a long hike back to the vehicle isn't much fun. The best way is to park your car, walk downstream, and then work your way back up.

Most of the time the water worked is shallow, anywhere from knee to thigh deep. These streams often braid into narrow runnels. Every puddle from the start of a riffle to a plunge pool below a waterfall is worth prospecting. The water needs systematic working but don't overdo it. A small pool might be explored with half a dozen strategic casts, larger pools with more likely looking trout haunts will probably need more.

Always work to avoid spooking fish. Use natural cover to disguise your approach wherever possible. When this isn't possible, stand back and test your arm by making longer casts. In shallow stretches it is sometimes

species tip

TROUT

Most anglers know that trout adopt what are known as feeding lanes in rivers. They conserve energy by sitting where the current will bring food to them. But did you know that these fish are more often found feeding in low-pressure areas in front of rocks rather than behind them?

necessary to wind the lure the instant it hits the water to avoid snagging up on rocks or branches. Always remember to look up before you cast as many more lures snag up in tree branches than in the water.

The methods in rivers, as distinct from streams, are similar. Tiny bibbed minnows and Celtas are my favourite trout lures. In big rivers, these should be flicked upstream and down, working every square metre of likely holding water. And the retrieve should be varied, sometimes a quick strip back, other times twitch the lure hesitantly until you find what is working on that day.

You can cover a spot with three or four casts. If a fish has a go at the lure then you do the same again or else leave, work another part of the river and come back to that spot later. In my experience, the largest trout will be caught in the lower reaches near the estuary. These fish linger along the river edge, lying in wait under shelter of overhanging grass for shrimp, galaxias, and insects.

Shrimps are the most easily obtained bait. In many waters, all you need is a long-handled fine mesh net and a coffee jar with moist sawdust in it to keep them alive. Shrimps live in the submerged watercress overhanging the riverbanks.

To fish shrimp thread half a dozen of the little crustaceans onto a No. 4 hook. The shrimps are too small to thread longitudinally,

noise

Talking isn't a problem when fishing, as voice waves will not penetrate the water. Sounds that frighten fish are created below the surface, vibrations transferred from the bank, thumping sounds such as cattle, horses, or clumsy anglers would make.

Fly fishing for trout is more about the hunt than the size.

so the hook passes through the middle of the shrimp at right angles to its body.

Big river trout, such as those you find in the Gellibrand, Aire, and Curdies rivers in Victoria, feed as readily on other trout as they do big yabbies on the bottom, or elvers. Successful anglers use live baits, such as wood grubs with night the best time. The method is basic. The grub is hooked through the collar, cast to the middle of a pool, and allowed to sink. As it runs down with the current, the grub is slowly retrieved; the critical time is just as the grub is nearing the surface. The big trout have a habit of taking a vertical position in the water, tails up. The pull gives the impression of being snagged.

AUSTRALIAN BASS AND ESTUARY PERCH

Among freshwater anglers, a small group exists who specialise in Australian bass. In Victoria, most of these people are based in East Gippsland, but in Queensland and New South Wales, bass have been widely stocked.

Many bass specialists, who chase the wild fish as against the stocked variety, are prepared to go bush and search isolated areas for their quarry. Make no mistake; serious bass fishing isn't easy. It is a physically demanding exercise and a two-day canoe run isn't unusual. Many bass specialists are prepared to go off road for miles, and then carry their small canoes or 'bass boats' long distances through difficult bushland before launching. When they come out it is usually downstream in some accessible area where they have arranged to be picked up.

repellent

The mosquitoes may be annoying but anglers should try to avoid placing repellent on their hands as this will then be transferred to the bait, lure or fly and may prove a turn-off for the fish, particularly in freshwater environs.

shopping list
TROUT
BAIT FISHING:
OUTFIT: Two to 3 kg, small threadline reel balanced to suit a rod about 2 m long to make casting bubble floats easier. Solid tip rods work well when there is any sort of breeze.
HOOKS: No. 14 hook for mudeyes; straight shanked No. 10 hook for smelt or minnow, and a No. 6 to 8 hook for worms.
Spinning:
OUTFIT: One to 3 kg, small threadline reel balanced to a rod of about 1.67 m capable of casting lures up to 20 grams in weight.
LURES: Most bladed lures and small minnows—floating and mid-water—will work. Here are a few that have been regular producers: Tassie Devil, Rebel Baby Bass and Baby Brown Trout; Celta No. 1 and No. 2; Vibrax; Min Min; Rapala CD3.

FLY FISHING:
OUTFIT: Four to 6 wt rod, weight forward floating or sinking line.
TIPPET: 1 kg to 2 kilograms.
There are many ancillary items for fly-fishing such as fly vests, floatant for flies and leaders, line cutters, forceps, indicators and other items. I suggest you seek professional advice from a specialist flyfishing shop for the extras.
FLIES:
Wets: Nymphs, brown or black with gold bead heads, Tom Jones; Woolly Bugger; Bagfly; green and black Matuka and mudeye patterns.
Dries: Black Beetle (fished wet or dry), Coch-y-Bonddu, Rusty Dun and Orange Spinner, Adams, Royal Wulff, Red Tag, ant and grasshopper patterns.

Sing Ling with an estuary perch. The salt water cousin of Australian bass, perch are often caught in brackish water with low salinity levels and the two species often overlap.

Rod Harrison with a typical Queensland impoundmant bass.

Australian bass are the best fighting freshwater fish I have caught, although angling friends who have caught sooty grunter in Queensland rate bass second. Impoundment fishing for bass has enjoyed a huge growth in northern New South Wales and Queensland to the point where there is now a dedicated bass fishing circuit based on the U.S. Bass Pro circuit, complete with lucrative prizes. Victorian bass may not achieve that level of growth, but then again with lakes like Bullen

Merri being stocked with bass, you can never be certain.

Most Victorians know more about estuary perch, a close relative, than they do about bass. Both fish are hard, aggressive battlers that can be annoyed into attacking a lure. And both fish hang around similar ground, along weed beds or mangrove stands near gutters and drop-offs. In tight water, they will have a lair in a snag and keeping them away from this safe house is the main concern of anglers who hook up.

The main difference between the two species is where they are found: estuary perch like the lower, estuarine reaches and saline water, while the bass prefer brackish to fresh water further upstream. In Victoria resident populations of perch can be found in most coastal streams with the best known ones being the Glenelg,

species tip
ESTUARY PERCH

Trying to catch estuary perch on a fly is made easier if you stir the fish up first. To do this take a small Rattler, remove the treble hooks, cast, and retrieve it along weed beds and drop-offs. Estuary perch will follow the lure and often strike or slap at it and when this happens another angler in the boat casts a fly back towards the shore. The returning fish, angry and stirred up, see the fly and take it.

Hopkins, Curdies, Gellibrand, Aire and Barham in the west and the Nowa Nowa, Snowy, Bemm, Cann, Wingan and Wallagaraugh rivers in the east. In some of the East Gippsland rivers, populations of both bass and perch will be found.

Bass will attack lures like bibbed minnows, Spinnerbaits and soft plastics such as Sliders. The small StumpJumpers work exceptionally well. The idea is to cast into and around snags where bass take up residence. Sometimes you start the retrieve almost as soon as the lure hits the water to avoid hooking a log or branch. When the bass are fired up the rake will be sudden and hard.

In southern Queensland and northern New South Wales, I have trolled bass in several waterways. In these situations most of the trolling is along weed lines, points and bays. The lures are made to run deep along weed lines and braided line is used on the reels as this gives the lures more running depth than monofilament.

Some of the best fun though is working surface lures, such as the Halco Night Walker. These are cast into the same snag-ridden areas. Dawn and dusk are the best times. You allow the lure to sit a few seconds then work it hard for a short distance before pausing once again. This action can infuriate bass into attacking.

Fishing estuary perch is similar. Live baits such as small baitfish and shrimp that are allowed to drift past a likely weed bank or snag often attract a strike. Lures can be cast beyond the snag and brought past several times before a strike will be had.

If you are into fly-fishing then surface poppers work well, as do midwater flies and Clousers. The strip is short and sharp, with a pause in between as it is with lures. A trick that works in East Gippsland is to take a small Rattler, remove the treble hooks, then cast and retrieve it along weed beds and drop-offs. Estuary perch will follow the lure and often strike or slap at it and when this happens another angler in the boat casts a fly back towards the shore. The returning fish, angry and stirred up, sees the fly and takes it.

YELLOWBELLY AND MURRAY COD

In recent years, a lot of work has been put in to develop native fisheries in both rivers and impoundments. And, for the most part, the effort has been worthwhile. Australian bass, silver perch, saratoga, and barramundi are just a few species that have come to the fore because of stocking. Probably the two most sought after native fish though are Murray cod and yellowbelly.

species tip
YELLOWBELLY

There are two triggers to watch out for which activate yellowbelly to come on the bite. A rise in water temperature is the first. When the temperature of the water rises to about 24 degrees Celsius, you will see a sharp increase in feeding activity. This is especially so among the big females, and this is a time to fish hard. The second feeding prompt is a rise in river levels. Yellowbelly heed their natural instincts and head upstream when the water levels rise. Barriers often stop this movement, but you can expect to come across a congregation of hungry fish just downstream.

Lake Mulwala on the Murray River in southern New South Wales is an example of the quality of fishing that can be achieved when a stocking program is well thought out and managed successfully. The Murray cod and yellowbelly fishing in Mulwala is the best native fishing in southern Australia.

Trolling on the lake using lures such as the StumpJumper and Spinnerbait lures requires an

Norm Crouch holds a 4 kg yellowbelly caught at Lake Callide.

Author caught this 17 kg Murray cod at Curlwaa on the Murray River.

intimate knowledge of the various channels, as it is necessary to thread your way through a forest of dead red gum trees and along the old riverbed to avoid the worst of the snags. Alan Way of the Shoreline Caravan Park at Mulwala is one of the more successful anglers in this water and he knows it like the back of his

species tip

MURRAY COD

Murray cod head up the pecking order among native fresh water fish and are generally found first in line in a deep hole or snag. A good area to look is where there is a junction of water, the sudden speed up in current plays smaller fish right into the jaws of cod, which simply flare their gills and suck the food in. Hone your hooks and be prepared to swim lures at different depths and use alternate colours until you strike the right formula.

broad hand. He trolls and bait fishes for cod and yellowbelly.

Bardi grubs, sliced in half and set on a long shanked size 2–4 hook, are favourite cod bait. For yellowbelly the local shrimp, crustaceans about 75 to 100 mm long are popular. The rigs vary but for the most part anglers fish on the bottom with a running sinker rig or else lower their bait over the side of their boat, allow it to get to the bottom then wind it up half a metre or so.

If there is anything you want to know about catching yellowbelly or Murray cod on lures or flies I can think of no-one better to ask than Rod Harrison. An angler's angler who doesn't need guides or trick photography to produce the goods, for more than 20 years Rod's work in both salt and fresh water has been at the cutting edge of angling developments.

I have fished for the natives with Rod on several waters in New South Wales and Queensland. Native fish on lures requires specialised techniques. First you have to know where the fish are likely to be lurking and then-offer a lure with all the right attributes: colour, action and depth are the keys to success.

The trip I remember most was on Lake Copeton in New South Wales. On that trip, we started out by fine tuning, or 'retrofitting' as Harro says, our lures. Chemically sharpened treble hooks are preferred and Harro was the

first angler I'd come across who, as a matter of course, pulled out a ceramic stone and worked these hooks over. His retrofitting also involved putting a larger set of treble hooks (No. 2) at the front of the lure and a smaller set (No. 4)

shopping list
COD & GOLDEN PERCH
BAIT FISHING & SPINNING:

OUTFIT: Three to 6 kg, either threadline or baitcaster. Spool up with braid lines for trolling, as this will allow the lure to swim deeper.

BAIT: Bardi grubs, scrubworms, shrimp, and yabbies.

HOOKS: No. 2 – 4 long shank.

LURES: Deep bibbed lures like Halco Poltergeist and StumpJumper about 50 millimetres. Rattlin Spots and Rapala CD15s also work well. Colours to choose range from chartreuse to dark green, hot pinks and trout patterns.

FLY FISHING:

OUTFIT: Seven to 9 wt. Weight forward intermediate or floating line and use a minimum 3 kg tippet.

FLIES: Deep Clouser Minnow, Dahlberg Diver, shrimp patterns.

at the rear. He explained that this was because of the way native fish feed.

'Perch, and that includes Murray cod and yellowbelly, have a natural shape on the head that shipbuilders replicate; that is a bow and bulge below,' he said. 'This means the water in front of the fish's eyes is disturbed enabling it to flare its gills and suck in unsuspecting prey.

'Most fish are taken at the broadest surface. It is the same with lures, which is why I place special significance on the front treble.'

Baitcaster reels spooled with Harro's own brand of pink coloured Bionic Braid line were used to flick the 50 mm deep bibbed lures to the edge of rocks and alongside the skeletal remains of tree-tops. Our modus operandi was to work rocky points, snags, and drop-offs. The slightest irregularities in the shoreline or bottom are likely places, as are choke points where the water narrows and the current increases. A fish finder was constantly on as a backup to Harro's fish finding skill.

It was in a choke point when the action went from hot to hotter. It started with a yellowbelly of about 2.5 kg that was putting up a valiant struggle after taking a green, deep-bibbed lure. At the other end, Rod was coaxing it along through the current. We were drifting through a stretch of fast water in a small canyon and, even though the fish was making life difficult by using its deep flank to hold in the current, it was almost a regulation battle. And then everything changed as a huge flash of white emerged through the tannin coloured water as a big Murray cod rose from its lair to take a swipe at the struggling yellowbelly.

'Did you see the size of that bloody cod?' Rod asked. He was excited and so was I. We had been on the lake trolling and spinning for just such a fish since sunrise, more than eight hours ago. 'Well, at least you know they're here,' he said after I acknowledged the presence of Australia's most famous native fish.

Murray cod proved scarce on this trip, and after two and a half days we only managed two of the 'green fish' as Harro called them. Mostly we caught and released yellowbelly, fish that ranged in weight from 1 kg to 3.5 kilograms. Mixed in with these were redfin and silver perch.

'At this size the yellowbelly we caught were all males,' said Harro. 'The females grow much bigger and a lot of them are around 7kg.'

Our problem was that the females were in spawning mode and not feeding. Harro said that these fish need a flood to spawn (which doesn't happen at Copeton) so what the female fish do is reabsorb the roe into their system. Our best results came in narrow ravines. Native fish congregate where there is a confluence, an area where a canyon narrows and the water flow increases.

Harro had explained: 'There is a pecking order in these areas with the biggest fish, the cod, at the front.' This was exactly where we caught our cod and most of the yellowbelly.

The fishing was always intense and selective. There was a thought process that went into fishing each new location with constant attention being paid to flies and lures: size, colour, shape and presentation.

CHAPTER 13

FISH SEASONS CHARTS

The following state-by-state charts are a guide to some of the more popular species and the best times. It is not a definitive guide by any means as fishing seasons can vary due to weather and other factors. For example, mackerel can be caught year round in north Queensland, but Anzac Day is regarded as the traditional start of the serious run of fish. Snapper can be caught all year in Port Phillip Bay, but the best run of fish commences during spring.

VICTORIA

SPECIES	OPTIMUM TIMES											
	JANUARY	FEBRUARY	MARCH	APRIL	MAY	JUNE	JULY	AUGUST	SEPTEMBER	OCTOBER	NOVEMBER	DECEMBER
Flathead	███	███	███	███					███	███	███	███
Snapper	███	███	███						███	███	███	███
Whiting	███	███	███	███								███
Bream					███	███	███	███	███			
Mullet					███	███	███	███				
Trout	███	███	███						███	███	███	███
Redfin	███	███	███						███	███	███	███
Yellowbelly		███	███	███	███							
Salmon	BAYS			SURF ███	███	███	███	███	███	BAYS ███	███	███
Tailor					███	███	███	███				
Garfish	███	███	███									███
Barracouta	███	███	███									
Silver trevally	███	███	███								███	███

WESTERN AUSTRALIA

SPECIES	OPTIMUM TIMES											
	JANUARY	FEBRUARY	MARCH	APRIL	MAY	JUNE	JULY	AUGUST	SEPTEMBER	OCTOBER	NOVEMBER	DECEMBER
Herring				■	■	■	■	■				
Tailor	■	■	■								■	■
Sand whiting	■	■	■	■	■							
WA jewfish	■	■	■	■	■	■	■	■	■	■	■	■
Snapper					■	■	■	■	■	■	■	
Skippy				■	■	■	■	■	■	■		
Black bream	■	■	■	■	■	■	■	■	■	■	■	■
Garfish			■	■	■	■	■	■	■	■		
Salmon		■	■	■	■	■	■					
Samson fish	■	■	■	■	■	■	■	■	■	■	■	■
Spanish mackerel	■	■	■	■	■	■	■	■	■	■	■	■
Spangled emperor	■	■	■	■	■	■	■	■	■	■	■	■
Barramundi				■	■	■	■	■	■	■	■	■

SOUTH AUSTRALIA

SPECIES	OPTIMUM TIMES											
	JANUARY	FEBRUARY	MARCH	APRIL	MAY	JUNE	JULY	AUGUST	SEPTEMBER	OCTOBER	NOVEMBER	DECEMBER
Snapper	■	■	■	■	■					■	■	■
Whiting					■	■	■	■	■	■		
Mullet			■	■	■	■						
Tommy ruff					■	■	■	■	■	■	■	
Garfish	■	■	■	■	■							■
Yellowbelly	■	■	■	■	■							■
Redfin	■	■	■	■	■						■	■
Salmon			■	■	■	■	■	■	■			
Mulloway	■	■	■	■	■						■	■
Bream	■	■	■	■				■	■	■	■	■

NEW SOUTH WALES

SPECIES	OPTIMUM TIMES											
	JANUARY	FEBRUARY	MARCH	APRIL	MAY	JUNE	JULY	AUGUST	SEPTEMBER	OCTOBER	NOVEMBER	DECEMBER
Bream	██	██	██	██								██
Mulloway	██	██	██	██							██	██
Flathead	██	██	██	██						██	██	██
Tailor	██	██	██	██						██	██	
Whiting	██	██	██								██	██
Dolphinfish	██	██	██	██								██
Marlin	██	██	██	██							██	██
Yellowtail kingfish	██	██	██	██	██							
Snapper									██	██	██	██
Trevally				██	██	██	██	██	██	██	██	
Yellowfin tuna	██	██	██	██	██	*Season earlier on north coast*				*South coast*	██	██
Albacore	██	██	██	██						*South coast*	██	██
Morwong				██	██	██	██	██	██	██	██	

TASMANIA

SPECIES	OPTIMUM TIMES											
	JANUARY	FEBRUARY	MARCH	APRIL	MAY	JUNE	JULY	AUGUST	SEPTEMBER	OCTOBER	NOVEMBER	DECEMBER
Flathead	██	██	██	██	██	██	██	██	██	██	██	██
Bream	██	██	██						██	██	██	██
Salmon	██	██	██								██	██
Snapper	██	██	██						██	██	██	██
Trout	██	██	██	██				██	██	██	██	██
Sea-run trout								██	██	██	██	
Tuna	██	██	██	██	██	██						
Barracouta	██	██	██								██	██
Sand whiting	██	██	██	██	██	██	██	██	██	██	██	██
Trevally	██	██	██								██	██
Trumpeter	██	██	██	██	██	██	██	██	██	██	██	██
Jackass perch	██	██	██									

QUEENSLAND

SPECIES	OPTIMUM TIMES											
	JANUARY	FEBRUARY	MARCH	APRIL	MAY	JUNE	JULY	AUGUST	SEPTEMBER	OCTOBER	NOVEMBER	DECEMBER
Whiting	■								■	■	■	■
Bream				■	■	■	■					
Flathead							■	■	■			
Tailor							■	■	■			
Mackerel				■	■	■	■	■	■			
Snapper						■	■	■	■			
Pearl Perch	■	■	■	■	■							
Longtail	■				■	■	■					■
Small black marlin	■ SOUTH QUEENSLAND	■	■		■ NORTH QUEENSLAND	■	■	■	■	■	■ SOUTH QUEENSLAND	■
Big black marlin									■	■	■	■
Barramundi									■	■	■	■
Swallowtail dart	■	■	■									
Golden trevally	■	■	■	■	■	■	■	■	■	■	■	■
Yellowbelly	■	■	■							■	■	■
Mangrove jack				■	■	■		■	■	■	■	■
Australian bass	■ IMPOUNDMENTS	■	■							■	■	■